The Polish Transformation

Studies in Critical Social Sciences Book Series

Haymarket Books is proud to be working with Brill Academic Publishers (www.brill.nl) to republish the *Studies in Critical Social Sciences* book series in paperback editions. This peer-reviewed book series offers insights into our current reality by exploring the content and consequences of power relationships under capitalism, and by considering the spaces of opposition and resistance to these changes that have been defining our new age. Our full catalog of *SCSS* volumes can be viewed at https://www.haymarketbooks.org/series_collections/4-studies-in-critical-social-sciences.

Series Editor
David Fasenfest (York University)

New Scholarship in Political Economy Book Series

Series Editors
David Fasenfest (York University)
Alfredo Saad-Filho (Queen's University, Belfast)

Editorial Board
Kevin B. Anderson (University of California, Santa Barbara)
Tom Brass (formerly of SPS, University of Cambridge)
Raju Das (York University)
Ben Fine ((emeritus) SOAS University of London)
Jayati Ghosh (Jawaharlal Nehru University)
Elizabeth Hill (University of Sydney)
Dan Krier (Iowa State University)
Lauren Langman (Loyola University Chicago)
Valentine Moghadam (Northeastern University)
David N. Smith (University of Kansas)
Susanne Soederberg (Queen's University)
Aylin Topal (Middle East Technical University)
Fiona Tregenna (University of Johannesburg)
Matt Vidal (Loughborough University London)
Michelle Williams (University of the Witwatersrand)

The Polish Transformation

Tadeusz Kowalik on the Epigonic Bourgeois Revolution of 1989

Grzegorz Konat

Translated by
Emil Tchorek
Gavin Rae

Haymarket Books
Chicago, IL

First published in 2024 by Brill Academic Publishers, The Netherlands
© 2024 Koninklijke Brill NV, Leiden, The Netherlands

Published in paperback in 2025 by
Haymarket Books
P.O. Box 180165
Chicago, IL 60618
773-583-7884
www.haymarketbooks.org

ISBN: 979-8-88890-353-7

Distributed to the trade in the US through Consortium Book Sales and Distribution (www.cbsd.com) and internationally through Ingram Publisher Services International (www.ingramcontent.com).

This book was published with the generous support of Lannan Foundation, Wallace Action Fund, and the Marguerite Casey Foundation.

Special discounts are available for bulk purchases by organizations and institutions. Please call 773-583-7884 or email info@haymarketbooks.org for more information.

Cover design by Jamie Kerry and Ragina Johnson.

Printed in the United States.

Library of Congress Cataloging-in-Publication data is available.

For Marta

Contents

Acknowledgements IX

Introduction 1

1 Tadeusz Kowalik's Thesis on the Polish Systemic Transformation as an "Epigonic Bourgeois Revolution" 37

2 Jan Baszkiewicz's Model of Bourgeois Revolutions 57

3 The Polish Systemic Transformation as a Bourgeois Revolution in Tadeusz Kowalik's Selected Works 92

Conclusion 152

References 189
Index 206

Acknowledgements

This monograph is a slightly modified version of my book entitled *Polska rewolucja. Tadeusz Kowalik o epigońsko-mieszczańskiej transformacji roku 1989*, which was published in Polish in 2021 by the Książka i Prasa publishing house (Konat, 2021b). Its content is a revised version of the doctoral dissertation entitled "Tadeusz Kowalik's Thesis on the Polish Systemic Transformation as a 'Bourgeois Revolution of the Epigones' in the Light of Jan Baszkiewicz's Model of Revolution", submitted and defended at the SGH Warsaw School of Economics in 2021. It would not have been completed without the patience, forbearance and, above all, invaluable substantive support of my supervisor, Professor Kazimierz Kloc, to whom I am immensely grateful.

I received a great deal of kindness and assistance during my research into Tadeusz Kowalik's thought from Professors Paweł Kozłowski, Henryk Szlajfer, and Jan Toporowski. As reviewers of my doctoral dissertation – the first critical recipients of the text – they gave me, also during numerous conversations, many valuable comments and suggestions. I am indebted to them in this respect, and my only regret is that I was only able to take into account some of these suggestions during the preparation of this book.

Another critical reader of my work was Professor Gavin Rae. I thank him for his valuable comments on it, but also for our many discussions and our joint work on Tadeusz Kowalik's thought, either searching Kowalik's archives at the Polish Academy of Sciences or organising a scientific conference dedicated to the achievements of Kowalik, which took place in July 2022 in Warsaw. Moreover, he agreed to join forces with Emil Tchorek to translate this book into English. Both of them have done a great job in this regard, for which they have my immense gratitude.

I have been engaged with Tadeusz Kowalik's thought since 2013. There is no doubt in my mind that the present book would not have been written if I had not been fortunate enough over these years to work in successive teams of scholars that created an atmosphere of free discussion and intellectual development. For this, I would like to thank all the colleagues with whom I had the pleasure of working during this period, in particular Ms Wanda Karpińska-Mizielińska, Dr Józef Niemczyk and Dr Piotr Ważniewski. However, special thanks are, above all, owed to Professors Tadeusz Smuga, Jacek Kulawik, Marek Gruszczyński, Elżbieta Adamowicz and Marek Rocki, who headed these teams.

I am also grateful to Professor Jerzy Osiatyński for the opportunity to learn from him the difficult art of researching the output of eminent economists, not only Tadeusz Kowalik, and my only regret is that I did not have the chance to show him the results of these teachings – i.e., this book – before his untimely passing in February 2022.

At various stages of work on the dissertation and book, I was able to count on the kindness of my colleagues who formed the seminar series entitled "Philosophy and Social Movements". In particular, I am indebted to Zbigniew M. Kowalewski, who, after reading the Polish edition of the book, provided me with many valuable comments, which I have tried to incorporate in this edition. I also received a great deal of help from Katarzyna Bielińska, Artur Maroń, Michał Siermiński, as well as Katarzyna Rakowska. I thank them all.

I am grateful to the family of the protagonist of my deliberations – Irena and Mateusz Kowalik – for allowing me to use the archives of Tadeusz Kowalik, and also to Ms Eliza Lewandowska, who generously provided me with access to her correspondence from the period when she was working on the translation of *Polska transformacja* into English.

I would also like to thank the Director of the Książka i Prasa publishing house, Stefan Zgliczyński, for agreeing to publish this book in the first place, and then for agreeing to republish it in English. What is more, he undertook the arduous task of editing the original manuscript, which undoubtedly benefited the text.

I am also very grateful to Professor David Fasenfest for accepting this text for publication in the *New Scholarship in Political Economy* series, and above all for the enormous patience he has shown with me. I would also like to thank the Brill editorial and production teams, and especially Judy Pereira, for all the work they put into this text. This whole endeavor, however, would not have come to fruition without the generous financial support of my university, SGH Warsaw School of Economics, for which I warmly thank its authorities.

Finally, the most important thing for me was always the support of my nearest and dearest. Throughout all these years, I could always count on the motivation and support of my Mum, Ewa Ligor. And my wife, Marta Konat, not only patiently put up with my constant work, but also read the entire original version of the text, removing many faults from it, and greatly improving its readability. To her I dedicate this edition.

Introduction

1

Tadeusz Kowalik (1926–2012) was a Professor of Economics and Humanities[1] who, in an academic career spanning almost 60 years, considered mainly the history of ideas, especially economic thought (or, as he sometimes called it, socio-economic thought),[2] also conducting comparative analysis of economic systems with particular attention to the Polish systemic transformation that took place in the final two decades of the 20th century. He was the author, co-author or editor of several dozen monographs and hundreds of scientific articles and book chapters.[3] His output's high scientific status is attested by translations of his work into several languages.[4] He also spent many years in important research centres all over the world[5] and his valued status is reflected in the opinions of many academic economists at home and abroad.[6]

Jan Toporowski describes Tadeusz Kowalik as "one of the great political economists of the twentieth century", placing him "alongside … Oskar Lange, Michał Kalecki and, of course, Rosa Luxemburg" (Toporowski, 2012: 14). He goes on to add that "Tadeusz Kowalik not only laid out the foundations of twentieth century political economy. He has also provided us with a political economy for the twenty-first century" (Toporowski, 2012: 14). Rajko Bukvić expresses a similar opinion, describing Kowalik as "one of the greatest Polish economists of the

---

1   As Kozłowski (2012) explains, "that was the terminology and full titularity once used" (p. 567).
2   See, for example, (Kowalik, 2012d: 71).
3   A competent though, as the authors themselves admit, an incomplete bibliography of Kowalik's works by can be found in (Karwowski, Szymborska & Toporowski, 2014).
4   As is generally acknowledged in the literature, Kowalik's most important work is a monograph entitled *Róża Luksemburg. Teoria akumulacji i imperializmu* [Rosa Luxemburg: Theory of Accumulation and Imperialism] (Kowalik, 2012b). It was translated into English (Kowalik, 2014), Italian (Kowalik, 1977b) and Spanish (Kowalik, 1979). There is also a translation of Kowalik's book *Polska transformacja* (Kowalik, 2009b) into English, as *From Solidarity to Sellout: The Restoration of Capitalism in Poland* (Kowalik, 2012a). The original Polish title of the latter book translates into English as "the Polish transformation". It was clearly the inspiration for the title of this book.
5   For more on Kowalik's activities with foreign academic centres see for example (Kowalik, 2005a), where he writes: "Although … I do not refer to them [in the text of the book – G.K.], my direct observations during my work (more than ten years in total) in the research centres of six Western countries (Austria, USA, Canada, England, Sweden, Switzerland) were an important addition to the book's content" (p. 6).
6   The most comprehensive tributes to Tadeusz Kowalik and his work are the two-volume *festschrift* (Bellofiore, Karwowski & Toporowski, 2014a; 2014c) and forthcoming intellectual biography of his (Rae, 2024).

second half of XX and the beginning of XXI centuries" (Bukvić, 2013: 201).[7] The editors of the scientific journal *Warsaw Forum of Economic Sociology* consider Kowalik to be "the most outstanding Polish economist of social-democratic convictions in the post-1989 period" (Kowalik, 2012e: 9). This is in line with Ewa Bińczyk's opinion that Kowalik "is widely recognized [in Poland] as one of the most important social economists in our country" (Bińczyk, 2015: 792).

For Karol Szwarc, "professor Tadeusz Kowalik was an eminent Polish left-wing intellectual, a man of dialogue, who was open to listening to any argument" (Szwarc, 2012: 13). As Riccardo Bellofiore, Ewa Karwowski and Jan Toporowski point out, Kowalik's main scientific purpose "was not to interpret the world but to change it with an honest, unsentimental understanding of capitalism and socialism" (Bellofiore, Karwowski & Toporowski, 2014b: 8).

Similarly, according to Zdzisław Sadowski, Kowalik is

> an economist, an outstanding historian of economic and social thought, an unparalleled researcher of social systems, a great expert in social democratic literature and, at the same time, a social and political activist, a tireless fighter who devoted his life to the fight against social and economic injustice.
>
> SADOWSKI, 2012: 547

Paweł Kozłowski also pays great respect to Tadeusz Kowalik as a scientist, noting both his method ("he knew that, in fact, every scientific reflection has some values at its core" (Kozłowski, 2012: 567–568)), as well as, like Sadowski, his broad research interests ("he studied economic thought, economic systems, the Polish transformation and earlier transformations" (Kozłowski, 2012: 567–568)).

Jerzy Osiatyński emphasises how Kowalik was "very prolific academically" (Osiatyński, 2012: 9). Edward Łukawer, in his book dedicated to outstanding 20th century Polish economists, mentions Kowalik as among the "top class" referring, in particular, to his works on systemic transformation (Łukawer, 2008: 138–142); the transformation, of which, as Karol Modzelewski characteristically pointed out, Kowalik was one of the "few bitter critics" (Modzelewski, 2013: 402). In a similar vein, Mirosław Bochenek writes: "Tadeusz Kowalik ... [was] known [especially] for his uncompromising fight for 'civilised' capitalism" (Bochenek, 2020: 74), and Wacław Stankiewicz concludes that "Kowalik's

---

7 Throughout the book, my own omissions are indicated by ellipses, and omissions in indirect quotations are indicated by ellipses in square brackets.

attitude as an academic and activist [after 1989 – G.K.] can be described with reference to the title of his essay *Dystrybucyjna sprawiedliwość w transformacji polskiej* [Distributive Justice in the Polish Transformation]" (Stankiewicz, 2007: 498).[8]

As Gavin Rae points out, Tadeusz Kowalik "managed to reach across political boundaries and perhaps like no other figure on the left in Poland was welcomed and invited by groups and parties from different traditions. ... the body of work he has left, the example he has set and the tradition from which he has come is one that should inspire the present generation" (Rae, 2012: 102). This opinion is echoed by John Bellamy Foster, who emphasises that "briefly meeting Kowalik in Toronto in the early 1980s" was "a big moment" in his life (Konat & Foster, 2018: 10).

Finally, appreciation for Tadeusz Kowalik and his work is also expressed in empirical studies of the community of Polish academic economists. In interviews conducted in 2015 with prominent Polish economists, eight out of twenty indicated Kowalik as an authority (Konat & Smuga, 2016).[9] Thus, all these voices are quite clear that, for those who came into contact with his work, Tadeusz Kowalik was an important figure in 20th and early 21st century Polish economics. In my opinion, this justifies undertaking research on the thought of this scholar.

2

Tadeusz Kowalik's output may be divided into three main areas:[10] works (i) devoted to the thought of Ludwik Krzywicki and, to a lesser extent, Stanisław

---

8   Stankiewicz means (Kowalik, 2002a).
9   It is therefore all the more surprising that, in a survey conducted in the same year and addressed to Polish academic economists with at least a PhD degree, to an open question "Which outstanding (foreign or Polish) economists have exerted the greatest influence on the directions of your academic work and your research interests?", only five out of 309 respondents (1.6%) indicated Tadeusz Kowalik in their answer. Interestingly, the respondents who did mention Kowalik as an authority listed him alongside economists like John Maynard Keynes, Joseph E. Stiglitz, Adam Krzyżanowski, Edward Taylor, Grzegorz W. Kołodko, John Kenneth Galbraith, Douglas C. North and Amartya K. Sen. In three out of five cases, Tadeusz Kowalik was mentioned together with Joseph Stiglitz. A discussion of both the references to the person and work of Kowalik in the aforementioned interviews, as well as his name in the questionnaire survey is presented in (Konat, 2019). More about the survey, its methodology and results in: (Konat et al., 2019).
10 The typology presented below differs slightly from the division proposed by Toporowski (2013b), who distinguishes in the political economy of Kowalik: (i) works on Kalecki and

Krusiński and the so-called "Krusińskites";[11] (ii) on the history of Polish economic thought, in particular on the theories of Rosa Luxemburg, Oskar Lange and Michał Kalecki[12] and (iii) on the analysis of economic systems and systemic transformation, including those devoted to the problems of convergence (e.g. theses on the "crucial reform" of capitalism and socialism), distributive justice and socio-economic inequalities.[13] At this point, it is worth noting that there are fundamental differences in Tadeusz Kowalik's output regarding his adopted research method (instruments characteristic for the history of ideas, economic history and comparative studies), the generally understood object of interest (political economy of capitalism, problems of real socialism[14])

Lange, (ii) opposition activity in Solidarity and related theoretical achievements (in particular, the thesis on the convergence of systems), (iii) the "campaign" against neoliberal capitalism.

11   See especially (Kowalik, 1959), and also (Kowalik, 1958; 1965; 1975; Kowalik, Hołda-Róziewicz, 1976; Falkowski, Kowalik, 1957). Kowalik was also one of the editors of Ludwik Krzywicki's *Dzieła* [Works] (Krzywicki, 1959).

12   There are far too many to try to list them all. Most of them are included in the aforementioned bibliography of works by Tadeusz Kowalik (Karwowski, Szymborska & Toporowski, 2014). It seems, however, that two monographs should be regarded as the most important: (Kowalik, 2012b) and (Kowalik, 1992a). In close connection with his work on the achievements of Lange and Kalecki was undoubtedly the fact that in the 1970s Kowalik headed the research group tasked with editing the works of Oskar Lange and Michał Kalecki at the Institute for the History of Science, Education, and Technology of the Polish Academy of Sciences (see (Konat, 2021a: 2)). He was also, among other things, editor of a selection of Oskar Lange's writings published in English (Lange, 1994). According to his own account, 20 years earlier Kowalik had written a monograph on Lange, but it was never published ("I consider it fortunate that the book on Lange I submitted to the management of the department [at the Institute for the History of Science, Education, and Technology of the Polish Academy of Sciences] in 1974 was never published. It was rejected by several publishing houses, sometimes without being read" (Kowalik et al., 2013: 631)). Many authors consider the part of his output devoted to Luxemburg, Lange and Kalecki as Kowalik's most important achievement. For example, Jan Toporowski writes that "The Lange *Works*, along with his collaboration with Kalecki and his studies of Luxemburg, remain Kowalik's most monumental achievement" (Toporowski, 2013a: 42).

13   The most important works by Kowalik in the field of economic systems analysis include (Kowalik, 2000; 2002c; 2005a; 2009b). One of his last undertakings in this area was the publication of documents from Stanisław Gomułka's private archive devoted to the Polish transformation (Kowalik, 2010b; Gomułka & Kowalik, 2011). As regards systemic convergence, Kowalik's works on "crucial reforms" are undoubtedly the most important (Kalecki & Kowalik, 1991; Kowalik, 1989).

14   Further on in the book I will use this particular term. For a similar decision, preceded by a brief discussion of alternatives see (Kozłowski, 1997: 10). In one of his works (of a textbook character), Tadeusz Kowalik summed up the richness of terminology in this

as well as the accepted set of axioms (Marxism, Kaleckianism or institutionalism).[15]

Tadeusz Kowalik's most important scientific contribution to what may be considered as his political economy,[16] is probably his demonstration of the essential elements of theoretical continuity between the works of Karl Marx, Rosa Luxemburg and Michał Kalecki in the monograph entitled *Rosa Luxemburg. Theory of Accumulation and Imperialism* (Kowalik, 2014). Here he proved that as Kalecki was not so much a "left-wing Keynesian" as was usually assumed, but an economist who should be included in the broad current of Marxist thought. This is, for example, the opinion of Jan Toporowski, who claims that

> The reconstruction of capitalist political economy on the basis of Marx's reproduction schemes led ... Kowalik ... to reject the thesis that Kalecki was a precursor of [John Maynard] Keynes. Keynes simply saw, in an

---

respect as follows: "The socio-economic system that prevailed in Poland [from the 1940s to the end of the 1980s], as well as in the entire so-called Soviet bloc and several Asian countries, was called variously: e.g. the 'real socialist' economy, the 'command economy', the 'centrally planned economy'. The latter name was used as the most politically neutral by *UN agencies* [emphasis T.K.]. Critics used a variety of more or less pejorative terms. Leszek Kołakowski introduced the term 'despotic socialism'. Jan Drewnowski popularised the term 'sovietism'. Western socialists and social democrats defined the social and economic system as state or bureaucratic capitalism, and if as socialism at all, as a rule with the addition: 'state', 'bureaucratic', 'absolutist', etc. Due to the dominant and sometimes monopolistic role of the communist parties both in the system of political power and in the economy, this system was often simply described as communist" (Kowalik, 2002e: 615).

15 More on this subject can be found in the sketch of Tadeusz Kowalik's biography contained in the introduction to the already mentioned two-volume *festschrift* (Bellofiore, Karwowski & Toporowski, 2014b) as well as in the forthcoming intellectual biography of Kowalik (Rae, 2024).

16 I take this definition of Tadeusz Kowalik's scientific activity from Jan Toporowski. Kurt Rothschild points to four conditions that, in his opinion, must be met in order to speak of "political economy". These are (i) an awareness that political and non-economic factors play an important role in shaping economic processes and outcomes, (ii) special attention to problems of power and conflicts of interest, the role of institutions and institutional change, and globally changing political and economic structures, (iii) an active interest in the theories and approaches of neighbouring social sciences and (iv) an interdisciplinary approach (Rothschild, 1989). In my opinion, the work of Tadeusz Kowalik meets all the above criteria. Interestingly, Kowalik had the opportunity to get to know Rothschild at a very early stage of his academic career. As he mentioned in an (unpublished) conversation with Kazimierz Łaski: "I met Kurt Rothschild during my stay in Vienna in 1959" (Łaski & Kowalik, 2007).

imperfect way, something of which Kalecki was much better aware based on Marxist discussions around the work of Rosa Luxemburg.

TOPOROWSKI, 2012: 12–13[17]

Among Tadeusz Kowalik's most important scientific achievements are, in my opinion, (i) identifying Ludwik Krzywicki as a precursor of the Monopoly Capital School and Rudolf Hilferding's concept of the "general cartel,"[18] (ii) offering an original synthesis of the history of economics in Poland, indicating that for at least several decades Marxist political economy was a current in world economic research to which Polish economists made an original and important contribution,[19] (iii) presenting his own concepts of the development of capitalism through structural crises and the convergence of capitalism

---

[17] The same author, together with Bellofiore and Karwowski, stress that "Tadeusz Kowalik was a key figure in challenging the framing of Kalecki within a Keynesian theoretical and policy agenda" (Bellofiore, Karwowski & Toporowski, 2014b: 3). It is worth noting that the monograph by Kowalik on Luxemburg very quickly received a warm welcome among representatives of the so-called Monopoly Capital School. Henryk Szlajfer recalls in this context: "when, in the early 1970s, Tadeusz Kowalik's book about Rosa Luxemburg, *which I value highly* [emphasis mine – G.K.], came out, I wrote to Paul [Sweezy, editor-in-chief of *Monthly Review*] about it, that there was this text in which Kalecki's theory was closely linked to the concepts of Luxemburg and certain threads of Marx's theory. *He received this information with great interest* [emphasis mine – G.K.]" (Konat & Szlajfer, 2019: 43). For more on the relationship between the Monopoly Capital School and Polish economics see (Foster, 2014) as well as texts in the volume (Konat & Wielgosz, 2018).

[18] See (Kowalik, 1959), especially chapter 3 (pp. 209–257). I first raised how pioneering Kowalik's findings were in this regard in a conference presentation entitled "Krzywicki, Kalecki, Kowalik: Monopoly Capital in Polish Economic Thought" (Konat, 2014). For a more contemporary, extended discussion on the issue of Krzywicki's precursorism vis-à-vis Hilferding and its development, see (Toporowski, 2022) and (Szymborska & Toporowski, 2022).

[19] See (Kowalik, 1992a), which Stankiewicz (2007: 498) describes as an "outstanding achievement" and Marek Tabin (2014: 63) – as "monumental". The proposal for the interpretation of Kowalik's work presented here I originally put forward in a conference paper entitled "Tadeusz Kowalik: the Founder of the Polish School in economics?" (Konat, 2015). It is worth noting that the first synthetic treatment of the problem of the contribution of Polish Marxism to world economics by Kowalik are the chapters by him in (Górski, Kowalik & Sierpiński, 1967). Years later, Kowalik described the dramatic fate of this book with some bitterness "In 1967 a textbook on the History of Economic Thought after 1870 was published by three authors including me. After the March 1968 'anti-revisionist/zionist' (*antyrewisyjonistyczny*) campaign, a new edition was published without my name [(Górski & Sierpiński, 1972)], and additionally with the assurance that it was the first textbook of its kind in socialist countries" (Kowalik et al., 2013: 624).

and socialism towards an undefined intermediate form of welfare state[20] and (iv) consistently applying what I call *value disclosure*[21] in his works.

---

[20] The former especially in (Kowalik, 1977a) and (Kowalik, 1978), while the latter is primarily in texts about "crucial" reforms (Kalecki & Kowalik, 1991; Kowalik, 1989). I am extremely grateful to Professors Jan Toporowski and Gavin Rae for drawing my attention to the significance of this part of Tadeusz Kowalik's work. In one of the latter's most recent works, one can find a detailed analysis of the issue of the relationship between "crucial reform" and the "welfare state" in Kowalik (Rae, 2022).

[21] This is my term, essentially equivalent to what Gunnar Myrdal (1969: 55–56) described as *bringing the valuations out in the open* or *exposing the valuations to full light*. Kowalik succinctly presented the basis of his version of *value disclosure* in (Kowalik, 2006b), where he began the discussion of method by stating that "a somewhat more extensive introduction revealing certain general premises of the author's reasoning is necessary [in this work]. The point ... is not so much the otherwise correct general statement of the philosophy and sociology of science that all scientific works are tainted by subjectivism, nor even the fact that in the social sciences it is usually greater than in the natural sciences, but above all the exceptionally high degree of subjectivism in works from the field of contemporary history, and that of one's own country. The author's biography, his ideological sympathies are somehow encoded in the choice of subject matter, the choice of sources (of which only some are available) and even in the language he uses. This is the case with all works in this field, including those by authors who say or even believe that they practice 'pure' science and only science" (p. 14). The remedy proposed by Kowalik (leaving aside the doubtful possibility of its application in cases of "belief in practising 'pure' science" signalled by Kowalik, which can be identified with the lack of self-awareness; on this subject see e.g. (Carr, 1990)) can be found in (deleted from the second edition, appearing only in the first edition of the book (Kowalik, 1980)) the following passage: "I think, therefore, that *authors of works on recent times should* – in addition to the professionally mandated striving for possible objectivity – *openly reveal their political or ideological sympathies* [emphasis mine – G.K.]. This is because it is tantamount to revealing 'the kind of glasses' through which they see reality. From the very beginning the reader can put on different 'glasses' – of a different colour and a different prism" (p. 4). Then, in a paragraph present again in both editions, Kowalik presents something that I consider to be the essence of *value disclosure* – he expresses his views and their evolution in time. He writes about himself: "The author of this work was from spring 1948 a member of PPR [Polish Workers' Party] ... then of PZPR [Polish United Workers' Party]; from 1956 he was among those who demanded radical – in our understanding of the time – reform of the system and its democratisation; he was finally expelled from the party [i.e. PZPR] in 1968, both for his opposition to repressions against students, as well as for 'the totality of his views'. And the second piece of information: he still [in 1980] believes in the sense of striving for democratic socialism based on parliamentarism and freedom, although he is not so sure that he is right as to convert others to his faith. At present he is more concerned with ensuring that the intellectual output of what is called the current is not completely forgotten" (Kowalik, 2006: 14). The congruence of the position of Kowalik presented here with the proposal of Myrdal is striking. The latter wrote that "every study of a social problem, however limited in scope, is and must be determined by valuations. A 'disinterested' social science has never existed and, for logical reasons, can never exist. However, the

However there is one more of Tadeusz Kowalik's theoretical proposals to be added to the above list: suggesting the possibility of treating the Polish systemic transformation from real socialism to capitalism as an "epigonic bourgeois revolution."[22]

---

value premises that actually and of necessity determine social science research are generally hidden. ... They are ... left implicit and vague, leaving the door open to biases. The only way in which we can strive for 'objectivity' in theoretical analysis is to expose the valuations to full light, make them conscious, specific, and explicit, and permit them to determine the theoretical research" (Myrdal, 1969: 55–56). The fact that Kowalik has followed the principle of *value disclosure*, understood in this way, to a far-reaching extent in numerous works deserves to be emphasised, given that, as Bo Sandelin, Hans-Michael Trautwein and Richard Wundrak note, "Myrdal's solution ... [postulating that] researchers should always make their norms explicit – is simple in principle, but ... difficult to practice" (Sandelin, Trautwein & Wundrak, 2014: 78). Establishing whether and if so, to what extent Tadeusz Kowalik's views were inspired by those of Myrdal (whose work Kowalik was familiar with; see for example (Kowalik, 2005b)) is beyond the scope of the book.

22 Due to the interpenetration of the terms "revolution" and "transformation (systemic)", their possible inclusion in another: "transition" and also – or perhaps above all – because Tadeusz Kowalik himself wrote about both transformation and revolution in the context of the Polish events of the 1980s and early 1990s, I will use them interchangeably (unless the context requires me to be more precise in my terminology). For the sake of accuracy it should be added that in the literature, especially in the field of the so-called "transitology", one can find many attempts to resolve this issue. For example, Andrzej W. Tymowski, in the context of the "logic of 1989" writes that while revolution means "a sharp rupture with the old order and breakthrough to a new one ... '[t]ransition' is also progressive, but evolutionary, articulated in step-by-step process, not polarizing, but based on continuity and consensus" (Tymowski, 1993: 176). Kowalik, it seems, recognised the terminological complications in this respect, pointing out, for example, that the "transformation in the economic sphere" alone (the use of which for the first time, in the context of "socio-economic evolution", he attributed to Karl Polanyi), can be ascribed at least three meanings: "a) the transformation of one mega-system into another, for example feudalism into capitalism, b) the transition from one variety of capitalism (one socio-economic system) to another, for example, the transition from free-market capitalism to the system called 'Scandinavian', or from the fascist war economy to the social market economy in West Germany after the Second World War, c) a continuous process of institutional transformation, guided consciously by reforms or spontaneously, to which all, even the most stagnant economies are subject" (Kowalik, 2007: 267–268). In light of the content of subsection (a), Kowalik's "epigonic bourgeois revolution" should probably be regarded as precisely such a "transformation in the economic sphere".

INTRODUCTION 9

3

The thesis content of the "epigonic bourgeois revolution", put forward by Kowalik in 1996 (Kowalik, 1996b)[23] and maintained by him in subsequent (at least a dozen) publications[24] until the end of his life,[25] is well expressed in the following excerpt from one of these works:

---

23   This article was also included in a collection published after Kowalik's death (Kowalik, 2013i), and has been translated and published in English at least twice (Kowalik, 1997a; 1997c). In addition, over the last quarter of a century, different authors writing in English have used different terms when referring to this concept of Tadeusz Kowalik. Consequently, we have in the literature, among others, "bourgeois revolution of the epigones" (Kowalik, 1997c), "bourgeois epigone revolution" (Kowalik, 1997a; 2012a), "epigonic bourgeois revolution" (Morawski, 1998) or even "bourgeois revolution of the latecomers" (Karwowski, Szymborska & Toporowski, 2014). In this book, the term "epigonic bourgeois revolution" will generally be used.

24   Among others, (Kowalik, 1997a; 1997c; 1997d; 2001b; 2003; 2005a; 2006a; 2008; 2009b; 2011a; 2011c; 2013b; 2013h). In (Kowalik, 2006a), Kowalik himself referred to the place of the thesis in his output, writing that he had evaluated "the Polish Solidarity revolution as epigonic and bourgeois" "for a long time and repeatedly" (p. 147). This repetition of Kowalik's thesis did not, however, seem to have provoked any debate on its subject, as it has been discussed in detail in the academic literature so far only at most in a few concise summaries. A representative example of the latter can be found in a text by Marek Tabin (2014), published after Tadeusz Kowalik's death, where the thesis is summarised as follows: "The 'Solidarity' revolution is described [by Kowalik] as epigonic bourgeois (of course, it is not about the political-freedom aspect of this revolution, but about what happened soon afterwards to the economy). It was bourgeois because it resulted in the restitution of the bourgeois state and the recognition as a propaganda dogma that the entire PRL [Polish People's Republic] period was nothing but a black hole in Polish history. Epigonic because mass unemployment and strong social inequalities, which had once made it possible to carry out rapid primary accumulation, are completely unnecessary today as there are more effective and less painful methods. And the question returns: why did Solidarity – the workers' organisation – agree to such a development? According to Tadeusz Kowalik (who refers here to a text by Jacek Kuroń), the years 1989–1993 saw the destruction of Solidarity as a popular and reformist movement. And the authorities which emerged from this 'Solidarity' considered it their first duty to make the greatest possible distance to the PRL in every respect" (p. 64).

25   It should be emphasised here that Kowalik decided to include his article from 1996 (Kowalik, 1996b) in the collection *O lepszy ład społeczno-ekonomiczny* [For a Better Socio-Economic Order] (Kowalik, 2013d) published after his death. The fact that he included this text in – as it turned out – his last work, in my opinion strengthens the argument that Kowalik considered it an important achievement until the end of his life, regardless of the way in which his attitude to the thesis presented there evolved (in the context of such an evolution, it is worth recalling his opinion expressed when discussing the works of Joseph E. Stiglitz: "as a historian of thought, I know that subsequent editions no longer accurately reflect the author's current thought" (Kowalik & Sierakowski, 2005: 200)). That *O lepszy ład społeczno-ekonomiczny* was "the last book written and prepared by Tadeusz

> the bourgeois, capitalist revolution [in Poland] was the work, as it once occurred [Kowalik has in mind especially the year 1918 – G.K.], of a mass movement of workers. As a result, paradoxically, a version of capitalism emerged [at the turn of the 1980s and 1990s in Poland] that I have no hesitation in describing as one of the most unjust social systems of the second half of the 20th century. ... The politically victorious struggle was to mean an acute social and economic defeat for the victors themselves [i.e., the workers – G.K.].
>
> KOWALIK, 2003: 225

The revolution thus understood had, according to Kowalik, its direct causes in the following combination of circumstances: "The temporary alliance of the workers with the intelligentsia, which was entrusted with programmatic matters, the highly important support of the [Catholic] Church, together with international financial organisations, made possible the peaceful transformation of a workers' revolution into a bourgeois one" (Kowalik, 1997a: 51).

The particular significance of the thesis stating that the Polish transformation process of the 1980s and the beginning of the 1990s were to be an "epigonic bourgeois revolution" or a "capitalist revolution" (by which Kowalik meant, as I will argue later, a bourgeois revolution) results, I believe, from its novelty manifested on two levels. Let us start with its originality against the background of the literature on the subject.

The term "bourgeois revolution" was first used, it seems, in the context of the transformations taking place in Eastern Europe in the late 1980s, in the spring of 1989. In a text published in the *Monthly Review*, Daniel Singer wrote: "We are simply watching the beginning of a vast upheaval in Eastern Europe: *A bourgeois revolution* [emphasis mine – G.K.] in institutions combined with a still uncertain economic reform, in countries where the bulk of private property had been eliminated" (Singer, 1989: 34). Singer maintained this opinion in, among others, an article written a little over a year later in the same periodical, where, referring to the situation in the Soviet Union, he stated that "in its first years *perestroika* offered the exhilarating experience of a country awakening from its slumber ... the Soviet Union became an altogether different country. All these freedoms of speech or assembly, it will be objected, are merely *the*

Kowalik", as well as the fact that the selection was made by Kowalik himself and not by Paweł Kozłowski, who edited this volume ("The selection [of texts for the book] was not ... an easy task. It was done by the author"), we learn from the "Introduction" to this work (Kozłowski, 2013b: 11).

bourgeois revolution come to Russia two centuries late [emphasis mine – G.K.]" (Singer, 1990: 83).

However, Singer was not alone in using the term "bourgeois revolution" to describe the changes in Central and Eastern Europe in the 1980s and 1990s: over the next few years a number of authors, in different contexts, expressed a similar view. Thus Iván Szelényi wrote that "The East European intelligentsia is conducting *a bourgeois revolution* [emphasis mine – G.K.] in a society without a bourgeoisie in order to create the bourgeoisie" (Szelényi, 1991: xii),[26] Joachim J. Savelsberg noted that "The late twentieth century witnessed ... the burial of hope and expectations of a communist utopia, and *bourgeois revolutions in*

---

26 This thought was later repeated several times. For example, the 1995 text reads "In 1989, a fraction of the intelligentsia seized power in Central Europe, their intention is to lead a bourgeois revolution without a bourgeoisie, but with the express desire to create a bourgeoisie" (Szelényi, Szelényi & Kovách, 1995: 720). The belief that the peculiarity of the Central European 'bourgeois revolutions' of the late 1980s and early 1990s was that they had to perform the task of creating a bourgeois class was in fact more widespread. For example, as early as 1992, J.M. Kovács, reporting on various types of 'constructivist' views of systemic transformation in the region, wrote: "In the absence of a strong middle class (entrepreneurs, civil society, etc.), the state must act as its temporary substitute. At the same time, it has to produce and train the natural agents of capitalist development. This is not the first time this will happen in this region – as demonstrated by Gerschenkron and Polányi. Once again, a bourgeois revolution has to be launched with the subsequent approval of the emerging bourgeoisie" (Kovács, 1992: 48). Zygmunt Bauman makes a similar point, beginning his reflections in this regard by quoting a statement by Andrzej Machalski, a Polish senator known for his extreme free-market views, from January 1990: "*What we have to do now is spread a bourgeois revolution which absolutely requires the creation of a bourgeois class* [emphasis mine – G.K.], characterized by an energetic approach to life, by creativity, readiness to expand and by individualism in economic thinking. There are such people. They only have to be woken up" (unsourced statement by Machalski, quoted in Bauman, 1993: 143–144). Bauman comments on this statement as follows: "Machalski spoke of the 'bourgeois revolution', but all bourgeois revolutions in history merely liberated fully formed bourgeois societies and the incipient capitalist economy from political constraints. The Polish bourgeois revolution must *create* [emphasis Z.B.] what other revolutions simply set free. As if we have not seen yet enough paradoxes, this particular variety of the *bourgeois* [emphasis Z.B.] revolution set itself a task which thus far has been known as the trade-mark of the *communist* [emphasis Z.B.] one: the task of constructing a social structure whose interests will (hopefully) offer the revolution, *ex-post-facto,* its legitimation and *raison d'etre*. Though distinguished by being a non-contrived, authentically indigenous product and thus far enjoying an overwhelming popular approval, this revolution (much like the imported and unwanted communist upheaval of 1945) had to be carried out by the visionaries from the ranks of *intelligentsia, using mostly ideological levers* [emphasis Z.B.] – and carried through fast, as long as there was enough capital of popular patriotic euphoria left to finance politically the economic costs of the dismantling of the patronage state" (Bauman, 1993: 144).

socialist societies [emphasis mine – G.K.]" (Savelsberg, 1995: 206), while Eboe Hutchful wrote simply of "Eastern Europe with its ... 'bourgeois' revolution" (Hutchful, 1991: 55).

Sometimes, as in Melanie Tatur's work, the term itself underwent some modification in the process: "In a different manner from the bourgeois revolutions, which released new structures which had already developed within the shell of the old order, the *quasi-bourgeois revolutions* [emphasis mine – G.K.] in Eastern Europe reveal a social vacuum" (Tatur, 1992: 68). And in some cases, like the article by Olga Kryshtanovskaya and Stephen White devoted to, as in Singer's pieces, the changes that took place in the USSR/Russia, the use of the phrase "bourgeois revolution" was even fortified with some argumentation:

> The redistribution of power ... appears to have been completed and with it the "second Russian revolution" has come to an end. It was a revolution in which a younger generation of the nomenklatura ousted its older rivals. In effect *it was a bourgeois revolution* [emphasis mine – G.K.], in that it led to a change in the sociopolitical system in the direction of private property and political pluralism. And it involved a redistribution of political power towards a group of younger, more pragmatic nomenklatura members, some of whom became politicians and some businessmen. In the economy there was a corresponding shift of power into property, based upon the privatization of the key sectors of the infrastructure: finance, retail trade, international economic relations, and the most profitable sectors of industry (especially the energy and mining complexes).
>
> KRYSHTANOVSKAYA & WHITE, 1996: 724

Apart from the explicit use of the term "bourgeois revolution" in the literature, one can also find a number of authors referring to it in the discussed context in a somewhat more subtle, but still sufficiently direct manner.[27] For example, in

---

27   I omit here, for obvious reasons, texts in which authors suggest that the bourgeois revolution in Poland took place at a different point in the 20th century than the turn of the 1980s and 1990s, as well as those written after the publication of Kowalik's 1996 article. (The latter still appear in the literature today; for example, Jacques Rupnik (2018) states that "The year 1989 stood for a 'bourgeois revolution' without a bourgeoisie" (p. 24)). Undoubtedly one of the most original theses, fulfilling both of the above criteria, is the one put forward by Andrzej Leder in his book *Prześniona rewolucja. Ćwiczenie z logiki historycznej* [An Over-Dreamed Revolution: Exercises in Historical Logic] (Leder, 2014), the content of which is well summarised by a critical reviewer of this work: "the thesis of *Prześniona rewolucja* is that, *contrary to popular belief, a bourgeois revolution took place in Poland* [emphasis mine – G.K.]. However, it did not take place after 1989, and even

a *New Left Review* article from 1990 Jürgen Habermas described the revolutions of 1989 as "rectifying":

> In Poland and Hungary, in Czechoslovakia, Romania and Bulgaria ... as revolutionary changes [of 1989] gather force and become revolutionary events – is also where one finds the clearest articulation of the desire to connect up constitutionally with the inheritance of the *bourgeois revolutions* [emphasis mine – G.K.], and socially and politically with the styles of commerce and life associated with developed capitalism, particularly that of the European Community.
>
> HABERMAS, 1990: 4–5

It is with reference to this very text by Habermas that two years later Krishan Kumar was to state "1789, the classic 'bourgeois revolution', is ... one obvious point of reference for the 1989 revolution" (Kumar, 1992: 318). Ernst Nolte, on the other hand, in his *Frankfurter Allgemeine Zeitung* article in 1991, wrote of a "conservative" revolution in the sense that it favours the bourgeoisie ("rehabilitates it", as the title says (Nolte, 1991: 27)). And Andrew Arato, in a 1993 text, states that "the revolutions of 1989 ... like all 'European' revolutions but unlike the Communist ones ... stop at the threshold of the *bourgeois* and the *nation* [emphasis A.A.], seeking presumably to preserve rather than to eliminate them" (Arato, 1993: 613).

---

less so before 1939; its proper epicentre was between 1939 and 1956. The problem is that, although the Polish masses were to be the ultimate beneficiaries, the proper subjects were first the Germans (who exterminated the Jewish bourgeoisie) and the Stalinists (who carried out the agrarian reform). The trauma of transpassive complicity in the extermination of the Jews and the expropriation of the land was to set in motion a process of erasing all memory of these crimes. The contemporary middle class, in denial of its own historical origins, is today pursuing either peculiar fantasies about its noble past or hyper-global models, the most grotesque embodiment of which is 'the dizzying career that sushi eating has made in the Polish bourgeoisie'" (Pospiszyl, 2013: 206). Interestingly, Stalinism in Eastern Europe is also considered a bourgeois revolution by Neil Davidson. Thus, in one of his articles, we read, for example, that "Russia experienced a counter-revolution as early as 1928, transforming a society which had been transitional to socialism into one based on an extreme form of state capitalism. [I] ... will show that it was this Stalinist model which was imposed by the USSR *in most of [E]astern Europe ... where it constituted neither counter-revolution nor the socialist revolution, but rather the modern form of the bourgeois revolution* [emphasis mine – G.K.]" (Davidson, 2015: 111). Due to the very different argumentation used to support such a thesis by Leder and Davidson, however, it seems that their proposals have little in common.

It seems that it was the relative popularity of statements like this that led a researcher in the middle of the first decade of the 21st century to conclude that "The revolutions in [E]astern Europe, as often stated, were bourgeois revolutions without a bourgeoisie" (Bohle, 2006: 75).[28] These "oft-made claims" were not limited to brief mentions, as some authors showed ambition to treat the problem in more depth. I am referring here in particular to the work of two authors representing the theoretical tradition of "state capitalism", Colin Barker and Colin Mooers, who presented their version of the thesis on the revolutionary-bourgeois character of 1989 in Eastern Europe and the arguments to support it as early as in 1994 (Barker & Mooers, 1994).[29] They were, however, apparently the only authors besides Kowalik to do so.

This brief review of the literature, leads to the general conclusion that Kowalik's "epigonic bourgeois revolution" thesis belongs to an unusually narrow group of authors who not only described the changes of the 1980s and 1990s in Eastern Europe as a "bourgeois revolution" but also tried to support this claim with argumentation. Perhaps it was for this reason that Jane Hardy counted Tadeusz Kowalik among the *co-authors* of the concept of "a bourgeois revolution without the bourgeoisie."[30]

Moreover, it is worth remembering that Kowalik formulated and presented his thesis for the first time in Polish. I have not been able to find any indication that anyone explicitly did so before him. And, last but not least, no one seems to have done so since, nor has Kowalik's authorship of the proposal

---

28 A similar, though somewhat less precise, opinion was expressed as early as 1994 by Elmer Hankiss: "The difficulties encountered by the transition process and the mistakes made by the new elites have given a new momentum to Marxist thought inside and outside the region. Most of the Marxist, Post-Marxist, Neo-Marxist critics welcome the defeat of Bolshevism and the introduction of the basic institutions of democracy and market economy. But their overall assessment of the transition process is radically negative. They state that a counter-revolution, and not a genuine revolution, has taken place in East Central Europe since 1989. *A kind of bourgeois revolution* [emphasis mine – G.K.] which is the best way to establish a nineteenth-century-type of free market capitalism à la Chicago in this region" (Hankiss, 1994: 536).

29 A few months after the publication of the text by Kowalik in *Nowe Życie Gospodarcze* [New Economic Life], Barker and Mooers' paper, in an expanded version, appeared as (Barker & Mooers, 1997). I will discuss its content in the book's conclusion.

30 "Neo-Gramscians and other radicals, however, have reinserted class analysis into the transformation agenda, but in arguing that there was a bourgeois revolution without the bourgeoisie suggests the absence of a capitalist class in Poland (and the rest of CEE) before 1990" (Hardy, 2009: 48). For the sake of accuracy, it should be noted that Hardy refers in this passage to Kowalik's comments from a text later than the article published in *Nowe Życie Gospodarcze* (Kowalik, 1996b) – chapter of the monograph of 2001 (Kowalik, 2001b).

been questioned. It therefore seems justified to assume that Tadeusz Kowalik's thesis was completely original in Polish-language literature. Kowalik himself seemed to be convinced of this. Thus in 2003, he wrote: "I justify *my* [emphasis mine – G.K.] thesis (which I have been proclaiming for six years) that August 1980 was an epigoneic-bourgeois revolution" (Kowalik, 2003: 225), while in a paper from 2007 he claimed: "the peculiarities [of the Polish transformation] that persisted for a long time, albeit in different tensions, led me to express the opinion in 1996 that one of the most unjust socio-economic systems of Europe of the second half of the 20th century had been established in Poland. This *empowered me to describe the Polish (counter)revolution as epigonic* [and] *bourgeois* [emphasis mine – G.K.]. The further course of events only strengthened my conviction" (Kowalik, 2013h: 189).

The view that Kowalik's thesis is completely original in Polish-language literature is supported by the findings of Piotr Borowiec, who reviewed the terms used to describe the Polish revolution of 1989. He finds references to

> "rationed revolution" or ... "controlled revolution". ... the neologism "refolution" was also coined by Timothy Garton Ash. ... [It appeared] ... that Solidarity's activity was called a "revolution of common sense". ... Adjectives that were added at the time to the metaphor "revolution" ... included [also]: "peaceful", "revolution in the majesty of the law", "velvet", "gentle", "quiet", "self-limiting", "bloodless", "negotiated", "legal and constitutional". ... terms have [also] appeared in the discourse: "creeping", "democratic", "[revolution] of Solidarity", "revolution of 1989", "peaceful revolution of Solidarity", "Polish", "[revolution] of freedom", "evolutionary", "systemic", "civilisational", "liberal", "personnel", "market", "moral". ... In the same context the formulations were used: "anti-communist revolution of 1989", "peaceful revolution of 1989", "[revolution] of a new beginning".
>
> BOROWIEC, 2013: 376–378, 381[31]

---

[31] To Borowiec's list, we should add at least one more term, which was used to describe the Polish revolution, as Kowalik himself drew attention to it by quoting the following fragment of an article by Janusz Surdykowski from 1990: "in Poland returning to Europe, an economic and psychological *liberalist revolution* [emphasis mine – G.K.] must first take place (that is, a formation of almost nineteenth-century capitalism with its original accumulation, exploitation and inequalities must arise), so that we can speak of more modern forms of organisation of the state and economy" (Surdykowski, 1990: 6; quoted in Kowalik, 2013a: 247). Borowiec's list, for obvious reasons – as it is based solely on the Polish discourse – does not take into account many terms functioning even only in the English-language literature, such as Habermas's (already mentioned) "rectifying"

Thus, among the terms collected by Borowiec, there is no "bourgeoisie" or "burghers."³²

In my opinion, the second fundamental originality of Kowalik's thesis lies in the fact that, like Barker and Mooers, he tackled the tough theoretical task of attempting to apply the concept of bourgeois revolution to the transformation from real socialism to capitalism, i.e. not, as was usually the case in the literature, from feudalism (or other historical modes of production, especially tributary)³³ to capitalism.³⁴ For a better understanding of the unusual nature of such attempts, it is worth briefly to cover the main contemporary theoretical positions on the bourgeois revolution as a notion itself.

As Neil Davidson explains, the term "bourgeois revolution"³⁵ was "first employed by the very moderate socialist Louis Blanc, who proclaimed in

---

revolutions (Habermas, 1990), "technocratic" revolutions (Eyal, Szelényi & Townsley, 1998) or "anti-revolutionary" revolutions proposed by Sakwa (2001).

32　However, this argument is somewhat weakened by the noticeable (and undoubtedly unavoidable) omissions to Borowiec's list. In his search he did not reach, for example, Tadeusz Kowalik's works devoted to the "epigonic bourgeois revolution" in Poland. Interestingly, the work of Kowalik is not alien to Borowiec as he mentions him as the author of the description of the Polish transformation as a "revolution from above" (Borowiec, 2013: 523).

33　Perhaps the shortest definition of it is given by Neil Davidson (2012) when he mentions "a mode of production ... [in which] the state acts as the prime extractor of the surplus" (p. 541).

34　For more on this subject, see (Davidson, 2012).

35　Here, it is necessary to draw attention to the distinction, considered legitimate by some authors, between *bourgeois* and *bourgeois-democratic* revolutions. The latter are, most generally speaking (especially according to Russian Marxists of the late 19th and early 20th centuries), revolutions that "would be both bourgeois in content (that is, ... [they] would establish the unimpeded development of capitalism) and ... [they] would introduce democratic politics that the working class could use to further its own demands" (Davidson, 2012: 207). In this book, however, following Jan Baszkiewicz, I will ignore such a distinction. He wrote that "[d]epending on the degree of activity of the people and their influence on events, many scholars distinguish between bourgeois and bourgeois-democratic revolutions: in the latter the role of the masses is particularly significant. However, Lenin made no such distinction: for him *bourgeois and bourgeois-democratic revolutions are synonyms* [emphasis mine – G.K.]. Precisely because in every genuine bourgeois revolution the presence of the people is the rule, in each of them he saw that element of democracy, although, of course, with very different intensity in different times and countries". And further on: "it is always a revolution that is both bourgeois and democratic. The first of these adjectives defines its tasks and the limits of its possibilities; the second – its character resulting from the active presence of the popular masses" (Baszkiewicz, 1981: 30–31). For an extensive discussion of the attitude of Lenin and other Marxist authors to the division between bourgeois and bourgeois-democratic revolutions, see (Davidson, 2012: 201–214 et seq.).

1839: 'Behold the bourgeois revolution of [17]'89!'" (Davidson, 2012: 117). Since then, the term has generated numerous theoretical disputes, which boil down to a lack of "agreement about what the essential qualities of the concept are" (Davidson, 2012: 487).[36] These have led to the development of several main positions, among which the three most important that deserve to be singled out are *revisionism*, *Capital-centric Marxism* and *consequentialism*.[37]

The revisionist approach to bourgeois revolutions was, as Davidson argues, by the end of the 20th century a

> consensus that can be summarized as follows: prior to the so-called bourgeois revolutions, the bourgeoisie was not "rising" and may even have been indistinguishable from the feudal lords; during the so-called bourgeoisie revolutions was not in the vanguard of the movement and may even have been found on the opposing side [of the conflict]; after them [the bourgeois revolutions], the bourgeoisie was not in power and may even have been further removed from control of the state than it had previously been; *above all, these revolutions had nothing to do with either*

---

36 The same is true of revolution in general. Eric Hobsbawm (2004) notes in this context that "[the] meaning of [the term] 'revolution' remains profoundly controversial, as the historiography of the subject demonstrates ..." (p. 455). Similarly writes Przemysław Sadura, whose "analysis of the ways in which 'revolution' is defined has revealed a complete lack of consensus on the criteria for this concept" (Sadura, 2015: 83).

37 Apart from Davidson, this division is recognised for example by Benno Teschke (2005) and Alexander Anievas and Kerem Nişancioğlu (2015). In doing so, the latter strongly advocate one of the aforementioned currents: "The 'consequentialist' interpretation of bourgeois revolutions subverts revisionist and Political [i.e. *Capital*-centric] Marxist critiques of the concept while providing a more apposite framework to understand their effects in their domestic and international dimensions" (p. 176). A polemic against their position can be found, for example, in (Post, 2018). In this book, I use the term *Capital*-centric Marxism (the capitalisation and use of italics is due to the reference to Karl Marx's *Capital* and not a common noun), preferred by some of the representatives of this current to the usual Political Marxism (see e.g. (Post, 2019: 158)). The latter article by Post is one of three that appeared in that issue of *Historical Materialism* devoted to the discussions around the notion of bourgeois revolution triggered by the publication of Neil Davidson's book (Davidson, 2012). The other two texts are (Gerstenberger, 2019), and (Davidson, 2019). They illustrate well the current state of discussion on the issue at hand. It should be noted, however, that the theory of bourgeois revolutions, as developed by the authors mentioned above, in many ways runs counter to theoretical considerations of revolution in general. This seems to be the reason why comprehensive monographs on bourgeois revolutions by Orsi (2009) or, especially, Davidson (2012) have so little in common with, for example, Chodak's (2012) work on revolutionary theory (in the latter, bourgeois revolutions appear explicitly only in the context of Barrington Moore's views (Chodak, 2012: 121–126)). This is, of course, true in both directions: theorists of bourgeois revolution do not usually refer to revolutionary theory in general.

> *the emergence or consolidation of capitalism* [emphasis mine – G.K.]. Depending on which version of the argument was in use at any time, this was either because capitalism had already fully developed before the revolutions and so did not require them or because capitalism only developed too many years after the revolutions for there to be any causal connection between them, or even ... because it was impossible to define feudalism or capitalism in the first place. Instead, revisionists claimed, these revolutions – if indeed they could be called revolutions – were just what they appeared to be and what participants said they were: *expressions of inter-elite competition for office, differences over religious belief and observance, or movements in defense of regional autonomy* [emphasis mine – G.K.].
>
> DAVIDSON, 2012: 366[38]

For quite different reasons, the use of the term 'bourgeois revolution' in the social sciences is opposed by the *Capital*-centric Marxists. Their position is presented by Charles Post, starting with an explanation of the genesis of the disputed concept itself:

> the notion of the bourgeois revolution is rooted in the early Marx's vision of the transition to capitalism. ... Marx argued that capitalism began in the medieval cities with the activities of merchants and artisans. The growing cities provided both a haven for peasants escaping serfdom and a market for agricultural goods. The growth of markets encouraged peasants to specialise output, innovate technologically and accumulate land and tools. Precapitalist propertied classes' hold on political power maintained old and created new impediments (legal coercion of direct producers, state-taxation and monopolies, etc.) to the deepening of markets. The bourgeoisie ... [therefore] leads its revolution and destroys these precapitalist remnants, allowing the free development of their new mode of production.
>
> POST, 2011: 247

However, according to Post,

---

[38] The revisionist position is similarly summarised by Bailey Stone (2020), according to whom "[revisionists] deemphasized long-term revolutionary causation and regarded European revolutions as originating in fortuitous convergences of short-term factors and also continuing on the basis of unpredictable contingencies" (p. x).

the growth of market-"opportunities" are not sufficient to disrupt the "rules of reproduction" of non-capitalist social-property relations. Instead, the *unintended consequences* [emphasis C.P.] of non-capitalist social classes pursuing the reproduction of their forms of social labour in very specific conditions of crisis and sharpened class-conflict *potentially lead to the emergence of capitalist social-property relations* [emphasis mine – G.K.].

POST, 2011: 247–248

In this context, Post also quotes an excerpt from the work of Robert Brenner, according to whom the concept of bourgeois revolution turns out to be unnecessary in a twofold sense:

First, there really is no *transition* [from feudalism to capitalism – G.K.] to accomplish: since the model starts with bourgeois society in the towns, foresees its evolution as taking place via bourgeois mechanisms, and has feudalism transcend itself in consequence of its exposure to trade, *the problem of how one society is transformed into another is simply assumed away and never posed* [emphasis mine – G.K.]. Second, since bourgeois society *self-develops and dissolves feudalism, the bourgeois revolution can hardly claim a necessary role* [emphasis mine – G.K.].

BRENNER, 1989: 280; quoted in POST, 2011: 248

Brenner's position (and that of other *Capital*-centric Marxists after him) is well summarised by Ellen Meiksins Wood. In her account, Brenner "argued that the 'bourgeois revolution' was a question-begging formula which ... assumed the very thing that needed to be explained by attributing to the bourgeoisie a capitalist rationality that needed only to be released from the bonds of feudalism" (Meiksins Wood, 1996: 221).

Thus "Brenner ... has demonstrated that the traditional conception of bourgeois revolution as an account of the transition to capitalism is circular and self-defeating. It cannot explain the emergence of a social form whose pre-existence it must assume" (Meiksins Wood, 1996: 223–224).

The third of the positions on bourgeois revolutions is consequentialism. Davidson, who counts himself among its representatives, explains that in this approach

individual bourgeois revolutions ... can be identified, not by the structural forms that they took, nor by the social forces that brought them about, but by their consequences, their outcomes [emphasis mine – G.K.]. Decisive among these consequences is the transformation of the state into one that – depending on where in the overall cycle a particular bourgeois revolution took place – *either initiates or consolidates the period of capitalist dominance* [emphasis mine – G.K.].

DAVIDSON, 2017: XIII[39]

He adds that this definition "does not commit us to a position that holds that the bourgeoisie has never been a revolutionary class; only that they are not required to be for the theory of bourgeois revolution to be coherent" (Davidson, 2017: XIII).[40] Thus, in the consequentialist view, not only is the bourgeoisie not necessary for bourgeois revolution to occur, but it can also happen that in the process of revolutionary change a social group fundamentally changes its socio-economic function. Davidson explains that

in some cases the personnel of a former ruling class remained in place while their role in the social relations of production changed – where, for example, slave owners became feudal lords or feudal lords became capitalist landowners.

DAVIDSON, 2012: 495[41]

Interestingly, even some representatives of the *Capital*-centric Marxism are inclined, at least as regards certain historical events, to accept the use of the term "bourgeois revolution" as proposed by the consequentialists. In this context, Charles Post, quoted above, provides what he calls a "minimal definition" according to which a bourgeois revolution is "a revolution that creates state-institutions capable of promoting the development of capitalist social-property relations. ... A revolution is *bourgeois* ... to the extent that it,

---

39 Similarly, Barker and Mooers (1997) write: "What gives a revolution its 'bourgeois' character is that it creates the conditions for capitalist development. This definition says nothing about the social background of those who carry out the reconstitution of the state. Bourgeois revolutions need not be carried out by actors who are capitalists or who are consciously acting in the interests of capitalism, though they may be" (p. 36).

40 Hobsbawm (2004) has a similar attitude to this issue. For him, "[revolutions] or at all ... such major sociopolitical upheavals as the French Revolution, belong to the class of historical phenomena whose significance is not to be judged by the intentions or expectations of those who make them, or even those which could be imputed to them by subsequent analysis. Such intentions are not, of course, irrelevant to the study of the phenomenon. However, they cannot determine it, because uncontrollability of process and outcome is its essential characteristic" (p. 457).

41 Baszkiewicz (1981) succinctly expresses essentially the same view: "revolution changes the classes that participate in it" (p. 186).

intentionally or unintentionally [emphasis C.P.], advances capitalist development in a given society" (Post, 2011: 249–250).[42]

In the light of the main presented contemporary positions on the question of bourgeois revolutions, the theoretical originality of Kowalik's "epigonic bourgeois revolution" thesis seems unquestionable. Revisionists and *Capital*-centric Marxists fundamentally deny the notion of bourgeois revolution any cognitive value and even consequentialists, it seems, reject its application to contemporary events like the transformation of real socialism into capitalism.[43] It is worth noting here that, in this respect, Marxist approaches

---

42   At this point it is also appropriate to indicate the approaches to the problem of bourgeois revolutions that have been developing, especially in recent decades, on the borderline between the two Marxist positions discussed above (*Capital*-centric Marxism and consequentialism) and which pay particular attention to the problem of international relations. As Benno Teschke, perhaps the most important exponent of this line of research, writes: "The international enters as an intervening moment in the determination of revolutionary origins, courses and outcomes – either in terms of revolutions triggered by wars, outside intervention, the export of revolution, multilateral attempts to contain or re-admit the revolutionary state into the society of states, or, indeed, by revolutionising the very principles upon which the international order operates" (Teschke, 2005: 22). Bertel Nygaard believes similarly and, writing about the French Revolution, proposes an original reinterpretation of this event as a bourgeois revolution precisely in the international dimension: "But national states and societies cannot be seen as developing in a void, according to formally universal standards. They develop within concrete totalities of international contexts. The same turmoil that produced a delay in French industrial development [in the 18th century] also provided Britain with the crucial opportunity to cement its competitive advance on its main commercial rival, thereby giving impetus to the industrial revolution and the immense strengthening of that country's economic position during the 19th century. *Within an international framework the [French] Revolution produced capitalist results without delay, even though these results were geographically displaced and, in an immediate sense, contradictory to the development of French national capitalism* [emphasis mine – G.K.]. Also, the French revolutionary centralization and rationalization of the state [during and immediately after the revolution – G.K.] had enormously significant international effects on the developments of states in other parts of continental Europe" (Nygaard, 2007: 167).

43   This is the case with Davidson, who, in the context of the events in Eastern Europe between 1989 and 1991, writes: "Rather than describe them as bourgeois revolutions, they seem to me to be far better understood as examples of the broader category of *political* revolution [emphasis N.D.]" (Davidson, 2012: 380). Elsewhere in his book, however, Davidson argues that "As capital increasingly sweeps away even the remnants of previous modes of production and the social formations that include them, the pattern of revolutions has increasingly tended toward the 'political' rather than the 'social' type, starting with the revolutions of 1989 in Eastern Europe that swept away the Stalinist regimes and began what Chris Harman called the 'sideways' movement from Eastern state capitalism to an approximation of the Western trans-state model" (p. 464). Let us add that by political revolutions Davidson means "struggles within society for control of the state,

(*Capital*-centric Marxism and, at least in part, consequentialism) are based on a classic interpretation of historical materialism.⁴⁴

This does not change the fact that, for my further analysis, consequentialism will be of particular importance. Not only because, as I have shown above, it is the only one of the three main approaches that is open to using the concept of bourgeois revolutions in historical and sociological research (without which my considerations would become pointless). It is also because, in view of its reliance on final consequences as the sole criterion for classifying revolutions as bourgeois, it is so inclusive that – at least hypothetically, and in isolation from the actual views of the scholars representing this current – it makes it possible to analyse, in terms of bourgeois revolutions, events even far removed from the accepted conventions in the literature.⁴⁵

4

As a result of the originality of Kowalik's thesis on the Polish "epigonic bourgeois revolution" as described above, at least two important problems immediately emerge. First is whether Kowalik was right to describe the transformation as a bourgeois revolution at all. Tackling this requires a serious exploration of the theoretical debates between, in particular, the *Capital*-centric Marxists

---

involving factions of the existing ruling class, which leave fundamental social and economic structures intact" (p. 114). In contrast, "Social revolutions, ... are not merely struggles for control of the state, but struggles to transform it, either in response to changes that have already taken place in the mode of production, or in order to bring such changes about" (p. 114).

44 As Nygaard (2007) explains, "both Engels and Marx rejected the views ... that the orthodox conception of the concept [of bourgeois revolution] could be viewed as a universally applicable model for historical analyses and political strategy. According to them, it would be illegitimate to transfer forms and specific historical stages derived from one historical totality (e.g., English society around the 17th century) to another (e.g., Russia at the end of the 19th century) Abstract concepts such as 'transition to capitalism' and 'bourgeois revolution' cannot exist in a theoretical void; they have to exist in and through particular historical settings" (p. 158).

45 This does not mean, however, that the substantive superiority of consequentialism has been acknowledged, for the criticism of this position seems to be justified. As was succinctly summarised by Teschke (2005): "if this revised concept of 'bourgeois revolution' is unsure about its causal agent, unsure about its results, and unsure about its duration, then why should we still adhere to it as an over-arching explanatory category? In other words, while the content of the concept has been progressively eroded, many Marxists still hold on to its semantic shell" (p. 6). Discussions around these and other problems with the concept of bourgeois revolution still seem far from being categorically resolved.

and the consequentialists, and if it is assumed that the transformation from real socialism to capitalism can be analysed in terms of a bourgeois revolution after all, then it is necessary to focus on the course of the transformation, its political, sociological and economic content. However, since the sole subject of my interest is the ideas of Tadeusz Kowalik and not the disputes over the concept of bourgeois revolution or the actual historical events of the late 1980s and early 90s, I will leave the question of the substantive validity of the thesis unanswered in this book: the considerations contained herein will not be aimed at determining whether Poland did in fact experience an "epigonic bourgeois revolution" or any other (counter)revolution.

The second problem, every researcher of Tadeusz Kowalik's thesis faces, is how to set about confirming it and whether this confirmation, understood here as pointing to concrete events, circumstances and phenomena that, forming a coherent whole, would exhaustively prove the thesis, can be considered sufficiently convincing. A review of Kowalik's output, however, immediately reveals that he did not present a comprehensive, exhaustive argumentation in support of his thesis, not only where the "epigonic bourgeois revolution" was the main concept but also in his other works, in particular in what is probably the most important dissertation on the Polish transformation of 1989, the book *From Solidarity to Sellout* (Kowalik, 2012a).[46]

Here we come to a fundamental issue. My study of Tadeusz Kowalik's contribution leads me to hypothesise that the argumentation supporting this thesis is present in his works, but is scattered in numerous texts, fragments of which also contain important reflections on the revolutionary character of the Polish transformation.[47] However, this immediately raises another question: if these scattered remarks were to be found, could they together serve as justification for the concept of an "epigonic bourgeois revolution"?

Answering this very question about whether the selected views of Tadeusz Kowalik on the Polish systemic transformation, after a reconstruction into a coherent argumentation, constitute a convincing hypothetical justification for

---

46 There seems to be a rather prosaic reason: an extensive and exhaustive justification of the thesis put forward in 1996 was never Tadeusz Kowalik's aim. Although he repeated it consistently in many subsequent works, it always took place either in very short texts or, if in longer ones, only as a passing reference in the context of other considerations. I will return to this issue in the book's conclusion.

47 Apart from (Kowalik, 2009b) and his other works already mentioned above, it is also worth mentioning (Kowalik, 2002c) and (Kowalik, 2013j). Of course, this is by no means a complete list.

his thesis on the "epigonic bourgeois revolution" in Poland, will be this book's central aim.

In order to properly carry out the objective outlined above, it will of course be a key task to determine whether, in the argumentation thus reconstructed, Tadeusz Kowalik has, in fact, justified his proposal convincingly. A hint as to which method of evaluation may turn out to be the most appropriate is provided, among others, in the aforementioned article by Barker and Mooers. In their approach, an answer to "how should we categorize the 1989 revolutions" or, in other words, whether they can be described as bourgeois, depends on an earlier explanation of "what *common features* [emphasis mine – G.K.] do they share with revolutions of the past" (Barker & Mooers, 1997: 28). A similar view was also expressed by Marcin Kula, who, in connection with Jan Baszkiewicz's book *Wolność. Równość. Własność. Rewolucje burżuazyjne* [Liberty. Equality. Property: The Bourgeois Revolutions] (Baszkiewicz, 1981) wrote

> The historian needs a measure ... to compare phenomena, also when he does not assume that the world has to develop according to a single pattern. Measurements are used by historians even without them being aware of it – for example by referring the events to earlier ones (probably there has not been a historian of revolution who would not refer the process analysed, even if only tacitly, to the French Revolution). Concepts such as "the bourgeois revolution" (but equally well, for example, "fascism" or "intermediate system") are measures abstracted like this from reality. They are constructs, if you prefer models, ideal types, built on the basis of reality, but they fit to it (or it to them) in a graded manner and rarely in 100%. Of course, it may happen that some real *set of phenomena* [emphasis mine – G.K.] will become the "model" so characteristic that it will be recognised as a fully typical designator of the "model". Yet, because of the diversity of social phenomena, this hardly ever happens. *We compare the construct obtained by means of a mental operation to reality (or vice versa) and only then can we ascertain its diversity, the deviation of real processes from those considered most characteristic of a given class of, dare we say, typical phenomena. Only by means of comparison like this can we trace the frequency of particular features of the phenomenon's occurrence* [emphasis mine – G.K.].
>
> KULA, 1984: 145–146[48]

---

[48] I am leaving aside here entirely whether Kula and Baszkiewicz are right to regard the French Revolution as bourgeois. Probably the best-known example of the polar opposite position is the work of the *Capital*-centric Marxist George Comninel (1987).

And further, in direct reference to the methodology of research on bourgeois revolutions:

> The concept of "bourgeois revolution" is needed in research ... as a benchmark. In the actual reality we detect some degree of approximation to this pattern, or, more often in practice, some elements of it. Reality will become easier to understand. ... In the case of the French Revolution there is the greatest, though certainly also incomplete, correspondence between theoretical construct and reality. In the case of other processes, the correspondence between theoretical construct and reality is lesser or selective, and the whole series of European revolutions could be arranged in a scaled continuum according to their distance from the strict, otherwise non-existent, conceptual designator. Baszkiewicz, in fact, follows this procedure; of the French Revolution he says that that it was bourgeois "par excellence", and then he traces the history of other countries, *wondering what fragments are elements of transformations of the type being sought* [emphasis mine – G.K.]; and to what extent and in what aspects of reality these transformations took place.
>
> KULA, 1984: 146

These passages rightly point to the necessity of finding argumentation in support of the thesis for making an "epigonic bourgeoise revolution" an appropriate *point of reference* – some *model* of bourgeois revolutions that would identify the set of phenomena required to characterise revolutions of this kind.[49] However, since there it is no point seeking any indications like this in Tadeusz Kowalik's works – in particular, he has never presented his own, nor referred to any other theory of bourgeois revolutions (it seems that he may never have studied this issue in depth) – it is necessary to choose a point of

---

49 Strictly speaking, the research procedure described in the cited fragments of Kula's text belongs to the instruments of *Comparative Historical Analysis* (CHA) in the sense of Comparative-Historical Sociology. Jack A. Goldstone (2003) distinguishes "two main approaches used in CHA: *process tracing* and *congruence testing* [emphasis mine – G.K.]" (p. 47). Of these two, direct application in my book will be the latter, which "provides the basis for claims regarding 'common patterns' ... The goal of congruence testing is therefore not to establish universal generalizations across a broad ... range of cases. Rather, congruence testing uses the fruits of process tracing to challenge and improve our understanding of how particular cases [here: revolutions – G.K.] of interest are related or different. ... *Using congruence testing, scholars make claims about the number of cases that 'fit' a particular causal sequence or pattern (or 'model')* [emphasis mine – G.K.]" (pp. 50–51).

reference from among the proposals beyond his work based on a certain set of selection criteria.

Therefore it should first be noted that as a point of reference I need a concept of bourgeois revolutions inclusive enough not to a priori eliminate the possibility of recognising in this category events other than just the transition from feudalism (or other historically contemporaneous modes of production) to capitalism.[50] Otherwise, its usefulness in analysing Kowalik's reconstructed argumentation regarding the transition from real socialism to capitalism could prove to be very limited at best. On the other hand, I will need a model containing an extensive and descriptive *set of criteria* of what can testify to the existence of a bourgeois revolution. Only a list of this kind will facilitate any comparison of perceptions of the characteristics of the Polish systemic transformation as a "bourgeois revolution" with the concept adopted as a point of reference. Finally, it seems justified to look for the point of reference in the works of thinkers who are as close as possible to Tadeusz Kowalik in an intellectual if not biographical sense.[51] Issues like a diametrically opposed system of professed values or a completely different biography of the creator of the concept juxtaposed with Kowalik's work could, in my opinion, become a source of not-quite obvious, but still substantively important mismatches in comparative analysis.[52]

Of the studies known to me, the criteria outlined above are best met, it seems, by the synthesis of the classic Marxist position on bourgeois revolutions (also described by me as a *model*)[53] by the eminent Polish historian Jan

---

50 As Sławomir Magala (1983) expressed it in another context: "Understanding the twentieth-century revolutionary experience is necessary to build a theory of revolution that does not treat events earlier than the French Revolution of 1789 and later than the 19th century class struggles in France as exceptions and anomalies from the point of view of ideological doctrine and research paradigm" (p. 153).

51 I am fully aware, however, that this condition is very restrictive and de facto limits the search for a point of reference to the works of Polish authors. Let us add, in fairness, that the works are not very numerous, because, as Jarosław Chodak (2012) points out, "Theoretical reflection on revolution has rarely been undertaken in Polish social sciences" (p. 10).

52 I see the acceptance of such a condition as a far-reaching but necessary realisation in practice of Quentin Skinner's (1969) principle of writing a history of ideas, according to which "no agent can eventually be said to have meant or done something which he could never be brought to accept" (p. 28).

53 By model I mean, following Sheila Dow (2002), "a particular expression of a theory which potentially allows the theory to be tested. ... the theory has different implications depending on what is assumed ... The models are acting as mediators between the theory and the evidence" (pp. 96–97). Baszkiewicz's work presents, as it seems, just such a model mediating between the theory of revolution and the history of such events. This was, for example, the opinion of Stanisław Salmonowicz (1983), who claimed that Baszkiewicz

Baszkiewicz (1930–2011),[54] presented in his monograph *Wolność. Równość. Własność* (Baszkiewicz, 1981).[55]

5

Baszkiewicz's views on bourgeois revolutions in *Wolność. Równość. Własność* are summarised by critical reviewers of this work as follows:

> In the terms of … [Baszkiewicz], bourgeois revolution is – in simple terms – *a mass anti-feudal movement …. in which the bourgeoisie took the leading role … and which led to transformations towards capitalism* [emphasis mine – G.K.]. The adjective "bourgeois" distinguishes this kind of revolution not only from agrarian revolutions …, but also, as Marxists usually want, from socialist revolutions.
> GRINBERG, KOCHANOWICZ & MELLER, 1983: 743

They then note that

> The bourgeois revolutions were …, according to Baszkiewicz, events as varied as the Peasants' War in Germany, the American Civil War, the Polish national uprisings, and even the Meiji Restoration reforms imposed from above in Japan (Bismarck is also described as a revolutionary from above). *At the same time, it does not seem that the course of events themselves or their social context play a greater role in the labelling practiced* [emphasis mine – G.K.].
> GRINBERG, KOCHANOWICZ & MELLER, 1983: 743

---

decided in *Wolność. Równość. Własność* to construct such a "*model of bourgeois revolution* [emphasis mine – G.K.], that it accommodates all the variants of social movements in history, even those quite distant from it" (p. 252), as well as Marcin Kula, cited earlier (Kula, 1984). Baszkiewicz does not seem to deviate significantly in this respect from the general tendencies in revolutionary studies. Indeed, as Chodak's (2012) review of the literature shows, it is quite generally accepted that "theorists of revolutions use specific models of the phenomenon" (p. 26).

54 Baszkiewicz was "a recognised international-level authority on general history of state systems, political and legal doctrines, the Polish state and law, and the history of ideas, law and political systems in France, especially during the Enlightenment and the 19th century" ("Doktorat", 2008: 227). For more on Baszkiewicz's scientific and intellectual biography see (Banaszkiewicz, 2011; Olszewski, 2009; 2011).

55 In my reflections I will also take into account the findings of at least one polemic around this book (Czarnota & Zybertowicz, 1983; Baszkiewicz, 1983).

Stanisław Salmonowicz sees the same tendencies in Baszkiewicz's essay:

> For the author [of *Wolność. Równość. Własność*] Poland is also a country of bourgeois revolutions: [as Baszkiewicz writes] "Actually, all the national uprisings in Poland fall within the concept of bourgeois revolution" [p. 105]. .... The question arises: *how much do we have to expand the notion of bourgeois revolution to accommodate, for example, the November Uprising?* [emphasis mine – G.K.].
>
> SALMONOWICZ, 1983: 250

Marcin Kula, on the other hand, states that the definition of bourgeois revolutions adopted by Baszkiewicz "allows its application more broadly than in relation to a single, isolated historical period", concluding "There is an unstated assumption in Baszkiewicz's book about ... the universality of the phenomenon under consideration" (Kula, 1984: 135).

Baszkiewicz's concept is therefore, as the above assessments suggest, not only very inclusive, but also consequentialist.[56] It is not difficult to find arguments to support this view in his works. He claimed, for example, that it is "not by the social forces that caused them" that we recognise bourgeois revolutions, and that although "it would seem that the natural hegemon of a bourgeois revolution is the bourgeoisie; very often ... this does not prove to be the case. Very often ... the bourgeoisie, actively participating in the revolution, recedes ... into the background or shares the hegemony" (Baszkiewicz, 1981: 33–34). Finally, he went on to write explicitly: "What is important is the direction in which the revolution is oriented, how it resolves social contradictions; *direct, active participation of the bourgeoisie is not, as history teaches us, a condition sine qua non of bourgeois revolution* [emphasis mine – G.K.]" (Baszkiewicz, 1981: 33–34).

Moreover, the quoted reviewers' remarks concerning the inclusiveness of Baszkiewicz's work also turn out to be accurate; its author not only approached bourgeois revolutions in a consequentialist manner, but also did not exclude the possibility of considering reformist activities as such. For example, he wrote that "deep (structural) *reforms are not the "opposite" of revolutions,* [emphasis mine – G.K.] ... [because] as Engels clearly explained – every revolution ... next to storming the Bastille and beheading kings, consists precisely of reforms"

---

56 In other words, Jan Baszkiewicz's views can be classified as close to the position Teschke (2005) calls "associated with the [Marxist] orthodoxy" (p. 5), and he includes in this group Christopher Hill, Lawrence Stone, Perry Anderson, Geoff Eley, Richard J. Evans, Eric Hobsbawm, Alex Callinicos, Colin Mooers and Neil Davidson.

(Baszkiewicz, 1983: 146). And in *Wolność. Równość. Własność*, he explicitly stated that

> if … the bourgeois revolution does not gain the upper hand, if it is bogged down in a prolonged power struggle or if it fails, the reforms for which the social situation is ripe will also occur. The old regime will carry them out under the pressure of the revolution or out of fear of it. Even the dramatic defeat of the revolution will not block the bourgeois transition: counter-revolutionary terror is incapable of stabilising the situation for any length of time. Reactionary regimes must also resort to structural reforms, which become a component of the broad process of revolutionary change. … *Thus revolutions and reforms are intertwined throughout the revolutionary cycle.* … *Sometimes … this process of reform "from above" is accelerated by violent means. Then we are dealing with a "revolution from above" controlled by the authorities.* [emphasis mine – G.K.]. Not every, even very important, structural reform can be described thus. *Revolution from above is a violent, brutal narrowing of the process of change and differs from evolutionary reformism. The classic example of revolution from above is Bismarck's actions in 1866–1871* [emphasis mine – G.K.].
> BASZKIEWICZ, 1981: 26

This is all the more important because, as we will see later, for some time Tadeusz Kowalik also used the term "revolution from above,"[57] in his case: in reference to the Polish transformations of the late 1980s and early 1990s.[58]

---

57 A term introduced, it seems, by Frederick Engels, and denoting, in the most general terms, fundamental political and social changes imposed by the elites on a subordinated population. In the Introduction to Marx's *Class Struggles in France 1848–1850*, Engels, in the context of Louis Bonaparte's gaining power in December 1851, writes that "The period of revolutions from below was concluded for the time being; there followed a period of *revolutions from above* [emphasis mine – G.K.]" with the following comment: "The gravediggers of the Revolution of 1848 had become the executors of its will" (Marx & Engels, 1990: 513). Alex Callinicos (2010) points out the affinity of this concept with Antonio Gramsci's concept of *passive revolution*: "the mode of passive revolution fits well the 'revolutions from above' that instituted the dominance of modern industrial capitalism across the 19th-century world" (p. 495).

58 He was not alone in this. As Chodak (2012) points out, "The political developments of the late 1980s and early 1990s in Eastern Europe prompted a revision of the notion of revolution. Apart from the absence of violence, the most noticeable feature of these events was the progressive blurring of the boundary between reform and revolution. These transformations were [therefore] associated with earlier cases of *revolutions from above* [emphasis mine – G.K.] or revolutions of elites" (p. 21).

What is probably most important in this context, however, is that Baszkiewicz did not rule out the possibility of interpreting not only his contemporary events but even future ones relative to the time of writing in terms of the bourgeois revolution (or, in the minimum variant: in terms of "the realisation of its tasks"). In *Wolność. Równość. Własność* we read, for example, that "even today [in 1981] in many Third World countries the realisation of the democratic tasks fulfilled by the bourgeois revolution is the order of the day. ... This gives the reflection on the bourgeois revolution a special feature of topicality" (Baszkiewicz, 1981: 29). And in the rest of the book, we learn that "the tasks of the bourgeois revolution – democratisation of the system and emancipation from the rule of foreign capital – are still waiting to be realised today in many countries of Latin America and, more broadly, of the Third World" (Baszkiewicz, 1981: 236).

Baszkiewicz's work also seems well suited to the needs of this book to present a list of features of bourgeois revolutions. As the author of *Wolność. Równość. Własność* explains "all historical works on revolution can be divided into two categories: they either deal with the aetiology or the anatomy of revolution. *My essay obviously belongs to the second category* [emphasis mine – G.K.]" (Baszkiewicz, 1983: 142).[59] The first chapter of Baszkiewicz's book, followed by chapters three to six, discuss exactly this "anatomy", systematically, thoroughly and with examples, referring to the constitutive features of bourgeois revolutions (such as revolutionary consciousness, the detonator of revolution, the problem of hegemony or revolutionary terror). Many valuable organising remarks can also be found, as we shall see, in some of the polemics around *Wolność. Równość. Własność*.

Finally, Baszkiewicz's work has, I believe, another advantage as a point of reference: the intellectual and biographical "kinship" between its author and Tadeusz Kowalik. Both wrote primarily in Polish with all the possible consequences. Both belonged to the same generation born a few (Baszkiewicz) or a dozen (Kowalik) years before Second World War, which they lived through as children. Most of their professional life was in the Polish People's Republic, including, in particular, the formative period in the 1940s and the first half of the 1950s. Both Baszkiewicz and Kowalik were for many years members of the Polish United Workers' Party (Koredczuk, 2015: 280; Kowalik et al., 2013: 631) for ideological reasons as is quite clear from the statements of both. What is probably most important, however, is that both for a long time counted themselves

---

59 Baszkiewicz seems to have borrowed the term "anatomy of revolution" from the title of Crane Brinton's book (Brinton, 1938), to which he refers in *Wolność. Równość. Własność* (Baszkiewicz, 1981: 30), even titling a subsection of his essay in this way (pp. 30–42).

among the representatives of Marxism in the broad sense of the term and later, after parting with it, both continued to draw on it.[60] The fact that Baszkiewicz was a contemporary of Kowalik's, Polish and openly Marxist, in a way shields my investigations against the accusation that the result of the comparative analysis is from the adoption of an inadequate point of reference, a theory written tens or hundreds of years prior to Kowalik's work in a completely different linguistic and cultural environment etc.[61]

However, let us pause for a moment at the question of both authors' Marxism. I have already signalled the connections of Tadeusz Kowalik's thought with this current, and I will also return to them in the conclusion of this book. On the other hand, Stanisław Salmonowicz comments on the relationship between the works of Jan Baszkiewicz and Marxism, as follows: "the author has used much of his artistry as a researcher and astute comparatist to prove that nineteenth-century views still retain their full value" (Salmonowicz, 1983: 252), only to specify elsewhere that "the only support for the analysis carried out [by Baszkiewicz in *Wolność. Równość. Własność*] are carefully collected quotations from the writings of Marx-Engels [sic!]" (Salmonowicz, 1983: 250). Similarly, Daniel Grinberg, Jacek Kochanowicz and Stefan Meller write that Baszkiewicz's book is "clearly situated in the current of Marxist deliberations" (Grinberg, Kochanowicz & Meller, 1983: 739), and Mikołaj Banaszkiewicz summarises its content as "faithfully reflecting the views of the classics of Marxism" (Banaszkiewicz, 2011: 38). Finally, in the context of his essay, Tadeusz Łepkowski describes Baszkiewicz simply as a "rigorous Marxist" (*marxiste rigoureux*) (Łepkowski, 1983: 232).

Baszkiewicz himself was open about his appreciation of Marxist thought. In his book we read, for example, that "Marx, Engels and Lenin's general theory of revolution contains explications of the revolutionary process that are applicable to all revolutions and concern their deep causes, the revolutionary situation, the motor forces of revolution and revolutionary hegemony" (Baszkiewicz, 1981: 11). Interestingly, his views in this respect have not changed

---

60 Despite outlining the similarities, it is also worth remembering the differences between the two scholars. For example, although I have included them in the group of Marxists, one cannot forget that Kowalik quite early – perhaps still during his studies at the Institute for Training Scientific Cadres (Instytut Kształcenia Kadr Naukowych, IKKN) in the 1950s became associated with a circle of revisionist intellectuals to which Baszkiewicz does not seem to have belonged.

61 It is worth noting at this point, however, that there is no indication that Tadeusz Kowalik was familiar with Jan Baszkiewicz's texts on the bourgeois revolutions, or at least that he used them when writing his work. A more thorough examination of this issue would of course require in-depth archival studies.

fundamentally over the years; in the text originally published in 1998 we read, therefore, that "the basic theses [in the field of revolutionary theory] of these [nineteenth-century] thinkers [Alexis de Tocqueville and Karl Marx] have *remained up-to-date* [emphasis mine – G.K.] (in particular the distinction between revolution as a complete social transformation and political revolution)" (Baszkiewicz, 2009a: 799).

The quoted fragments from Baszkiewicz's work also indicate a more general feature of his writing, which at the same time constitutes another link to Tadeusz Kowalik. The author of *Wolność. Równość. Własność*, similarly to Kowalik with his *value disclosure*, did not hide his political views and sympathies, which he expressed, for example, in the following commentary:

> While I was writing my essay [*Wolność. Równość. Własność*], I received a letter from an anonymous reader. He informed me that he had bought a biography of [Georges] Danton I had written and had even begun to read it, but had immediately thrown it into a dark corner when he found that at the very beginning I had referred to "Herr Marx" [sic!]. I confess that this encouraged me to make particularly intensive use of the socialist classics. *Please also pay attention to the metric of my essay: it shows that it was published in October 1981. It is not worth recalling what the attitude of a large part of our intelligentsia towards Marxism and Marxists was then* [emphasis mine – G.K.]. Is it so difficult to understand that *an abundant reference to "Herr Marx" can simply have the character of a world-view and ideological declaration? For I believed – and I still believe – that the negative attitude towards "Herr Marx" manifests, apart from political obstinacy, a pathetic provincialism, which weighs so heavily on our intellectual life* [emphasis mine – G.K.]. Of course, I understand very well that in science ideological declarations are not enough – what matters is results, not intentions.
> BASZKIEWICZ, 1983: 139

6

The proper realisation of the aim of my book depends on, I believe, the correct and strict definition of its framing analytical assumptions. A fundamental assumption (and only an assumption) is undoubtedly that the "bourgeois revolution" is a cognitively valuable concept of the social sciences. If we allow for the possibility, as do e.g. the representatives of revisionism and *Capital*-centric Marxism, that the set of bourgeois revolutions is in fact empty, and analyses in these categories are therefore usually devoid of substantive justification, the examination of Kowalik's thesis would immediately become obviously pointless.

Moreover, the aim and thematic scope of the book condition my adoption of consequentialism, in its most inclusive variant, i.e. the assumption that it is possible to also consider the transformation of real socialism into capitalism in terms of bourgeois revolutions. Related to this is another assumption that it is possible to apply to a specific socio-economic system, like real socialism, strictly defined historical categories, such as *class, bourgeoisie*, etc.[62] I also assume, as I have already explained, that among the available concepts of bourgeois revolutions, the synthesis (model) by Jan Baszkiewicz will be appropriate for the purposes of this book.

Two further assumptions relate directly to Tadeusz Kowalik's work. The first is the recognition that by writing about the "epigonic bourgeois revolution" Kowalik meant the bourgeois revolution and not any other type of revolution or, taking into account that he used, among others, the phrase "epigonic bourgeois counter-revolution" a counter-revolution (this will be discussed in detail later in the book). Secondly, in the absence of Kowalik's comprehensive argumentation that would support his thesis, it is assumed that my reconstruction of his selected views on Polish systemic transformation may be regarded as a justification of just this kind.

Finally, the third group of assumptions that condition my analysis are those concerning the applied method. They revolve around taking the position that the application of *Congruence Testing*, a procedure from the tool box of comparative historical sociology, is also possible in the case of research in the field of the history of ideas. This means, in particular, allowing for the use of a selected model of bourgeois revolutions to assess the conformity not so much of historical events, but of their description as interpreted by a selected thinker. I also assume the possibility of applying to the analysis of views on relatively contemporary events, theories developed (also or primarily) on the basis of experiences from the distant past.

Taking on these assumptions, in the further part of the book I will reconstruct, in turn, Tadeusz Kowalik's thesis on the Polish systemic transformation as an "epigonic bourgeois revolution" (chapter one), Jan Baszkiewicz's views on bourgeois revolutions (chapter two) as well as Tadeusz Kowalik's views on

---

62 Possible exceptions to this rule, resulting from their meanings in the context of events in Poland in the 1980s perhaps departing too far from those grounded in theory, will be discussed separately and in detail.

the Polish systemic transformation into an argumentation in favour of his thesis (chapter three). In the conclusion I will attempt to compare the reconstructions of the second and third chapters.

Significantly, all the aforementioned reconstructions will essentially fall into the *rational* category. Richard Rorty, recognising them as one of the four main ways of writing the history of ideas (alongside *Geistesgeschichten*, historical reconstructions and doxographies),[63] provides the following characterisation:

> Rational reconstructions typically aim at saying that *the great dead philosopher had some excellent ideas, but unfortunately couldn't get them straight because of "the limitations of his time".* They usually confine themselves to a relatively small portion of the philosopher's work [emphasis mine – G.K.]... They are written in the light of some recent work in philosophy which can reasonably be said to be "about the same questions" as the great dead philosopher was discussing. They are designed to show that the answers he [the philosopher] gave to these questions, though plausible and exciting, *need restatement or purification* [emphasis mine – G.K.] or, perhaps, the kind of precise refutation which further work in the field has recently made possible.
>
> RORTY, 1984: 56–57[64]

However, this is not, I think, the only account of the concept of rational reconstruction in contemporary philosophy of science that can be applied in my book. A slightly different understanding of it was presented, for example, by Imre Lakatos in *Proofs and Refutations* (Lakatos, 1976). As Harro Maas points out, in this work

---

63   It is worth noting at this point that this is not the only possible classification. In particular, with regard to economic thought, it is worth noting the "four broader categories in which HET [history of economic thought] can be classified" identified by Marcuzzo (2008): "textual exegesis", "rational reconstructions", "contextual analysis", and "historical narrative" (p. 108). Let us note here that in her article Marcuzzo subjects the use of "rational reconstructions" (here understood as attempts at "contemporary understanding of the issues addressed by past authors" (p. 109)) in relation to economic thought to well-deserved criticism. However, given both the purpose of this book and the material on which the considerations in it are based, it seems that this criticism does not apply in this case, and the use of Marcuzzo's proposed alternatives would be unwarranted.

64   The very concept of rational reconstructions is clearly much older than Rorty's work, and over the years, even considering only twentieth-century philosophy, various meanings have been attributed to it. For more on this, see (Sady, 1990).

> *a rational reconstruction presents a logical sequence of arguments, it does not present these arguments in their historical order of appearance* [emphasis mine – G.K.]; ... This was Lakatos's distinction between rational and historical reconstructions; *a rendering of the logic of the argument versus a rendering of the actual course of events* ... [emphasis mine – G.K.]. Lakatos's notion of rational reconstruction enables us to see how historical positions can be reconstructed as an exchange of arguments that may lead to the present, but do not need to be framed in modern vocabulary. ... For Lakatos, historical reconstructions were [instead] about the actual order of historical positions (that might differ from its rational reconstruction).
>
> MAAS, 2013: 78

In the light of the above definitions, it seems, first of all, that the reconstructions I make will fulfil all the criteria outlined by Rorty. Thus, I shall discuss problems raised by the "late great philosophers", but left unfinished by them (although not so much because of the "limitations of the times", but rather due to the fact that the thesis of the "epigonic bourgeois revolution" in Poland in the work of Kowalik, or Baszkiewicz's attempts to outline a model of bourgeois revolutions were not among the main concerns of the two authors). I will be discussing this thesis in the light of another work (by Baszkiewicz), and I recognise that the concepts I am dealing with require certain contemporary additions or commentaries in the case of both thinkers.

Moreover, it seems that, in view of the fundamental aim of my analysis – the juxtaposition with a point of reference of an argument reconstructed into a coherent, rather than historically continuous whole, I must abandon the discussion of the works of both Kowalik and Baszkiewicz in the order of their creation, in favour of focusing on the reconstruction of logical coherence, which in turn remains in line with Lakatos's view.[65]

---

[65] It is worth adding that my combined adoption here of both Lakatos's and Rorty's positions finds grounds in the literature. Indeed, Matthias Klaes (2003) argues that "Lakatos's rational reconstruction can be regarded as a particular interpretation of the rationalist commitment underlying ... Blaug–Rorty rational reconstruction" (p. 501). Interestingly, it seems that Tadeusz Kowalik could also be regarded, under certain conditions, as a proponent of rational reconstructions. He applied such a method, although not necessarily with the awareness of this fact, when writing his monograph on Rosa Luxemburg (Kowalik, 2012b), and when deciding on the layout of the book *O lepszy ład społeczno-ekonomiczny* (Kowalik, 2013d). As the editor of the latter, Paweł Kozłowski, reports: "We considered several issues. The most important was to decide which point of view should dominate the collection: historical or problem-based. Should the whole be a review of the evolution of the author's views and of the themes he chose, or should it show the importance of the

All this, of course, while remaining fully aware of the limitations of reconstruction in the history of economic thought, particularly in relation to the necessity of making selections and interpretations as well summarised by Rodolfo Signorino:

> The reconstruction of the economic theory embodied in the text of a past writer is influenced by the conscious or unconscious *a priori* value judgements of the interpreters. Interpreters have their own views on what constitutes *the* [emphasis R.S.] right economic theory or *the* [emphasis R.S.] correct procedure to distinguish good economic analysis from bad, or, more simply, on *the* [emphasis R.S.] exact solution to the analytical problem(s) tackled by the economist(s) of the past under scrutiny. No reconstruction can take place without selection and each selection implies evaluation.
>
> SIGNORINO, 2003: 332–333[66]

---

problems and themes, irrespective of the time of their presentation? I preferred the first, historical perspective. Tadeusz Kowalik opted for the second" (Kozłowski, 2013b: 11).

66 A similar thought was expressed much more briefly by Kozłowski (2014), who wrote that "a history of ideas, as belonging to the field of humanistic research, is based on interpretation" (pp. 50–51). However, this view, which seems to be well established in historiosophy, can be put perhaps even more plainly. Thus, Carr (1990) simply states that "history means interpretation" (p. 23), elsewhere in his essay, specifying that "The point of view of the historian enters irrevocably into every observation which he makes; history is shot through and through with relativity" (p. 70). Signorino's quoted claims about selection are also in line with Carr's views: "The historian is necessarily selective. The belief in a hard core of historical facts existing objectively and independently of the interpretation of the historian is a preposterous fallacy" (Carr, 1990: 21). In relation to the study of revolutions, such a view was expressed, exceptionally succinctly, e.g., by John Dunn (1972) when he wrote that "The value-free study of revolutions is a logical impossibility for those who live in the real world" (p. 2).

CHAPTER 1

Tadeusz Kowalik's Thesis on the Polish Systemic Transformation as an "Epigonic Bourgeois Revolution"

1

Kowalik begins his short article from *Nowe Życie Gospodarcze* (issue of 15 September 1996 (Kowalik, 1996b)) devoted to the "epigonic bourgeois revolution"[1] by drawing attention to what he considers to be the obvious fact that "the workers played the key role in the bourgeois revolutions of continental Europe" (Kowalik, 1997a: 49).[2] In order to confirm this, in this text and in several others in which he refers to the thesis, he quotes the following excerpt from a paper by Oskar Lange from 1931, entitled "Kryzys socjalizmu" [Crisis of Socialism] (Lange, 1990):

> When, after the war in all the countries of [C]entral Europe, in Germany, Austria, Hungary, Poland, the remains of the ancient regime collapsed and, on the wreckage of the Hohenzollern, Habsburg and Romanov monarchies, bourgeois democratic republics were created, it was the workers' movement which was the creator of these republics. Since the workers' movement did not have the strength to endow the newly created republics with a proletarian class character, it was unable to avoid the republics

---

1 Or, as he sometimes referred to it, the "epigonic-bourgeois revolution" (with a hypen). Kowalik used such a term, for example, in the title of a chapter from 2003: "Polska rewolucja epigońsko-mieszczańska na drodze do Europy" [Poland's Epigonic-Bourgeois Revolution on its Way to Europe] (Kowalik, 2003). However, this did not seem to have any bearing on the content of the thesis itself.
2 In the remainder of this chapter, I will mainly quote this particular translation of Kowalik's article, as the only complete and literal one. This is because the second of the previously mentioned translations of this text, published in *Dissent* as "The Polish Revolution" (Kowalik, 1997c), differs slightly from the original: apart from a few minor changes, such as the omission of some sentences referring to the details of the Round Table Agreements, in this version a paragraph in which Kowalik quotes a fragment of Edward Lipiński's work (see (Lipiński, 1981: 592–593), as quoted in (Kowalik, 1997a: 52)) was deleted and two paragraphs devoted respectively to the role of the Catholic Church in the Polish systemic transformation (and in public life in general) and to the influence of the nomenklatura on the course of the revolution described (Kowalik, 1997c: 27) were added.

> it had created becoming bourgeois states. This created [...] the tragicomic situation in which workers' parties created republics which were in their sociological content bourgeois states.
>
> LANGE, 1990: 93; quoted in KOWALIK, 1997a: 50

In each of the texts devoted to the "epigonic bourgeois revolution", Kowalik comments on this quote in a similar way, but perhaps most synthetically in *Systemy gospodarcze* [Economic Systems], where we read that

> the quoted opinion [of Lange] expresses a thought which fits the Solidarity revolution very well: *the bourgeois, capitalist revolution was the work of, as it used to be, a mass movement of wage workers* [emphasis mine – G.K.]. As a result of spectacular mass strikes, first in Lublin, then in Gdańsk, Szczecin and Silesia [the order of the strikes indicates that Kowalik has July and August 1980 in mind here – G.K.], they achieved a great political victory, often called a revolution. *However, in the summer of 1989, this victory quickly turned into their defeat* [emphasis T.K.]. *A "bourgeois class state" emerged* [emphasis mine – G.K.], which promoted the version of capitalism least favourable to the workers of Central Europe.
>
> KOWALIK, 2005a: 358[3]

According to Kowalik, this pattern of events was recreated in Poland "during the years 1980–1992" (Kowalik, 1997c: 27), "in virtually classic form" and the immediate causes of this revolution "dependent on mass unemployment, impoverishment and glaring inequality" (Kowalik, 1997a: 52) he sees in the following combination of circumstances

> The temporary alliance of the workers with the intelligentsia, which was entrusted with programmatic matters, the highly important support of the [Catholic] Church, together with international financial

---

3   Another version of this commentary reads: "I believe that in ... the opinion [of Lange] here there is a fundamental idea that vividly fits the Solidarity revolution. Namely: the bourgeois, capitalist revolution was the work, as it used to be, of a mass movement of wage workers. The result, and this is paradoxical, was one version of capitalism which I have no hesitation in describing as one of the most unjust social systems of the second half of the 20th century. ... *It is a peaceful transformation of a revolution into a counter-revolution, into the defeat of the victors* [emphasis mine – G.K.] ... The politically victorious struggle was to mean an acute social and economic defeat for the victors themselves" (Kowalik, 2003: 225).

organisations, made possible the peaceful transformation of a workers' revolution into a bourgeois one.

KOWALIK, 1997a: 51

In at least one text, Kowalik also adds that significant for the occurrence and course of such a revolution in Poland were the specific circumstances – due to the conditions of real socialism – in the social structure:

> The novelty of the situation in Poland is that the labour movement did not confront a stronger, better-organized force. A fully fledged *capitalist revolution* [emphasis mine – G.K.] took place under conditions where a *bourgeois class* [emphasis mine – G.K.] and its organized representation were non-existent. Thus the new rulers were anticipating the future in creating the foundations of a new system favourable to the *middle-class-to-be* [emphasis mine – G.K.].
>
> KOWALIK, 2001b: 224

Thus, from the above excerpts we learn that, for Tadeusz Kowalik, the essence of the "bourgeois revolution" or the "capitalist revolution" was the establishment of a "bourgeois class state", that is, the restoration of capitalism in Poland, in the version "least favourable to the workers" (it was based on "mass unemployment, impoverishment, and glaring inequalities"); that it came about as a consequence (at least initially) of the high activity of the wage workers; the nature of the final outcome was influenced by the "temporary alliance" of workers with the intelligentsia and the involvement of the Catholic Church and international organisations; and finally: that it all took place in conditions in which there was no real bourgeoisie and its organised representation.

The quoted statements, however, also show that Kowalik, by putting forward his thesis, left more questions open than he managed to answer. First of all, in the context of the above-quoted fragment of the 1996 article, the very formulation of the title is striking: *Sierpień – epigońska rewolucja mieszczańska*, which translates as *August: An Epigonic Bourgeois Revolution* (or, as in David Holland's translation, *August: A Bourgeois Epigone Revolution* (Kowalik, 1997a)), which clearly suggests that the author considers the events of August '80 (or, more generally, the years 1980–1981) to be a bourgeois revolution. In another work, Kowalik wrote straightforwardly: "I justify my thesis (which I have been proclaiming for six years) *that August 1980 was a bourgeois epigone revolution* [emphasis mine – G.K.]" (Kowalik, 2003: 225).

However, this position does not seem to be confirmed either by the *Nowe Życie Gospodarcze* article content or by Kowalik's views expressed in any of his other works on the subject. This formulation reveals a contradiction consisting not only, as I have shown above, in Kowalik's much broader definition of the framework of the events: in 1980–1992, but also in the unambiguous indication of the consequence of those events. Kowalik writes explicitly, in more than one work, that there was a transformation in Poland from a "workers' revolution into a bourgeois revolution" or from a "revolution into a counter-revolution" and thus, firstly, that in that period there were de facto two revolutions and not one, and secondly, that it was not the "workers'" August of '80 that was the "bourgeois revolution" (or "counter-revolution", I will return to this issue), it only came *afterwards*.[4]

What is more, Kowalik gives strong grounds in his works for recognising not only the Solidarity of 1980–1981 but also the later movement up to mid 1989 as a workers' movement, on behalf, and in the interest of, the workers. He comments on the events of that breakthrough year as follows in *Systemy gospodarcze*:

> politically victorious struggle was to mean an acute social and economic defeat for the *victors* themselves [i.e. the workers; emphasis mine – G.K.] ... Violent upheavals, and especially bloody revolutions, often bring unexpected and unwanted results. In Poland, however, the transfer of power took place peacefully, as a result of a compromise reached earlier. *The workers were supported by the intelligentsia* [emphasis mine – G.K.], which facilitated this compromise ...
> KOWALIK, 2005a: 358–359

If, as Kowalik claims, the workers in 1989 were "victorious", this means that at least until the middle of 1989 there could still be no talk of a "bourgeois" revolution, even if (and this is unclear in light of Kowalik's work) he no longer perceives the events of that time as a workers' revolution. What is more, since in 1989 Polish workers were, as we read, only "supported" by the intelligentsia,

---

4 This interpretation is confirmed not only in Kowalik's works but also by other authors writing about the same events. For example, Zbigniew M. Kowalewski in his article entitled strikingly similar to the text by Kowalik from 1996: "Sierpień – zdradzona rewolucja" [August: A Revolution Betrayed], states unequivocally that "these events [the 1980–1981 revolution] were a typical and classic *workers' revolution* [emphasis mine – G.K.]" which, however, "was broken by Martial Law" (Kowalewski, 2005: 9). A convincing argument in favour of the thesis that the revolution which broke out in Poland in 1980–1981 had a workers' (and therefore certainly not a bourgeois) character is developed in (Siermiński, 2020).

it means that, in Kowalik's opinion, they were still the subject (or driving force) of the events taking place.

Finally, Kowalik referred to the issue discussed here directly in at least one of his statements. In an interview with Krzysztof Lubczyński in 2006, he stated that he did not see a direct connection between the August Agreements and "later events leading to capitalism. The basic events and choices, the decisions that led to capitalism of the type of the primitive accumulation of capital, took place in the late spring and summer of 1989" (Kowalik & Lubczyński, 2013: 342). Thus, the title of the 1996 text, suggesting the "bourgeois" character of August '80, as well as some of Kowalik's statements (e.g. about the "bourgeois, capitalist revolution being the work of ... the mass movement of wage workers") should be regarded as, at best, rather unfortunate mental shortcuts.

2

The above considerations point to some problems requiring resolution with the thesis in question. The first is at what precise moment in Polish history, according to Kowalik, was the "epigonic bourgeois revolution" supposed to have taken place?

There are some hints in the two passages quoted above ("However, in the summer of 1989, this victory [of the workers] quickly turned into their defeat" and "The basic events and choices, the decisions that led to capitalism of the type of the primitive accumulation of capital, took place in the late spring and summer of 1989"). There are many more similar formulations in Kowalik's works.[5] In the first place, it is worth noting the following paragraph:

> At the beginning it might have seemed that the [parliamentary] elections of 4th June 1989 were a victory for the representation of a strong workers' movement, inspired by the idea of self-government, a movement – let us repeat – which was social democratic in its basis. And meanwhile, starting from this victory, *in the summer of that year there was a turn to the right* [emphasis mine – G.K.] that resulted in the creation of one of the most unjust socio-economic systems in 20th century Europe. *The*

---

5 I omit here the less strict statements by Kowalik (but entirely consistent with the line of argument I have presented) which point to 1989 in general as a revolutionary period. These include, for example: "in 1989 ... Poland embarked on the unfortunate path of political transformation" (Kowalik, 2013h: 186) or the formulation proclaiming that 1989 was the "Year of the Great Choices" (Kowalik, 2002a: 82).

> workers' revolt [sic!] *found its culmination in the bourgeois-epigonic restoration of capitalism on the Anglo-Saxon model* [emphasis mine – G.K.].
> KOWALIK, 2013b: 212

Apart from the very important last sentence, from which it once again follows that Tadeusz Kowalik equates the epigonic bourgeois *revolution* and the epigonic bourgeois *restoration of capitalism*, and that in his considerations we are dealing with de facto two revolutionary events (before and after the "turn to the right"), in the quoted fragment we also find an explicit statement that this turn to the right took place in the summer of 1989, *after 4th June* of that year.[6] This remains in line with Kowalik's more theoretical observation that "*Until late summer 1989* [emphasis mine – G.K.], however, all these reforms were kept within the limits of the former socio-economic mega-system [real socialism – G.K.]" (Kowalik, 2001b: 224). And finally, one more clarification: in *From Solidarity to Sellout* we read that "*in September 1989* [emphasis mine – G.K.] ... [a] leap to a private market economy was proclaimed, supposedly based on tried-out schemes" (Kowalik, 2012a: 189). It seems justified, therefore, to assume that – despite the general 1980–1992 timeframe – Tadeusz Kowalik regarded 1989, particularly the late summer of that year, as the "bourgeois revolution" that he had referred to.

At this point, however, another problem of a chronological nature becomes apparent with Kowalik's thesis. Since the strikes that, as Kowalik writes in one of the passages quoted above, led to the "political success" of the revolution, took place in 1980, and the "bourgeois revolution" only in the second half of 1989, how should we perceive the continuity (or lack thereof) between these events? In particular: did the "transformation of the workers' revolution into a

---

6 Kowalik writes about this in a similar way in at least several other works. In a text published in *Gazeta Wyborcza* in 2002, he states that for him "1989 was a time of great hope (*first half of the year*) [emphasis mine – G.K.] and equally great disappointment (*second half*) [emphasis mine – G.K.]", and further that in Poland in the same year "*suddenly in late summer* [emphasis mine – G.K.] the philosophy of jumping into the 'free market' began to take hold" (Kowalik, 2002b: 20). Furthermore, in a 2009 interview, he claims that "Solidarity went to the elections with the slogans of the Round Table Agreements, not contradicting the old Solidarity programme. *The change came in the summer of 1989* [emphasis mine – G.K.]" (Kowalik, 2009a: 11), and in the "Preface" to the first volume of Stanisław Gomułka's published documents (Kowalik, 2010b) we read that "the basis [of this publication] ... is the documentation of the *eventful second half of '89* [emphasis mine – G.K.], and its main content is the process of preparing what went down in history as the Balcerowicz Plan" (Kowalik, 2010a: 13). Finally, in *From Solidarity to Sellout* Kowalik notices that "*late in the summer* [of 1989; emphasis mine – G.K.] decisions were taken that determined the victory of the Anglo-Saxon version of capitalism, built through shock and sacrifice" (Kowalik, 2012a: 52).

bourgeois revolution", of which he writes, take place, as some of his statements suggest, only in 1989 itself, or did it perhaps encompass almost the entire decade of the 1980s?

Unfortunately, although, as we will see in the following chapters Tadeusz Kowalik referred several times to the changes which took place in Solidarity in the 1980s, he left too few indications, most often of a too general nature (and sometimes simply contradictory), to be able to attempt an unambiguous answer to the questions posed above. In particular, it seems that Kowalik never resolved whether the changes he described took place gradually and continuously throughout the 1980s, or whether there was a sudden breakthrough in 1989. This is well illustrated by two quotations from *Systemy gospodarcze*. First, Kowalik writes that "for a quarter of a century (since the first Solidarity, not 1989) our country has been undergoing processes of radical reforms and profound system changes" (Kowalik, 2005a: 6) and then, only a few pages later, he states that "in the late 1980s and early 1990s, the communist system unexpectedly collapsed" (Kowalik, 2005a: 12).

3

As I have already shown, Tadeusz Kowalik wrote in the context of the Polish transformation about a "revolution", a "counter-revolution" and even a "workers' revolt". In an article from 1996 he also referred to these events as a "social upheaval" (*przewrót społeczny*).[7] This is part of another problem with the discussed fragment of Kowalik's work, which is the lack of terminological precision. While I will not refer to the terms "upheaval" and "revolt" as only mentioned in passing,[8] it seems necessary to discuss the dichotomy of the terms "revolution" and "counter-revolution", which appears in Kowalik's work.

---

7 "The largest labor movement in Europe brought about a *social upheaval* [emphasis mine – G.K.] from which there emerged one of the most inequitable social systems that the continent has seen in this century" (Kowalik, 1997c: 27).

8 As an aside, it can only be noted that, as Jan Baszkiewicz explains, "the difference between an upheaval and a revolution is the absence of significant transformations in the class basis of the system. A putsch or coup d'état often only changes the personnel arrangements: this is usually the case with palace upheavals. ... A putsch or coup d'état can also mean a one-off violation of the principles of the system, after which everything returns to the old track ... and can finally overturn all political institutions without any change in class rule" (Baszkiewicz, 1981: 19–20). As for the distinction between revolution and revolt, Baszkiewicz points to the crucial importance of the class consciousness of the revolutionary masses, their organisation and the revolutionary project: "Consciousness and organisation: this is perhaps the key to explaining the 'sterility' of revolts. They generally lack a realist

In the literature on the subject, the problems of distinguishing between revolution and counter-revolution or one type of revolution from another are, one would think, quite common. For example, in the context of the transformations in Eastern Europe in the late 1980s and early 1990s, Catherine Samary mentions "the combined traits of 1989–1991: a challenge to the political and socioeconomic structure of the existing system in a capitalist sense (*revolutionary or counter-revolutionary, according to perspectives*) [emphasis mine – G.K.], but through reforms imposed from above" (Samary, 2020). Neil Davidson, on the other hand, points out that "Although it will no doubt astonish future generations, one of the persistent problems of the left for much of the twentieth century was an inability to distinguish between bourgeois and proletarian revolutions" (Davidson, 2012: XII).

Not surprisingly, Tadeusz Kowalik also faced similar difficulties. As the already quoted fragments show, he presented at least two different interpretations of the events that took place in Poland in the 1980s. According to the first, the workers' revolution broke out first, and later – the bourgeois revolution (Kowalik's "peaceful transformation of the workers' revolution into a bourgeois revolution"). According to the second, the country experienced only one revolution – a workers' revolution, which was followed by a bourgeois counter-revolution ("peaceful transformation of a revolution into a counter-revolution").

What is important, is that there is no indication that Kowalik attempted to make a decision on this issue. Thus, in his later works he wrote, for example, about the "epigonic bourgeois (counter)revolution" (Kowalik, 2013h: 189) thus avoiding the need to choose between the two interpretations. Of course, this does not mean that his works are completely devoid of reflection in this regard. For example, in the 2011 chapter we read:

"revolutionary project" – even when their leaders ... formulate a mature programme which goes beyond vague egalitarianism. Revolts also lack the ability to organise the conquered territory. These two weaknesses distinguish a revolt from a revolution, even an unsuccessful one" (Baszkiewicz, 1981: 22). However, this does not exhaust the issue, because, as the author of *Wolność. Równość. Własność* goes on to argue, it is actually quite easy to confuse a revolution with a putsch, upheaval or coup d'état. Baszkiewicz also points to what he calls a *pseudo-revolutionary situation*, which "only on the surface appears to be revolutionary. The classic example is the passion in France at the turn of the 20th century around the case of [Alfred] Dreyfus. It stirred up incredible passions, conflicts and polemics. It seemed to many people that the entire social order was breaking down and that the country stood on the threshold of revolution. However, the crisis almost exclusively affected the educated and well-off strata; its impact on the masses was negligible. Jules Guesde wrote that the workers saw in the Dreyfus affair only 'a civil war among the bourgeoisie'" (Baszkiewcz, 1981: 125).

> Bronisław Łagowski is ... right when he writes that Solidarity "in its deeper historical dimension was a counter-revolution, but empirically it proceeded like a revolution while also being self-limiting". I gave a similar meaning to the description of August 1980 as an epigonic bourgeois revolution.
> KOWALIK, 2011a: 15–16[9]

In Kowalik's works devoted to the Polish transformation, the fragment quoted above is probably closest to explaining how its author understood the term "counter-revolution" in the context of the systemic transformation in Eastern Europe. However, in other texts we find statements that cast doubt on whether Kowalik could have been inclined to such a "counter-revolutionary" interpretation. For example, he wrote in 2001

> [In 1989] workers lost in social as well as political terms. Was this because, as some argue, [in 1918] workers had had to be bought off at a time when the socialist revolution was knocking at the door, whereas 70 years later it was a period of *counter-revolution* [emphasis mine – G.K.]? *Obviously, there is something in this, but as an explanation it is too general. Also too simplistic, though not without a grain of truth, is the belief of many rank-and-file trade unionists that they were betrayed by the intellectuals* [emphasis mine – G.K.].
> KOWALIK, 2001b: 237[10]

Tadeusz Kowalik went a step further in *Polska transformacja*, where the possibility of counter-revolution was directly reduced from the level of theoretical considerations to merely a question of how a social group perceives the surrounding reality:

> [I don't feel I need to] repeat my highly critical assessment of the Polish transformation here, of its bourgeois epigonic character, *perceived by the workers, who were the main actors of the "Solidarity" revolution as an expression of counter-revolution* [emphasis mine – G.K.].
> KOWALIK, 2009b: 221[11]

---

9   In the passage quoted above, attention is also drawn to Kowalik's repeated reference of the term "epigonic bourgeois revolution" to August '80. The work he cites is (Łagowski, 2010).
10 What is interesting is Kowalik's suggestion that by counter-revolution we can mean the betrayal of a former ally, rather than the actions of an overt enemy known from the beginning.
11 The above sentence reveals at least one more paradox in Kowalik's statements. In the fragment quoted earlier – agreeing in this with Bronisław Łagowski – Tadeusz Kowalik seems

Finally, two more circumstances should be noted in this context. Firstly, Kowalik mentions the *primitive accumulation of capital*[12] as an important element of the transformational reality, supporting the thesis of a "bourgeois revolution" (this issue will be discussed later in this chapter). It seems very unlikely that Kowalik linked this classically Marxist concept with the conviction that there was a counter-revolution rather than a revolution in Poland. Secondly, it is worth referring at this point to the inspiration for Kowalik's considerations, already signaled earlier, which is a paper by Oskar Lange from 1931. In it, Lange wrote about "the role which the workers' movement fulfilled in Central Europe, the role of a continuator and finisher of the bourgeois revolution" (Lange, 1990: 92) at the same time suggesting that what was meant was a situation in which the workers' movement participated in the bourgeois revolution to the end (or even independently "finished" it) and therefore certainly not a transformation into a counter-revolutionary movement at some point in its course. All this together allows me to assume that Kowalik's thesis should be considered in the categories of revolution rather than counter-revolution.

---

to refer to Solidarity as a counter-revolutionary force. Here, however, the trade union and the entire social movement are presented (as we already know: not for the first time) as a de facto subject of the workers' revolution, against which this counter-revolution is directed. Interestingly, this passage, which in *Polska transformacja* constitutes the opening paragraph of one of the subsections of chapter 13, has disappeared completely from the English edition (see (Kowalik, 2012a: 302)).

12 Kowalik explained his understanding of the term "primitive accumulation" in several works. Thus, in an article from 1996, we read that "In the post-communist countries (PCC) several phenomena *reminiscent of primitive capital accumulation (mass and permanent unemployment, impoverishment of the majority of people, growing criminality) have emerged* [emphasis mine – G.K.]. ... One economic need of primitive capitalist accumulation was to create conditions for economies of scale, by introducing a technological division of labour, and by building modern transport and other elements of an integrated national economy" (Kowalik, 1996a: 289, 293). Most often, however, when referring to primitive accumulation, Kowalik meant only the impoverishment of the broad masses. This is how he wrote about it, for example, in a chapter from 2003: "in the current half-century [second half of the 20th century – G.K.] numerous countries have been industrialised, in Europe – e.g. Scandinavia and Austria, and in Asia (Japan, Taiwan) without the impoverishment of significant groups of the population, *without primitive accumulation of the British or even German type* [emphasis mine – G.K.]. However, following the 'principles' of English *primitive accumulation of capital, with its mass impoverishment and exploitation* [emphasis mine – G.K.] in more recent times it means the impoverishment of human capital" (Kowalik, 2013k: 136).

4

Tadeusz Kowalik's thesis raises at least two other terminological problems. Firstly, it seems necessary to establish why Kowalik wrote about a "burghers'" (*mieszczańska*) and not a "bourgeois" (*burżuazyjna*) revolution: indeed, in probably all his works on the subject published in Polish, including especially his 1996 article, Kowalik uses the term *epigońska rewolucja mieszczańska*, the very literal translation of which is "epigonic burghers' revolution". In particular, it is worth considering whether the author of *From Solidarity to Sellout* used the term "burghers" instead of "bourgeoisie" on purpose, taking into account the differences between the terms, or whether he considered them to be essentially the same, making the decision to use one and not the other for reasons other than rhetoric.

In this context it is worth noting what seems to be a fairly common view among scholars that the bourgeoisie is a term specific to capitalism, while burghers is a more general term, usually applied to pre-capitalist formations. This is how Ryszard Kołodziejczyk, for example, explains it:

> The word "bourgeoisie" comes from the French la bourgeoisie [sic!] or burghers. *However, these are not completely unambiguous terms* [emphasis mine – G.K.]. The term bourgeoisie is used colloquially today to describe the main [in the sense of dominating – G.K.] class of capitalist society. Thus the word bourgeoisie is not applied to the pre-capitalist epoch ... *The bourgeoisie ... includes only the wealthiest part of the burghers proper* [emphasis mine – G.K.] in the formative period of the victory of the capitalist economy. Therefore *the emergence of the bourgeoisie as a formed stratum or social class is connected with the development of the capitalist social and economic formation* [emphasis mine – G.K.]. It is thus a creation of modern times, being born together with capitalism.
>
> KOŁODZIEJCZYK, 1979: 138–139

It cannot be entirely ruled out that Tadeusz Kowalik – taking into account the absence of the bourgeoisie in real socialism (at least in the formal sense), to which he drew attention in one of the passages already quoted, where he wrote about "creating the foundations of a new system *favourable to the middle-class-to-be*" – used the word "burghers" in his thesis on purpose, wanting to avoid references to the bourgeoisie. It seems more likely, however, that he completely ignored the possible differences between the bourgeoisie and the burghers, and took over the reference to the latter from the authors whose works he used when writing the article for *Nowe Życie Gospodarcze*.

In the aforementioned paper by Lange from 1931, frequently quoted by Kowalik in works devoted to the "epigonic bourgeois revolution", the author, when referring to events commonly known in the literature as "bourgeois revolutions", consistently and without exception writes about "burghers' revolutions", even though he uses the term "bourgeoisie" many times in the text. Lange's identification of the "burghers" with the "bourgeoisie" is perhaps best illustrated by the following passage from "Kryzys socjalizmu":

> Austrian Social Democracy ... understood that the state which it had created, which it was ready to defend at any time against the return of the Habsburgs, was nothing more than *a burghers' class state* [emphasis mine – G.K.], *"eine Bourgeoisrepublik"* [bourgeois republic] (as Otto Bauer called it), that this state is, like every burghers' state, only an apparatus of class rule *in the hands of the bourgeoisie* [emphasis mine – G.K.].
> LANGE, 1990: 94

Thus, we are most likely dealing with a rather imprecise and anachronistic terminology adopted by Kowalik from Lange's text. It should be added here that the use of the words "bourgeoisie" and "burghers" interchangeably in Polish, including in scholarly literature, does not seem to be without precedent even among scholars studying the issue of bourgeois revolutions. It happened, for instance, to Jan Baszkiewicz[13] or Stanisław Salmonowicz,[14] which undoubtedly only strengthens the interpretation that Kowalik treated these terms as synonyms. Especially since, as one can assume, he did so not only in the context of the Polish "epigonic bourgeois revolution": from one of his texts we learn, for example, that the French revolution was "liberal-burghers'" (Kowalik, 2013l: 98).

Finally, when Kowalik presented his thesis in English, he simply used the term *bourgeois revolution*. This term can be found, among others, in the texts in *Labour Focus on Eastern Europe* and *Dissent* of 1997 and in *From Solidarity to Sellout*. Taking into account that, at least in the case of the latter work, we know for sure that Kowalik closely cooperated with the translator in the post-translation process,[15] it seems safe to assume that if his intention in using the

---

13 "For the bourgeois revolutions, undoubtedly the common denominator is the active presence of the popular masses. Without their intervention, a real *burghers' revolution* [emphasis mine – G.K.] is impossible" (Baszkiewicz, 1981: 30).
14 "[T]here can only be talk of a bourgeois revolution if it is actually *the burghers* [emphasis mine – G.K.] that grasp power" (Salmonowicz, 1983: 252).
15 I am grateful to Ms Eliza Lewandowska, translator of *Polska transformacja* into English, for providing me with valuable information on this subject.

term "burghers" in Polish was to differentiate between this social stratum and the bourgeoisie, he would have referred to it in some way.

The second terminological issue that needs clarification here is Tadeusz Kowalik's use of the term "epigonic". As he explained in his 2003 chapter, he regarded the Polish "bourgeois revolution" as

> epigonic in three ways.[16] Firstly, it drew on *patterns which had already disintegrated after the First World War* [emphasis mine – G.K.]. The revolutions ... [in Central and Eastern Europe in 1918–1919 – G.K.] meant a *political* defeat for the workers, but not a *social* defeat [emphasis T.K.]. From the social point of view, they meant the creation of the foundations of the welfare state (e.g. in Poland the eight-hour working day and many other workers' rights). In contrast, after 1989 we have both the political and social defeat of the working majority.
>
> KOWALIK, 2003: 226

Then Kowalik adds that, in his opinion, an epigonic revolution also took place in Poland,

> in the sense that ... [it was] *long overdue. In the second half of the twentieth century, a number of countries carried out industrial modernisation without the primitive accumulation of capital* [emphasis mine – G.K.]; without shifting income from the poor to the rich. Examples were Austria, Finland and even Spain. In none of these countries *was modernisation based on capital accumulation leading to the absolute impoverishment of large social groups* [emphasis mine – G.K.]. Rather, there was an uneven increase in incomes, but nevertheless an improvement in living and working conditions of all basic social groups. Apart from the countries mentioned above, this probably also applies to all the "Asian tigers".
>
> KOWALIK, 2003: 226

Finally, for Kowalik, the Polish "bourgeois revolution" of 1989 was also

> an epigonic revolution in the sense that it *promotes primitive accumulation of capital in conditions when it is not necessary* [emphasis mine – G.K.] because, with all reservations, Poland is at an average level of

---

16 In an article from *Nowe Życie Gospodarcze* an analogous sentence reads: "I define this [revolution] as an epigone revolution *in two senses* [emphasis mine – G.K]" (Kowalik, 1997a: 51).

> development. We are not in *the phase of transition from manual production to mass, factory production* [emphasis mine – G.K.] where the proverbial first million dollars was stolen to buy machines and establish factories. There is no such need. The quite rapid GDP growth in the years 1994–1999 proved precisely that a small modernisation and transfer of a part of the production apparatus into private hands was enough to make the economy much more efficient. It turned out that a high GDP growth rate was possible with small modernisation outlays and only a partial change of the ownership structure.
>
> KOWALIK, 2003: 226[17]

Kowalik's in itself clear and exhaustive argumentation requires, however, a few words of commentary. First of all, it seems that the statement made in the article from 1996, that the "bourgeois revolution" is "epigonic" in two senses, was much closer to the truth. The second and third arguments quoted above boil down to Kowalik's rejection of the necessity of a primitive accumulation of capital as an alleged condition of modernisation or improvement of economic efficiency. On the other hand, the first and second arguments essentially consist of a claim about a time mismatch – a "lateness" or "obsolescence" of ideas which, according to Kowalik, constituted the theoretical foundations of the Polish transformation. Therefore, it would not, I believe, be unreasonable to state that Kowalik presents the "epigonic" nature of the Polish "bourgeois revolution" only in de facto one, broadly conceived, dimension: the adoption of the long outdated view of the indispensability of primitive accumulation for the introduction of changes in the economy and society as the main principle of the systemic transformation.[18]

---

17 In article of 1996 Kowalik writes more briefly on the same subject: "But this was an epigone's revolution in another sense. This type of bourgeois revolution has already become increasingly a relic of the past. In many countries modern private market economies have been established without the primitive accumulation of capital on the American, English, or even German model. On the one hand, this makes possible the association of (equity) capital; on the other, the fact that these new revolutions took place in countries in which big industry (often too big) already existed meant that the accumulation of the proverbial first million through speculation, theft, or fraud was not necessary to assist the transition from manufacture to industrial production. For the same reason, the impoverishment of some to increase the capital of others was entirely unnecessary" (Kowalik, 1997a: 51–52).

18 The hypothesis that an *anachronism* understood in this way is an essential element of the epigonism of the "bourgeois revolution" in Kowalik's work is to some extent supported by the content of the (as I have already explained: slightly modified) translation of *Sierpień...*, which appeared in the journal *Dissent* in 1997 (Kowalik, 1997c). In a new paragraph, not present in the original, the phrase *imitative bourgeois revolution* is used

5

Tadeusz Kowalik inevitably came into contact with the issue of revolution in his academic and journalistic activity, from time to time taking the floor in discussions devoted to this topic. As early as 1957, in a text in *Życie Gospodarcze* [Economic Life] edited by Kowalik at that time, we read that "the popular masses make history. ... On a day-to-day basis, primarily as producers, but as the revolutionary ranks in periods of breakthrough" (Kowalik, 2013f: 429–431), and further on:

> For the mass revolutionary movement, scientifically expressed theses alone cannot suffice as ideology. They are spontaneously supplemented by beautiful ideals arising from the people's longing for a happy future and by their preferred slogans and mottoes. Is it any wonder that the simple soldiers of the revolution are dreamers and at the same time so often utopians?
> KOWALIK, 2013f: 430–431

Nor could he completely disengage from this issue in his study of Rosa Luxemburg. Thus, from *Theory of Accumulation and Imperialism* we learn, for example, that

> already during the first Russian revolution, Rosa Luxemburg popularized Marx's well-known thesis that in the conditions of a delayed bourgeois-democratic revolution (Germany, 1848) there is a possibility of its direct transformation into the socialist revolution. There is no evidence that she abandoned this opinion later on.
> KOWALIK, 2014: 125

And in the article by Kowalik with Włodzimierz Brus, we read that

> the problem of the changes in capitalism is broader than that of revolution or decline. The revolution may only be an unnecessary step in a process of reforms. And it is not merely a matter of those reforms that are implemented by the bourgeoisie in a conscious attempt to placate the

---

(Kowalik, 1997c: 29). In turn, the sentence which in the original reads "I define this as an epigone revolution in two senses" (Kowalik, 1997a: 51) in *The Polish Revolution* was changed to "I see Poland's revolution as a revolution of the epigones, as *a pale imitation of an earlier revolution* [emphasis mine – G.K.], in two senses" (Kowalik, 1997c: 27).

restive workers. Changes undertaken in the interests of the bourgeoisie may also pave the way for the other civilization.

BRUS & KOWALIK, 1983: 246

However, in the period of several years preceding Tadeusz Kowalik's thesis on the "epigonic bourgeois revolution" in Poland, one very specific issue from the theory of revolution appeared in his oeuvre, which seems to be of particular importance for my considerations. This is well illustrated in a text from 1991 entitled "Zmiana ustroju – wielka operacja czy proces społeczny?" [Regime Change: A Great Operation or a Social Process?] (Kowalik, 1991c) in which, incidentally, Kowalik included many elements that would later form the basis of his arguments in the most important works on the Polish systemic transformation[19] and, probably for the first time in such a developed way, he applied the notion of "revolution from above" to the events in Poland at the turn of the 1980s and 1990s. Discussing what he calls the "constructivism" of Leszek Balcerowicz and his team, Kowalik writes thus:

> The concept of *"revolution from above"* [emphasis mine – G.K.], of the state as the great demiurge, including the obsession with the great need for speed, is based on the deep conviction that society, or at least its majority, is, or is becoming, more and more opposed to designed transformations. In the best case, the "representation" of future social interests can be invoked, i.e. a kind of Lukácsian "potential consciousness", only this time not of the working class, but of a specifically conceived "civic society", or the much desired middle class. The constantly emphasised difficulty is that this longed-for middle class has yet to be created. ... And this is precisely what this *revolution from above* [emphasis mine – G.K.], or the revolutionary state, is supposed to do.
>
> KOWALIK, 1991C: 33

Kowalik dealt with the issue of the possibility of conducting a "revolution from above" in real socialism even before 1989.[20] However, it was due to the systemic

---

19   Among others, criticism of the Balcerowicz Plan and its creators' (especially Jeffrey Sachs), emphasis on the role of Waldemar Kuczyński and his influence on Tadeusz Mazowiecki for the shape of the Polish transformation, criticism of the claims about the "non-alternative" character of the Plan, references to the thought of Ralf Dahrendorf etc. (Kowalik, 1991c).

20   In an article on the "crucial reform" of real socialism, polemicising with Richard Lowenthal, Kowalik wrote, among other things: "I believe that the dependence of the economy on the political system has been too closely identified by Lowenthal with the

transformations that it occupies a permanent place in his texts. Thus, in a polemic with an article by Maurice Glasman (1994) we read: "As a programme for the stabilization of the economy, the Balcerowicz Plan had undeniable successes. However, as a programme for *revolution from above* [emphasis mine – G.K.], it was a failure" (Kowalik, 1994: 134). And in a chapter of the 1995 monograph, Kowalik wrote: "Even today, when the belief in the rapid building of capitalism has disappeared and the possibilities of *'revolution from above'* [emphasis mine – G.K.] have been exhausted, it is still assumed that there is no alternative to the initially formulated programme of transition" (Kowalik, 1995: 106).

Importantly, the differences between the revolution "from above" and the "epigonic bourgeois" revolution seem to be quite significant in Kowalik's work. When writing about the former in the context of the Polish transformation, he does not refer, for example, to August '80, nor to the dynamics of the events of 1980–1992, nor even only to those that took place in 1989. For Kowalik, the "revolution from above" in Poland, in the first half of the 1990s, was the Balcerowicz Plan alone.

Nonetheless, several years of considering the "revolution from above" were probably an important stage in Kowalik's work on the 1996 thesis. It is worth noting in this context the chronology: references to the transformation of the real socialist economy in terms of a "revolution from above" are present in Kowalik's work until the mid-1990s but not later. After 1996, he probably never uses the term, and when writing about the Polish transformation as a revolution he calls it exclusively "epigonic bourgeois" (in various variants). It seems, therefore, that the "revolution from above" preceded the "epigonic bourgeois" one in Kowalik's deliberations, and was then completely supplanted by the latter.[21]

But where did this change come from? The direct impulse, directing Tadeusz Kowalik's deliberations in the direction of the "bourgeois revolution",

---

mobilization functions of the state, and particularly with the frequent *'revolutions from above'* [emphasis mine – G.K.]. Direct mobilization of society by the party or by the state for the attainment of their different objectives may become less and less frequent, or even wither away. Those in power may give up making *'revolutions from above'* [emphasis mine – G.K.], yet under 'real socialism' the party and the state will exercise a much more extensive control over the economy, its organization and adopted goals than in any capitalist country, including those where the extent of state interventionism or paternalism – as in Japan – is high" (Kowalik, 1989: 47–48). The text that Kowalik is arguing against is (Lowenthal, 1970).

21 However, I am obviously not suggesting here, nor does Tadeusz Kowalik do it anywhere, that these notions are disconnected. Also, in Kowalik's approach they do not seem to be contradictory.

could have been the aforementioned article by Oskar Lange from 1931. In Kowalik's pieces devoted to the Polish transformation that appeared before the one introducing the "epigonic bourgeois revolution", references both to Lange and to the bourgeois revolution are absent. In other words, the term "bourgeois revolution" to describe the Polish transition to capitalism first appears in Kowalik's work in the very same essay in which he first refers to Lange's 1931 article filled with terms "burghers", "bourgeoisie", "burghers' revolution", etc. This does not seem to be a coincidence.

In Kowalik's work from before 1996 there is no indication that he was aware of any theories of bourgeois revolutions other than the rudimentary one presented by Lange in the aforementioned paper. We can therefore assume that "Kryzys socjalizmu" was Kowalik's only source of theoretical knowledge about bourgeois revolutions (at least directly, i.e. when he wrote the *Nowe Życie Gospodarcze* article) and their course (including in particular: about the participation of the working class in them).

What possibly struck Kowalik most in "Kryzys socjalizmu" in the context of Polish transformation was the similarity (real or apparent) between the situation in Poland in 1905–1918 and that in 1980–1989 (or even 1980–1992). That is, the possibility of constructing a "bourgeois class state" only through a workers' revolution immediately preceding such a construction. On the basis of this analogy, in *Sierpień – epigońska rewolucja mieszczańska?*, Kowalik introduced a novelty into his reflections: he fortified his earlier, more lax analyses with the concept of "bourgeois revolution". Perhaps influenced by some kind of intuition on the issue of a possible anachronism of his 1996 proposal, however, Kowalik supplemented the term "bourgeois revolution" with the adjective "epigonic" (or, as in *The Polish Revolution*, also: "imitative"), which may well be seen as an attempt to escape the serious theoretical problems that may arise from his use of this term, but nevertheless is clearly Tadeusz Kowalik's original contribution to the formulation of the thesis.[22]

In contrast to "revolution from above", which disappeared from Tadeusz Kowalik's analyses from 1996, primitive accumulation of capital, another important element of his research prior to the thesis of the "epigonic bourgeois revolution" in Poland, became the foundation of this proposal. A possible inspiration to use – always in a negative context (in the chapter from 1995 we even read about "loathsome traits of primitive accumulation" (Kowalik, 1995: 106)) – this old Marxist concept to describe the Polish transformation is

---

22 The question of the possible influence of Lange's essay on the formulation and shape of Kowalik's thesis on the epigonic bourgeois revolution in Poland I discuss in more detail in (Konat, 2022).

revealed in an article written by Kowalik with Ryszard Bugaj in 1990, where we read that:

> Privatisation, or more accurately quasi-privatisation, which had been taking place since 1988, brought about many pathological phenomena: first and foremost the so-called enfranchisement of the nomenklatura. ... It was ... a phenomenon so massive that it can be counted among the most characteristic features of the epoch of the dismantling of real socialism, *a new kind of primitive accumulation* [emphasis mine – G.K.].
> BUGAJ & KOWALIK, 1990: 3

And further:

> Despite its strikingly pathological features, the "enfranchisement of the nomenklatura" did not meet with an unequivocal assessment. It was argued that, although the procedure was morally dubious, it was worth paying the price for the change of political system. ... Jadwiga Staniszkis posed this issue in the *Tygodnik Solidarność* in the most "systemic" way ..., considering the nomenklatura companies as the basic form of capitalism development in Poland ... According to this author, "after 40 years we are back in the phase of *primitive accumulation* [emphasis mine – G.K.]".
> BUGAJ & KOWALIK, 1990: 3[23]

Finally, it is worth underlining one more element – besides considerations of revolution and primitive accumulation – which was also present in Kowalik's earlier works and was later used by him in formulating the thesis of the "epigonic bourgeois revolution": reflections on the role of the intelligentsia in the Polish transformation. I will return to this issue in more detail in chapter three, so here let us just draw attention to one of the most interesting characteristics that Tadeusz Kowalik presented prior to formulating his thesis:

> As for the intelligentsia ..., this group of opinion-shapers had never constituted one independent political force ... On the contrary, the intelligentsia was always "subservient" to the "guiding" political force of the time. To generalize very simplistically, the intelligentsia first served the communists and "Solidarity;" now [i.e. in the mid-1990s] it serves the Church at the ideological level and the emerging new "moneyed"

---

23   The text referred to by the authors is (Staniszkis, 1989).

class at the pragmatic level. Finally, only a minority among the intelligentsia was ever associated with the poor and the marginalized. The co-operation between the intelligentsia and the workers attracted worldwide attention precisely because it was – as defined by G.[ustaw] Herling-Grudziński – "an unusual phenomenon". Unusual phenomena cannot be entirely explained in a rational manner.

KOWALIK, 1995: 93

CHAPTER 2

Jan Baszkiewicz's Model of Bourgeois Revolutions

1

In his book devoted to the "anatomy" of bourgeois revolutions, Baszkiewicz (1981) makes no attempt to offer one definition of this concept.[1] Indeed, he approvingly quotes Vladimir Lenin, according to whom "A bourgeois revolution is a revolution which does not depart from the framework of the bourgeois, i.e., capitalist, socio-economic system. A bourgeois revolution expresses the needs of capitalist development" (Lenin, 1962: 49).[2] Elsewhere, however, he presents definitional dichotomies or even more far-reaching distinctions, without selecting between the possibilities discussed. Thus, for example, he states that

> we can ... understand the bourgeois revolution in two ways. In a broad sense, *bourgeois revolution is the whole cycle of capitalist transformations up to the full establishment of a new social system* [emphasis mine – G.K.] filled with revolutions ("from below" and "from above") and reforms. In a narrower sense, it will be *a particular revolution "from below"* [emphasis mine – G.K.]: Dutch, English, French. And thus, "one of the waves that beat against the old regime". Colloquially, bourgeois revolutions are usually referred to in the latter, narrower sense.
> BASZKIEWICZ, 1981: 26–27

---

1 One of the critical reviewers of the book, Tadeusz Łepkowski, points out that in the context of Baszkiewicz's struggle with definitions in his opinion the author did not quite "know how to distinguish definitively between several terms (phenomena and processes), such as counter-revolution, restoration (and the movement leading to it), conservatism and reaction" (Łepkowski, 1983: 235) [Translation from French by Zbigniew M. Kowalewski, to whom I am very grateful for this help].

2 Adam Czarnota and Andrzej Zybertowicz offer a terminological remark to this citation of Lenin by Baszkiewicz: "Simplifying, 'the need for the development of capitalism' is the immediate or far-reaching interests of those social groups whose actions (regardless of their realised aims) lead, as an objective result, to the development of capitalist relations of production. Thus, to 'express' the needs of capitalism can mean: to create more favourable conditions for the actions of groups of people developing capitalist relations of production" (Czarnota & Zybertowicz, 1983: 143).

Elsewhere, however, Baszkiewicz adds further, as he calls them, "scales and sections", noting, among other things, that "we can ... speak of an entire epoch of bourgeois revolutions, that is, of a transition to capitalist formation on a global scale. This epoch begins in the sixteenth century and proceeds along an ascending line until the European revolution of 1848" (Baszkiewicz, 1981: 29). We can at most guess, given that he did not in any way single out any of these definitions, that Baszkiewicz regarded them as equally valuable. However, this does not seem to be an obstacle to making use of his model for the purpose of the book.

In the Introduction I signalled that the publication of *Wolność. Równość. Własność* has met with wide interest in the scientific community. It is important to note that many of the papers that have appeared in connection with the publication of Baszkiewicz's book have contributed significantly to a better understanding of its content (perhaps also by the author himself, prompting him to engage in sometimes extensive polemics), or (at least some) have expressed certain thoughts in the essay more precisely. A good example of this is, I think, the article by Adam Czarnota and Andrzej Zybertowicz from *Colloquia Communia* of 1983 (Czarnota & Zybertowicz, 1983).[3] They made a successful attempt to clarify some fundamental issues raised by Baszkiewicz, which at the same time constitute a good starting point for my further considerations in this chapter.

In their article, Czarnota and Zybertowicz first define precisely the causes of bourgeois revolutions that figure in Baszkiewicz's book, and then present them in the form of the following scheme:

---

3 The use of this work seems legitimate particularly in the light of Baszkiewicz's own opinion of it: "[Czarnota and Zybertowicz] try to systematise the distinctive features of the bourgeois revolution that emerge from ... [my] arguments. ... For this, I am grateful to them" (Baszkiewicz, 1983: 146). As the author of *Wolność. Równość. Własność* rightly notes, the text by Czarnota and Zybertowicz is of an orderly nature particularly with regard to how he presents the list of features of bourgeois revolutions. It is worth pointing out also, however, that the list compiled by these authors is not without its shortcomings. This is especially true, it seems, of their, at times, insufficiently attentive reading of Baszkiewicz's essay. For example, Czarnota and Zybertowicz only found the issue of the "movement of the masses" in an interview given by Jan Baszkiewicz to the weekly magazine *Tu i Teraz* [Here and Now] (Czarnota & Zybertowicz, 1983: 141–142) whereas he writes about this issue in *Wolność. Równość. Własność*: "For bourgeois revolutions, the common denominator is undoubtedly the active presence of the popular masses. Without their intervention, a genuine bourgeois revolution is impossible" (Baszkiewicz, 1981: 30). Baszkiewicz himself rightly pointed out a certain, as he put it, "sloppiness" on the part of Czarnota and Zybertowicz in this regard (Baszkiewicz, 1983: 146).

(1) structural causes [*przyczyny głębokie*] → (2) direct causes [*przyczyny bliskie*][4] → (3) revolution (outburst). (The arrows denote the relation of generation, that is, the production of a successor by a predecessor). The scheme thus outlined looks logical; let us now see how it looks after concretisation: ... (1) tensions and contradictions in ... the mode of production → (2) revolutionary situation + revolutionary consciousness + detonator → (3) revolutionary outburst.
  CZARNOTA & ZYBERTOWICZ, 1983: 137–138

Baszkiewicz addressed this proposal as follows:

In my view "structural causes" refer to the bourgeois revolution in the broad sense of the term, understood not as a single "outburst" but as the constitution of a new capitalist society; as a process "dialectically linking overthrow and adaptation, revolutions and reforms". Thus the structural causes should be looked at from a broader perspective than the above-quoted scheme suggests. A revolution in the narrower sense (a single wave in a revolutionary cycle) is generated by these structural causes, *but it also usually exerts a powerful influence on them* [emphasis mine – G.K]: it changes the state of tension in the mode of production, influences the balance of social forces and transforms class conflicts and alliances. *These influences relate not only to the duration of the revolution itself, but also to the subsequent course of the "revolutionary cycle"* [emphasis mine – G.K]. This prompts us to consider the problem not in the context of a single outburst, but of a whole cycle.
  BASZKIEWICZ, 1983: 143

Correcting the scheme that his views were written into by Czarnota and Zybertowicz, Baszkiewicz thus seems to claim, firstly, that not all three phases they described are on the same level of analysis, but rather represent successive

---

4 The use by Czarnota and Zybertowicz of the "structural" and "direct causes" of the revolution, introduced by Baszkiewicz, requires explanation at this point. In *Wolność. Równość. Własność* we read that "one can distinguish the 'structural' causes of the bourgeois revolution conceived as a change of formation, the replacement of the old society by a new, capitalist one. These causes mature slowly. ... But this is only the basis for bourgeois revolution conceived as a long process dialectically linking overthrow and adaptation, revolutions and reforms. In this process, there are individual explosions: revolutions that crumble the old regime. There must be adequate fuel for these 'direct causes' or what we would define today as a revolutionary situation. And finally, there must be a spark that acts as a trigger for the revolutionary outburst" (Baszkiewicz, 1981: 120–121).

transitions from the most general level ("tensions and contradictions in the mode of production"), through the intermediate ("revolutionary situation" or "revolutionary consciousness") to the most concrete – the actual revolutionary "outburst".

Secondly, the author of *Wolność. Równość. Własność* makes a remark of fundamental importance on the mutual relations between the individual phases of the scheme proposed by Czarnota and Zybertowicz. He notes that, in his view, the interdependence between elements 1) and 2) is not so much the result of 2) from 1) as it is a two-way relation, in other words: *feedback*. It seems that it will not be an abuse to say that this correction, although Baszkiewicz did not express it explicitly, also applies to the interdependence between points 2) and 3) and 1) and 3).

When taking into account the comments of the author of *Wolność. Równość. Własność* we obtain a new version of the scheme: 1) structural causes (after concretisation: tensions and contradictions in the mode of production) ↔ 2) direct causes (revolutionary situation + revolutionary consciousness + detonator) ↔ 3) revolution (outburst) ↔ 1) (again) structural causes; the result symbol (→) has been replaced by one for feedback (↔). The introduced modification is of fundamental importance to my analysis, because the bidirectional relations, signalling the mutual influence of subsequent elements of the scheme, in practice make it very difficult (or even impossible) to attempt to demonstrate dependencies of this kind with concrete historical events (or, as in the case of this book, their descriptions in the output of Kowalik). This leaves me with a set of situations and phenomena to identify, without the possibility of making precise judgments on the cause-effect relations between them.

Czarnota and Zybertowicz's attempt at a synthetic summary of Jan Baszkiewicz's concept does not however end with this presented scheme. In another place in the article, they write that, in the light of Baszkiewicz's model, to recognise we are dealing with a bourgeois revolution, it is also necessary to establish the occurrence of the following phenomena:

> a) "a rapid change in the state", breaking the continuity of the law and creating its own legality; b) "significant transformations in the class basis of the system", "a change in class rule"; c) the setting of political and social tasks, "a realistic revolutionary project", the emergence of "an alternative to the social status quo"; d) "the ability to organise the conquered terrain" [by the revolutionaries – G.K.].
>
> CZARNOTA & ZYBERTOWICZ, 1983: 141

Moreover, according to Czarnota and Zybertowicz, things get even more complicated when

> we shall take a look at an interview conducted with the author [of *Wolność. Równość. Własność*] ... in the weekly *Tu i Teraz* [(Baszkiewicz, Rykowski & Władyka, 1982: 1, 4)] where J. Baszkiewicz stated, among other things: e) "a true revolution cannot take place without a movement of the masses"; f) "a revolution is a complete change of the political system and the social system combined with a change in the class substrate of power"; g) "the first manifestation of a revolution is a change of people, a change of personnel. Without this there can be no question of revolution". Point f) could be treated as an expression, in other words, of point b) [of the previously quoted passage – G.K.] ... Points e) and g), on the other hand, present elements that are quite new in relation to the characterisation contained in the book.
>
> CZARNOTA & ZYBERTOWICZ, 1983: 141–142[5]

The authors of the quoted article also raise two fundamental problems. The first stems from the above-quoted fragment ("Point f) could be treated as an expression of point b)") and boils down to the question: how many features of bourgeois revolutions does Baszkiewicz include in his model? The second, equally important, is of a methodological nature; the authors of the review ask: "is it only the *combined* [emphasis A.Cz. and A.Z.] occurrence of the listed phenomena that constitutes a revolution [bourgeois revolution in Baszkiewicz's terms – G.K.], or is the occurrence of only some sufficient" (Czarnota & Zybertowicz, 1983: 141).

Let us begin our attempt at an answer by listing all the features of bourgeois revolutions mentioned in the passages quoted, this time dividing them into those I will conventionally call *general* or *basic*, i.e. those arising from the scheme of causes of bourgeois revolutions (these will be: (i) tensions and contradictions in the mode of production, (ii) revolutionary situation, (iii) revolutionary consciousness, (iv) detonator and (v) revolutionary outburst) and those which I shall hereafter refer to as *detailed* (*auxiliary, additional*). These will be: (vi) a rapid change in the state, breaking the continuity of the law and creating its own legality, (vii) significant transformations in the class basis of the system, a change in class rule, (viii) the setting of political and social tasks, a realistic revolutionary project, the emergence of an alternative to the social

---

5 Earlier in this chapter I mentioned that in the case of point e), this is not a justified statement.

status quo (in short, the revolutionary project), (ix) the ability to organise the gained terrain, (x) activity ("movement") of the masses; (xi) complete change of the political and social system combined with a change in the class substrate of power and (xii) a change of personnel.

The set of features presented above requires, I believe, some modifications and additions, resulting both from the authors' own doubts and suggestions as well as from my own reflections. Accordingly, I shall make the following changes: firstly, I shall treat the "change of personnel" as part of a "rapid change in the state, breaking the continuity of the law and creating own legality"; secondly, following the suggestion of Czarnota and Zybertowicz, I shall combine into one point henceforth numbered (vii), the two concerned class transformations: "significant transformations in the class basis of the system, a change in class rule" and "a complete change in the political and social system combined with a change in the class substrate of power" and finally, "the ability to organise the gained terrain" will be discussed as part of a wider phenomenon, extensively described by Baszkiewicz in *Wolność. Równość. Własność* under the new term "hegemony".

The result gained is a list of ten features of bourgeois revolutions, which I have expanded to include others that were not mentioned in Czarnota and Zybertowicz's remarks but, in my opinion, are found in Baszkiewicz's essay and are worth taking into account. These include: (xi) the formation of "revolutionary staffs" (*sztaby rewolucyjne*)[6] and the huge role of the intelligentsia in them, (xii) the "external aspect", which encompasses "the relationship of the bourgeois revolution to the national problem", (xiii) the idea and practice of "completing the revolution" and the related role of revolutionary propaganda, (xiv) the "cult of revolutionary leaders", (xv) economic terror and (xvi) the quandary of religion and the clergy's "reactionary" role.[7] Importantly, these will fall into a distinct "detailed" features group.

This is how I address Czarnota and Zybertowicz's first question: about the number of features of bourgeois revolutions in Baszkiewicz's model. As for he second one, concerning the (dis)connectivity of criteria, in other words, which criteria as defined by the author of *Wolność. Równość. Własność* should be considered (and why) as necessary to speak of a bourgeois revolution in a given case, the answer, I believe, is implicitly contained in the presented division of "general" and "specific" features.

---

6 As in military staffs, not in the sense of staff personnel.
7 All numbering used is for ordering purposes only and in no way implies succession or prioritisation of features.

The first of these groups includes the features that, in my opinion, an historical process or event must necessarily possess in order to be called a bourgeois revolution in Jan Baszkiewicz's sense. This is an obvious assumption given that the category of "basic" factors includes, on the one hand, the fundamental causes without which a bourgeois revolution, in the light of the model, simply cannot take place and on the other, the revolutionary "outburst" itself, i.e. Baszkiewicz's "concrete revolution" in a "narrower sense."[8] Referring to the question of (dis)connectivity, I assume that the features from the basic list must occur in all cases, otherwise the scheme discussed above, from which they stem, would remain incomplete (not closed).

On the other hand, in the specific features group I include those that may, or may not, be identified for us to speak of a bourgeois revolution in Baszkiewicz's sense. This follows directly from reading *Wolność. Równość. Własność*, the author of which, as we shall see, repeatedly stresses that each of these criteria separately does not condition the recognition of an event as a bourgeois revolution.[9] This will apply in particular to revolutions "from above", where some of the "auxiliary" features, like the "activity of the masses", are obviously not applicable.

Finally, we must also remember that Baszkiewicz's model is de facto consequentialist, i.e. that the basic condition for recognising a revolution as bourgeois is in its result, which must "express the needs of the development of capitalism". This, however, raises the question: how does this principle harmonise with the list of features described above, none of which directly refers to events or phenomena that would indicate the capitalist character of the resulting effects? In light of the content of Baszkiewicz's work, the only possible answer seems to be to consider the *coincidence* of both these elements as necessary; that is, both the occurrence of the features and the transformation

---

8   At the same time, it must be remembered that in the case of a revolution "from above", an outbreak of this kind will have to be considered as quite different from the "classical" mass uprisings usually associated with a revolution "from below".

9   Thus, from the text of the essay we learn, for example, that although "It would seem that the natural hegemon of a bourgeois revolution is the bourgeoisie, *very often however, this does not prove to be the case* [emphasis mine – G.K.]" (p. 33), and in the thesis connected with Baszkiewicz's reflections on the revolutionary project, stating that "the moderate, liberal wing of the revolution opts as a rule for a constitutional monarchy, while the radical wing for a democratic republic", we learn that "*this rule is full of exceptions* [emphasis mine – G.K.]" (pp. 233–234). It is worth adding at this point that I will also apply the above principle to the *manifestations* of particular features of bourgeois revolutions in Baszkiewicz's model. If any of them can be manifested in several different ways, I assume that it is sufficient to identify only one in order to speak of the occurrence of that feature.

to (or towards) capitalism. In other words, when a revolution exhibits all the features discussed above, but its final, even distant in time or space result is not capitalism, it is not bourgeois in Jan Baszkiewicz's terms.[10]

2

The level of detail of the sixteen features of bourgeois revolutions identified in the previous section will obviously vary. Some, as Baszkiewicz indicates, will be deemed not to require more extensive commentary, while others will require more space. The latter undoubtedly includes "tensions and contradictions in the mode of production".

In his work on the bourgeois revolutions, Jan Baszkiewicz does not explain how he understands a "mode of production" and what is meant by the "tensions and contradictions" within it, limiting himself at most to general remarks like "the maturing capitalist system within the former society creates tensions and contradictions in the whole mode of production" (Baszkiewicz, 1981: 121). Consequently – especially given the fact that *Wolność. Równość. Własność* is, as I have already explained, a synthesis of the views of the Marxist classics – I take it that this author was using these categories in the meanings assigned by, in particular, Karl Marx and Friedrich Engels.

The former, in an excerpt from his *Contribution to the Critique of Political Economy* (Marx, 1987), explained that

> In the social production of their existence, men inevitably enter into definite relations, which are independent of their will, namely relations of production appropriate to a given stage in the development of their material forces of production. The totality of these relations of production constitutes the economic structure of society, the real foundation, on which arises a legal and political superstructure and to which correspond definite forms of social consciousness. *The mode of production of material life* [emphasis mine – G.K.] conditions the general process of social, political and intellectual life. It is not the consciousness of men that determines their existence, but their social existence that

---

10   One can, of course, also imagine a hypothetical opposite situation, i.e. when a revolution leads to capitalism but does not display any of the characteristics mentioned. In practice, however, it would be extremely difficult to identify a case where revolutionary systemic change has occurred in the absence of at least the main categories discussed in this chapter.

determines their consciousness. At a certain stage of development, the material productive forces of society come into conflict with the existing relations of production or – this merely expresses the same thing in legal terms – *with the property relations within the framework of which they have operated hitherto* [emphasis mine – G.K.]. From forms of development of the productive forces these relations turn into their fetters. Then begins an era of social revolution. The changes in the economic foundation lead sooner or later to the transformation of the whole immense superstructure. ... *In broad outline, the Asiatic, ancient, feudal and modern bourgeois modes of production may be designated as epochs marking progress in the economic development of society* [emphasis mine – G.K.].

MARX, 1987: 263

The passage quoted above shows firstly that, according to Marx, the growing contradictions in the mode of production between the material productive forces of society and the existing relations of production or, more specifically, the property relations in which they have hitherto developed, lead to a "period of social revolution."[11] Secondly, however, it reveals that we are dealing here with a long-term, multi-faceted and large-scale process. An elaboration of the above argumentation can be found in Engels, who referred his considerations in the *Anti-Dühring* both to the (actual) transition from feudalism to capitalism and to the (potential) transition from capitalism to socialism:

> the new productive forces ... can only be maintained and further developed by *the introduction of a new mode of production* [emphasis mine – G.K.] corresponding to their present stage of development; that *the struggle between the two classes* [emphasis mine – G.K.] engendered by the hitherto existing mode of production and constantly reproduced in ever sharper antagonism has affected all civilised countries and is daily becoming more violent.
>
> ENGELS, 1987: 254

He thus points to the class struggle as a manifestation of the contradictions discussed here.[12] There are indications that Baszkiewicz shared this view. In

---

11 In fact, this is a view that, at least for some Marxists, has survived to this day. For example, at the end of the 20th century, Perry Anderson briefly summarised the same thought in the following way: "modes of production change when the forces and relations of production enter into decisive contradiction with each other" (Anderson, 1992: 17).

12 A similar suggestion, though not explicitly, was made by Karl Marx in a passage in the third volume of *Capital*, which Susan Himmelweit describes as "a working definition

Wolność. Równość. Własność we read, for example, that it is "the *structure of class forces changing with economic development* [emphasis mine – G.K.] – the industrial revolution is of primary importance here – that determines the capitalist transformation by way of revolution" (Baszkiewicz, 1981: 121).

Elsewhere in his polemic with Dühring, Engels notes, however, that the tension in the mode of production ("the contradiction between socialised production and capitalist appropriation"), which is at the heart of it, "*In ... crises ... ends in a violent explosion* [emphasis mine – G.K.]. ... The mode of production is in rebellion against the mode of exchange, the productive forces are in rebellion against the mode of production which they have outgrown" (Engels, 1987: 263). The plural "crises" used by Engels is not without significance. For, as it seems, what is meant is not so much each individual crisis (these find a more "macroeconomic" explanation in Marxist theory), but their whole cycle, a *chronic* crisis.[13]

The excerpts from the works of the Marxist classics presented above thus point, in my opinion, to two possible manifestations of the "tensions and contradictions in the mode of production" leading up to the bourgeois

---

of the 'mode of production'" that "[a]ll sides in the debate would be happy to accept" (Himmelweit, 1991: 381). Marx writes there that "The specific economic form, in which unpaid surplus labour is pumped out of direct producers, determines the relationship of rulers and ruled, as it grows directly out of production itself and, in turn, reacts upon it as a determining element. Upon this, however, is founded the entire formation of the economic community which grows up out of the production relations themselves, thereby simultaneously its specific political form. *It is always the direct relationship of the owners of the conditions of production to the direct producers* [emphasis mine – G.K.] – a relation always naturally corresponding to a definite stage in the development of the methods of labour and thereby its social productivity – which reveals the innermost secret, the hidden basis of the entire social structure" (Marx, 1998: 777–778). This view survived, moreover, among some Marxist scholars at least until the end of the 20th century. Thus Teschke, in his "textbook version of the concept 'bourgeois revolution' within Marxism" (to which current, as I have already signalled in the Introduction, Baszkiewicz and his book can be counted) distinguishes four essential elements, one of which is the identification of "*a growing class antagonism* [emphasis mine – G.K.] between a 'retrograde' feudal nobility and a 'progressive' bourgeoisie that had grown in the interstices of the feudal-absolutist régime" (Teschke, 2005: 4–5).

13   A chronic crisis like this was, moreover, already written about by Engels himself. Thus, in the preface to the 1892 English edition of *The Condition of the Working Class in England*, we read "we have had [in England], ever since 1876, a chronic state of stagnation in all dominant branches of industry. Neither will the full crash come; nor will the period of longed-for prosperity to which we used to be entitled before and after it. A dull depression, a chronic glut of all markets for all trades, that is what we have been living in for nearly ten years. How is this?" (Engels, 1990b: 266).

revolution: the class struggle and the chronic, recurring economic crisis.[14] The above argument, however, requires some comment.

The question of what the "mode of production" is and to what historical socio-economic systems this term can be applied is a matter of controversy in contemporary Marxist literature beyond the scope of this book.[15] Let us just note that there are convincing positions according to which real socialism, the system functioning for several decades in the Soviet Union and the countries of the Eastern Bloc, cannot be considered a mode of production. For example, Zbigniew M. Kowalewski, presenting his own definition of the mode of production,[16] also states that "the *mode of exploitation* [emphasis mine – G.K.] persisting in … [real socialism] does not constitute any *relatively stable and permanent mode of production* [emphasis mine – G.K.]" (Kowalewski, 2020: 356). Kowalewski further develops this thought as follows:

> No "new form of class society" that has ever appeared in history has lasted only a few decades. The very short duration, as well as the radical instability of this "new form" [i.e. real socialism – G.K.], testifies to the fact that in *the USSR, and later the Soviet bloc, neither a new mode of production emerged* (e.g. of the enigmatic "bureaucratic collectivism" kind), *nor did the old one revive in any form* [emphasis mine – G.K.] (e.g. of some kind of chimerical "state capitalism" in its various theoretical variants).
>
> KOWALEWSKI, 2020: 409–410

The above remarks seem to be of great importance for my analysis. In the Introduction, I signalled that, in the case of some of the Marxist terms used, the specific nature of the application of Baszkiewicz's model to the analysis of

---

14 This approach, moreover, was perpetuated by Marxism. Simon Clarke, with reference to theorists of the second half of the 20th century, notes that "The distinctiveness of the Marxist approach was the attempt to establish that this *crisis expressed the contradictory foundations of the capitalist mode of production* [emphasis mine – G.K.], and that the resolution of the crisis could not be achieved by reform, but only as the outcome of an intense class struggle" (Clarke, 1994: 7).
15 The main positions on this issue are briefly discussed by Susan Himmelweit (1991).
16 "[A] mode of production is a unity of relations of production and productive forces. … all (antagonistic) modes of production are certain modes of exploitation, while not all modes of exploitation are modes of production – these are very few. A given mode of exploitation is at the same time a mode of production only when the corresponding relations of exploitation and productive forces constitute a unity. That is, when the labour processes, and with them the productive forces (the productive powers of social labour), including the labour power of the direct producers (their capacity to work), are formally and really subsumed under the relations of exploitation" (Kowalewski, 2020: 414–415).

Kowalik's views on the transformation from real socialism to capitalism may require clarification or revision. In view of Kowalewski's comments above, it is very possible that in the case of the "mode of production" we are dealing with just such a requirement.[17]

On the other hand, these observations do not seem to apply to the manifestations of "tensions and contradictions" we have identified in the writings of the classical Marxists. Therefore in the following discussion, I will look for descriptions of class struggle and chronic crisis in real socialism in Kowalik's works, ignoring whether or not it was a mode of production. For the sake of greater terminological precision, however, I shall abandon writing about the "mode of production", referring from now on in the context of this section to "tensions and contradictions in the functioning of the socio-economic system".

3

Another basic criterion for identifying bourgeois revolutions in Baszkiewicz's terms is the occurrence of a "revolutionary situation" (which sometimes he referred to as a "revolutionary crisis" (Baszkiewicz, 1981: 38)). Discussing this issue, the author of *Wolność. Równość. Własność* first points to the inseparable link between the situation, the revolutionary project and the activity of the masses. He then points out that although revolution without a revolutionary situation is impossible, not every such situation must necessarily lead to the outbreak of a revolution.[18] Finally, Baszkiewicz points to several manifestations of a revolutionary situation: *"political crisis* [emphasis mine – G.K.] – 'the real disorganization of the government', 'confusion in the government', 'the desperate situation of the government' – and a *social crisis* [emphasis mine – G.K.],

---

17   It is worth noting that, as it seems, neither Tadeusz Kowalik nor Jan Baszkiewicz used the term "mode of production" to refer to real socialism anywhere in their works.

18   "The revolutionary situation does not determine ... the success of the revolution; it is a necessary condition for the outbreak of the revolution, but it gives no guarantee of its victory. 'There has never been, there is none, there will not be, nor can there be a revolution which did not stand some risk of defeat'. The success of a revolution is by no means determined by the initial situation alone, but also by the dynamics of the revolutionary process, the changes in the balance of forces, the maturation of whole groups and social classes, their growing experience, but also their growing weariness, their political weaknesses, their mistakes and betrayals" (Baszkiewicz, 1981: 122). The sentence quoted by Baszkiewicz in this passage comes from (Lenin, 1965: 371). Note that in his book, the author of *Wolność. Równość. Własność* provides the sources of the excerpts he quotes only for the works of Marx, Engels and Lenin.

[as well as] ... a considerable increase in the *activity of the masses* [emphasis mine – G.K.]" (Baszkiewicz, 1981: 121–122). All of these require some discussion.

As for the political crisis, according to the author of *Wolność. Równość. Własność* it is

> inherent in the revolutionary situation consisting of a stalemate, that is, in the blockage of political institutions, in the bankruptcy of the politics of the ruling classes, in the collapse of respect for "normal" political rules, in violent disputes among the power elite – and more broadly among the possessing classes – around the need for reforms, their pace and their extent.
> BASZKIEWICZ, 1981: 128–129

The social crisis, on the other hand, consists, in Baszkiewicz's opinion, of "a feeling of oppression or impulse towards vigorous protest against it", because, as he points out, "the growth of oppression, poverty, a sense of hopelessness and frustration goes hand in hand with the politicisation of the masses. There is a link between social and political revolutions. ... Social crisis in a revolutionary situation is not simply a feeling of misery, the agitations inherent in this situation are not simply 'hunger riots'. Then even poverty becomes politicised" (Baszkiewicz, 1981: 128).

Finally, the "activity of the masses", the "growth" of which,[19] according to Baszkiewicz, is to be expected within the framework of a revolutionary situation, does not have to appear as active resistance to the authorities. On the contrary,

> in the revolutionary process ... *passive resistance plays a significant role* [and] *can be an important component of the revolutionary situation* [emphasis mine – G.K.]. It is not only a refusal to approve of existing institutions, but also a refusal to carry out the orders of authority. ... Marx [in the context of the Spring of Nations in Germany – G.K.] pinned great hopes on a resolution of the Prussian Assembly (15 November 1848) that the people of Prussia should refuse to pay taxes to the government. He even called it the "bourgeois manner" of fighting reaction and believed in its effectiveness.
> BASZKIEWICZ, 1981: 243

---

19   The emphasis on the dynamics of the phenomenon described (not just the "activity of the masses" but its "growth") distinguishes this *manifestation* of one feature in Baszkiewicz's model ("growth") from another separate feature ("activity").

The author of *Wolność. Równość. Własność* then goes on to discuss the processes and phenomena that, in his opinion, may lead to the occurrence of the revolutionary situation thus characterised. The first of these is, as he notes, not so much the "absolute" misery of the masses[20] but rather the deepening of socio-economic inequalities: "Among the objective premises of the revolutionary situation Lenin mentioned 'the suffering and want of the oppressed classes [which] have grown more acute than usual'" (Baszkiewicz, 1981: 38).[21] Elsewhere in the book, Baszkiewicz adds that,

> the symptom ... of a [revolutionary] situation is not always an economic crisis. For what is a good economic situation, for whom is it good? Yes, it favours the bourgeoisie and strengthens it; but it can significantly *worsen the position of wage labour* ... [emphasis mine – G.K.]. Even in periods of prosperity there is no lack of poverty and deep frustration.
> BASZKIEWICZ, 1981: 127

The revolutionary situation may also stem from, according to Baszkiewicz, the "financial bankruptcy of the state". Using the example of late feudalism, he points out that in "the modern era the needs and costs of maintaining the state are constantly increasing, but it is usually the 'third estate', the bourgeoisie and the peasantry, that bears the main burden of fiscal pressure..." (Baszkiewicz, 1981: 129).

However,

> *the financial capabilities of these potentially revolutionary classes ... are as limited as their patience* [emphasis mine – G.K.]. A government caught between its class relations with the privileged, which does not allow it to burden them, and its needs, which the third estate cannot and will not fully satisfy finds itself in a no-win situation.
> BASZKIEWICZ, 1981: 129

On the other hand, according to the author of *Wolność. Równość. Własność*, the causes of the political crisis constituting the revolutionary situation may

---

20   "[T]he claim by some Western scholars that Marxists derive revolutions simply from the misery and hunger of the masses is a gross oversimplification. [According to Lenin] 'Oppression alone, no matter how great, does not always give rise to a revolutionary situation'" (Baszkiewicz, 1981: 38). The sentence quoted by Baszkiewicz is taken from (Lenin, 1963: 221).

21   The sentence quoted by Baszkiewicz is taken from (Lenin, 1964c: 214).

be "a crisis in the top echelons of power" (e.g. dynastic crisis), "the effects of war" (especially of defeat),[22] and finally particularly intense "corruption and contempt for the rules of decency and public opinion among the ruling elite" (Baszkiewicz, 1981: 130).

Completing his reflections on the revolutionary situation, Baszkiewicz adds one more element, which, he claims, conditions the others:

> However, the various manifestations of social and political crisis – economic disasters, the bankruptcy of the treasury, lost wars, corruption of power, etc. – need not, after all, be the prelude to a revolutionary situation. They will not become so if the ruling elites and the classes behind them have not lost their ability to respond to the challenge. Therefore *the key issue here is the reformist impotence of the old order in the face of states of crisis* [emphasis mine – G.K.].
>
>   BASZKIEWICZ, 1981: 130–131

4

Another of the basic criteria for including events in the category of bourgeois revolutions is, in Baszkiewicz's model, "revolutionary consciousness."[23] The author of *Wolność. Równość. Własność* stresses that if the great social forces have not acquired revolutionary consciousness, then "the revolutionary situation will not cross the threshold of becoming an actual revolution" (Baszkiewicz, 1981: 35). He defines this consciousness as the "readiness and ability for revolutionary mass action", noting at the same time that it is formed "on the soil of the experience of great social groups and classes" (Baszkiewicz, 1981: 135).

---

22   "The Crimean and Japanese war defeats contributed in no small measure to the revolutionary situations of 1859–60 and 1904–05 in Russia. ... a lost war ... tends ... to expose the incompetence, recklessness and corruption of the regime and the negative selection of the state cadre. ... [the revolutionary situation] is also mobilised by the lost war of the national oppressor: the defeats of the Austrians at Magenta and at Solferino (in 1859) caused a revolution in the Central Italian states they controlled" (Baszkiewicz, 1981: 129–130).

23   Since the question of how "revolutionary consciousness" relates to "class consciousness" is a marginal issue for the purpose of the book, at this point, I refrain from discussing it in detail. A concise introduction to the Marxist understanding of the latter term can be found in (Fetscher, 1991).

Next, he explains that:

> The revolutionary consciousness is expressed in the recognition that the "established order" is fundamentally wrong. It is not that the rulers violate the rules of law or morality, but that the social order has completely degenerated. It is a state from which one must leave, regardless of the risk of this *exodus*, just as one flees from a city infested with plague or from a house on fire. ... It is not, however, to be an escape to nowhere, without wondering whether another society is at all possible. The revolutionary consciousness is the triumph of alternative thinking: people stop believing that the reality in which they have been living is "natural", and is the "best of all possible worlds". *The conviction that another society is possible, that people do not have to repeat for centuries the same rules, gestures, behaviours, paves the way. That they have an influence on social institutions, the thorough transformation of which is within the reach of human capabilities* [emphasis mine – G.K.]. Of course, in order to demolish the old slave house, it is not necessary to have plans for a new building, but revolutionary consciousness is not only oriented towards destruction. Destroying the old prison is only half the job and sometimes not the most difficult at all.
> BASZKIEWICZ, 1981: 136–137

The issue of revolutionary consciousness was also addressed by Baszkiewicz in his polemic with Czarnota and Zybertowicz, though with a more critical approach:

> revolutionary consciousness retains a great deal of independence from the processes of longue durée that make up the structural causes of social transformation. This consciousness is peculiar to overestimating solidarity, fraternity, harmony of aspirations and interests of the revolutionary community, ... the "WE" aggregate. The violent delegitimization of the prevailing social order is often accompanied by the belief that the bad regime is to blame for "everything" (including the economic collapse or demographic imbalance). The revolutionary consciousness boldly crosses all barriers of possibility. There is a rapid leap from the feeling of helplessness and powerlessness to the conviction of the almost unlimited influence that "WE" have on socio-political reality. All it takes is one more effort.
> BASZKIEWICZ, 1983: 144–145[24]

---

24 We can only assume, given that Baszkiewicz's works on bourgeois revolutions seem to have been written under the influence of the socio-political mood of Poland in the early

As far as the "detonator" for the revolutionary outburst is concerned, Baszkiewicz defines it as "the crossing of the threshold between a revolutionary situation and revolution, the moment when the old superstructure 'cracks'" (Baszkiewicz, 1981: 122) before adding that Lenin referred to this crossing as the "revolutionary moment" (Baszkiewicz, 1981: 122). As the author of *Wolność. Równość. Własność* claims, in most cases, it is possible to create a "model scenario" for the moment:

> The detonator of the revolution is a mass demonstration in the capital, armed or peaceful, more or less clearly inspired by the political movement of the bourgeoisie, but growing out of the irritation of the masses. The demonstration meets with an armed reaction of the army and the police, there is shooting, and sometimes even a massacre, sometimes the building of barricades, the storming of strategic points of the city ... The most favourable course of events is the rapid collapse of the *ancien regime's* resistance, forcing the authorities to capitulate or be driven out. ... It is a different situation if a popular demonstration is massacred and crushed. Despite keeping the capital, the government may face a generalised rebellion as the massacre turns out to be the start of a nationwide movement.
> BASZKIEWICZ, 1981: 139–140[25]

Baszkiewicz also points out that "The apparent disproportion between the immediate cause of such a sudden explosion and its consequences resulted in confusion among observers; indeed, it could often seem that the revolution had broken out over a trifling matter" (Baszkiewicz, 1981: 140). And he concludes his very brief reflections on the "detonator" with an observation that "sometimes there are many such sparks falling on accumulated gunpowder and *only one of a series of detonators triggers the explosion* [emphasis mine – G.K.]" (Baszkiewicz, 1981: 139).

Finally, the last basic feature of bourgeois revolutions in Jan Baszkiewicz's model is the "outburst". The set of auxiliary criteria, on the other hand, opens with the point: "a rapid change in the state, breaking the continuity of the law and the creation of its own legitimacy; a change of personnel". What both categories have in common is that the author of *Wolność. Równość. Własność*,

---

1980s, that the catalytic role of the views of the author of *Wolność. Równość. Własność* was fulfilled here by the events of the Polish "Solidarity Carnival" of 1980–1981, as well as by martial law.

25 This description clearly takes into account only the "from below" variant of the revolution.

considers them to be so obvious that they do not need to be discussed in detail. Thus, all we learn about the revolutionary outburst (apart from what has already been mentioned above in the context of the "detonator") is that Baszkiewicz refers to it as "a single wave in the revolutionary cycle" (Baszkiewicz, 1983: 143) or, in other words, that he identifies it with a single event defined as a revolution.[26] The decision of the author of *Wolność. Równość. Własność* not to discuss in detail the revolutionary outburst and the violent changes in the state seems right, given that in both cases the understanding of their designations is immediate and probably not controversial.

5

Baszkiewicz also pays little attention to "the significant transformations in the class basis of the system, a change in class rule" or "a complete change in the political and social system combined with a change in the class substrate of power". Interestingly, the first of the above formulations comes entirely from a single passage in *Wolność. Równość. Własność*, where Baszkiewicz does not so much discuss the transformation as points to it as a factor that makes it possible to distinguish between revolutions and putsches, upheavals or revolts:

> An upheaval differs from a revolution in that there is no *significant transformation in the class basis of the system* [emphasis mine – G.K.]. ... A putsch or coup d'état can ... overturn all political institutions without any *change in class rule* [emphasis mine – G.K.].
> BASZKIEWICZ, 1981: 19–20

The second of these elements comes, as already explained, from a brief mention in an interview published in the weekly *Tu i Teraz* (Baszkiewicz, Rykowski & Władyka, 1982). However, Baszkiewicz does not elaborate on these remarks, probably also in this case considering them to be quite obvious in themselves. Thus, in the book, he merely mentions that the idea of fundamental class transformations as a condition for recognising events as a revolution is already present in the Marxist classical writings[27] and adds that *"the change in class rule*

---

26   "[In the revolutionary cycle] there are individual *explosions – revolutions* that crumble the old regime [emphasis mine – G.K.]". At the same point in the essay, Baszkiewicz also refers to them simply as "revolutions *sensu stricto*" (Baszkiewicz, 1981: 121).

27   He cites Engels (1989: 43) in this context ("Every real revolution [...] brings a new class to power and allows it to remodel society in its own image") and Lenin: "The passing of state

should be ... understood broadly [emphasis mine – G.K.]. ... it must be remembered that the bourgeoisie is divided into groups and strata with very different levels of aspiration and interest" (Baszkiewicz, 1981: 20).[28] Let us just note that, as we know from other fragments of Baszkiewicz's work, in his model the presence of the bourgeoisie in a given society is not necessary for the revolution taking place to be considered as bourgeois. Analysing the "change in class rule" (or in the "class substrate of power") it is therefore, I believe, also necessary to allow for the possibility that this class only comes into being or consolidates itself *as a result* of such a revolution, and then, as a consequence, takes over the said "rule".

Unlike the several features discussed above, Baszkiewicz describes at length the question of the "movement of the masses" and "the active presence of the masses" as the "common denominator" of the bourgeois revolutions. Significantly, according to the author of *Wolność. Równość. Własność* without the involvement of the popular masses "a real bourgeois revolution is simply impossible" (Baszkiewicz, 1981: 30).[29]

This obviously raises the question of "revolutions from above". The apparent contradiction in Baszkiewicz's position disappears, however, when we realise that, firstly, he understood "the activity of the masses" very broadly, not limiting his use of the term solely to cases of spontaneous and turbulent demonstrations and, secondly, that he referred the indispensability of the activity to the entire "revolutionary cycle" rather than to a single outburst (the equivalent

---

power from one class to another is the first, the principal, the basic sign of a revolution" (Lenin, 1964a: 44).

28   Baszkiewicz continued these considerations in one of his later texts, but also there he did not propose any clear-cut solution. Attention is drawn only to a passage in which the author, based on his reading of Karl Marx's writings, seems to distinguish quite strictly between class "rule" and power in the state: "the ruling class determines the 'direction of travel', power 'chooses the route'. ... The state makes class goals a reality, but the means of achieving them must be subject to choice and political decision. A certain flexibility in the action of power in the sphere of day-to-day politics, its relative freedom, also in its relations with the ruling class, is thus simply a condition for the effective execution of its class tasks. ... this autonomisation of power by no means invalidates the class character and class tasks of the state" (Baszkiewicz, 2009b: 383–384).

29   And elsewhere in the book we read: "It is clear that revolutions – including bourgeois revolutions – can only be made by the masses being moved by deep social needs" (Baszkiewicz, 1981: 125). It is worth noting that in this, as in many other cases (as has been hinted at before), Baszkiewicz directly refers to the work of the classics of Marxism. For example, on the same subject Engels wrote "The bourgeoisie is, at best, an unheroic class. Even its most brilliant achievements, those in England in the seventeenth century and those in France in the eighteenth, were not gained in battle by the bourgeoisie itself, but won for it by the popular masses, the workers and peasants" (Engels, 1988: 401).

of which, in the case under discussion here, are events described as revolutions "from above"). Baszkiewicz's broad understanding of the "mass movement" may in a sense be demonstrated as follows:

> the masses, especially the more politicised urban masses, are keenly interested in, and sometimes fascinated by, the overthrow of despotism, the abolition of social privileges, freedoms (although economic freedom raises doubts and criticisms), equality of rights, including political rights, the election of authorities, and often, finally, the vision of a republic. After all, the petty bourgeoisie and the workers had long believed that political democracy would solve the "social question". Indeed, even the young Marx identified the popular vote with the political rule of the proletariat, or at least of the people.
> BASZKIEWICZ, 1981: 146–147

However, in Baszkiewicz's opinion, there were some significant cracks in the common vision and interests of the bourgeoisie (at least the petty bourgeoisie) and the people, as outlined in the above quotation:

> The masses could not meet the bourgeoisie in all ... political postulates though, in many issues, there was ... a concordance of views at least in the formal sense. The bourgeoisie, moreover, excelled at substituting itself for the notion of the people and in exploiting the theme of popular sovereignty. The play with these words – the people, the rights of the people, the rule of the people, the people's principles – was sometimes even perfected: behind the screen, however, lay the sovereignty of the bourgeoisie and bourgeois principles. But let us not immediately start shouting, as some do, about lies and manipulation: many revolutionary activists sincerely believed that they were the people ([Maximilien] Robespierre: "I am not the defender of the people, I am myself of the people").
> BASZKIEWICZ, 1981: 147–148

Perhaps the most important contradiction was, however, according to the author of *Wolność. Równość. Własność*, that although "the movement of the masses" was necessary to deliver the revolution, at the same time the bourgeoisie was often terrified by this activity. As he put it: "the bourgeois revolutionary oscillates between two attitudes. He counts on the strength of the people in the fight against reaction and would not like the revolutionary zeal of the people to weaken while, at the same time, fearing the popular element might get out of his control" (Baszkiewicz, 1981: 143). Then Baszkiewicz explains:

> The fear of the popular element, tinged with contempt, stems from firmly rooted features of the bourgeois mentality. The bourgeois is used to giving orders but not receiving them from the people ... The bourgeois is a rationalist and hates whatever seems irrational in the popular movement; it is in favour of order and discipline, and therefore afraid of the "rampant anarchy" inherent, in the bourgeois view, in the mass movement. Important consequences follow from this as the bourgeois wants to close the chapter of revolutionary "chaos" as soon as possible, to return to social stability even at the price of compromise with the forces of the old order (in an extreme situation even at the cost of capitulation before them) and, if necessary, by surrendering political power to his protector like William of Orange [the Silent], [Oliver] Cromwell, [Napoleon] Bonaparte ... And as long as the revolution lasts, the bourgeois will exert all its strength to keep events under control.
> BASZKIEWICZ, 1981: 144

Generalising the conclusions from the course of the revolution in Germany in 1848, Baszkiewicz puts forward a thesis on the "regularity" of the development of the mass movement in the revolutionary cycle. As a rule, the workers' movement shapes itself under the influence of the "general democratic" movement and then slowly moves away from it (Baszkiewicz, 1981: 52). According to Baszkiewicz, the fatigue of the popular masses with revolution is not without influence on this dynamic:

> The bourgeois revolutionaries speak so many fine words to the people, and make so many promises to them – and this is repeated at every turn of the revolutionary events. But how many times can one calmly accept successive disappointments instead of rewards for struggle, effort and sacrifice? *The people's weariness is all the more understandable because the belief in the possibility of immediately repairing the world is one of the very lasting components of popular consciousness* [emphasis mine – G.K.].
> BASZKIEWICZ, 1981: 204

Finally, in addressing the issue of popular activity, Baszkiewicz could not but refer to the strike, which is, as he argued, one of the most important manifestations of the "mass movement" in the bourgeois revolutions:

> The working class brings to the cycle of bourgeois revolutions its own forms of struggle, above all the *political mass strike* [emphasis mine – G.K.]. ... The mass strike in an already industrialised country was able

to disorganise or even paralyse the functioning of the state (production, transport, supply, communications). The workers' strike movement radiated out in the form of agrarian strikes and the rural movement in general; it was imitated by various intellectual groups (strikes of certain free professions, school strikes...). *Most importantly, however, the political strike is not usually a simple passive resistance. Elements of active struggle appear in the great strike movement. This is because striking workers do not sit passively at home: they gather, demonstrate and fight the army and the police* [emphasis mine – G.K.].
BASZKIEWICZ, 1981: 244–245

6

Another feature of bourgeois revolutions, which is explained at greater length in Jan Baszkiewicz's work, is the "very intricate" (Baszkiewicz, 1981: 38) question of the "revolutionary project", which the author of *Wolność. Równość. Własność* defines as

the ideas of the great social forces (and not only of individuals) about the aims, tasks and limits of the revolution. A project is less than a programme, because it does not have such a detailed, concrete character but is also more than a programme because it embraces a vast horizon, presenting bold alternatives to what was.
BASZKIEWICZ, 1981: 38

Baszkiewicz then briefly discusses the fundamental problems a researcher faces when attempting to make any generalisations about the revolutionary project:

It is relatively easy to analyse the project of one revolution ... It is impossible to reduce to a common denominator the projects of all bourgeois revolutions. They occur during more than four centuries, in countries with different traditions, at different levels of development of capitalist relations and in different international contexts. And even when we look at one selected revolution, we soon see complications. ... different situations correspond to a radicalisation of the revolutionary project or to an intensification of its conciliatory character. In view of the pluralism of revolutionary projects and their changeability, *any generalisations are only very approximate* [emphasis mine – G.K.]. Generalisations include, for example, the thesis that the moderate, liberal wing of the revolution opts, as a rule, for a constitutional monarchy, while the radical wing opts for a democratic republic. But this rule is full of exceptions.

BASZKIEWICZ, 1981: 222–224

Moreover, in Baszkiewicz's view, it cannot even be said that a common feature of revolutionary projects is to favour the development of capitalist social relations. As an example, he cites the French Revolution, during which "many revolutionary 'planners' neither wished for, nor even anticipated in, the abyss of misery, exploitation and debasement that the unfettered development of capitalism would create" (Baszkiewicz, 1981: 224). According to the author of *Wolność. Równość. Własność* the following conclusions can be drawn from this:

> When ... we look at various revolutionary projects, including those formulated by the radical left and the extreme left, we come to the conclusion that it is necessary to show the two sides of bourgeois revolutions: an anti-feudal revolution is not always, at the same time, a capitalist revolution *in intent* [emphasis mine – G.K.]. "Both of them, the bourgeoisie and the proletariat, constituted the new society and stood together in one camp against the old feudal society". The anti-feudal content is common to all the projects, although their consistency in rejecting the feudal regime or its relics is uneven. *However, not all re-invention projects are capitalist in the sense of consciously postulating capitalist development and bourgeois rule. Undoubtedly, the class interests of the bourgeoisie were best served by the liberal project, although the need to win over the popular masses sometimes forced it to make concessions to the radical-democratic programme* [emphasis mine – G.K.]. However, the opening up to free capitalist development was not always immediately and fully expressed even in the liberal project.
>
> BASZKIEWICZ, 1981: 226[30]

Baszkiewicz devotes particular attention to two other elements that appear often enough in revolutionary projects though are not necessarily common to all. Firstly, as he argues, in "the sphere of systemic and political issues, revolutionary projects commonly formulated *the abolition of despotism and the overthrow of social privileges* [emphasis mine – G.K.]" (Baszkiewicz, 1981: 229).

---

30 The sentence quoted by Baszkiewicz in this passage comes from (Engels, 1990a: 306).

Secondly, he points out that the status quo ante, to which some of the leaders of the bourgeois revolutions postulated a return, "is a mythical or idealised past, which makes it possible to insert bold visions of a new and better world into the idea of a 'return to the roots'. In this way, going back into the distant past actually means a *total and usually utopian questioning of the present* [emphasis mine – G.K.]" (Baszkiewicz, 1981: 210).

In his book, Baszkiewicz explains that "The class that plays a leading role during a revolution (or one of its phases) in relation to the other revolutionary classes, we shall call the *hegemon* [emphasis J.B.] of the revolution". Then he adds that although "It would seem that the natural hegemon of a bourgeois revolution is the bourgeoisie; very often, however, this does not prove to be the case. Many times the bourgeoisie, actively participating in the revolution, removes itself ... into the background or shares hegemony" (Baszkiewicz, 1981: 33). This does not, however, change the fact that the question of hegemony is one of the decisive features of revolution, and despite the reservations Baszkiewicz makes, the exercise of hegemony by the bourgeoisie, however limited in time, circumstances or the co-hegemony of other classes, can be an important distinctive feature in this respect.

Discussing the issue of hegemony, Baszkiewicz refers to the thought of Antonio Gramsci, one of the most important theorists of this issue:[31]

> To equate hegemony with political power would be inaccurate. When analysing the bourgeois revolution in Italy, Gramsci distinguished between domination (*dominio*) and direction, intellectual, moral and political hegemony (*direzione, azione egemonica*). He also recognised that these two types of class relations could intertwine and combine. ... *Let us therefore not identify revolutionary hegemony with power* [emphasis mine – G.K.]. In 1789 the French bourgeoisie was already the hegemon of the revolutionary movement before it gained and consolidated its power; in 1793 it temporarily lost its role as hegemon of the revolution, but retained power; the workers and petty bourgeoisie had hegemony in the first weeks of the revolution in France 1848, but their participation in power was modest and secondary; the Russian working class exercised hegemony in the revolution of 1905, although it did not gain power at all.
>
> BASZKIEWICZ, 1981: 145

---

31 On Gramsci's concept of hegemony see, for example, (Bates, 1975).

Then the author of *Wolność. Równość. Własność* links the ability of the bourgeoisie to exercise hegemony in the revolutionary process especially, but not exclusively, in the face of growing adversity (including, in particular, competition with other social groups for revolutionary hegemony),[32] to distinctive features of this class. According to Baszkiewicz, "the bourgeoisie imposes its point of view on the mass movements, channels it, realises its hegemony over the more ardent and much more revolutionary classes", all due to the "numerous advantages at its disposal" which "enable it to occupy a hegemonic position" (Baszkiewicz, 1981: 149). It is not only about the "material resources" at the bourgeoisie's disposal, but also about "its compactness, which makes it easier to agree on positions and to organise" (Baszkiewicz, 1981: 149). In this context, Baszkiewicz states that

> when its elementary class interests like the protection of bourgeois property, the elimination of feudal reaction or the keeping of the popular movement in check are at stake, the bourgeoisie is able to forget its quarrels, to take decisions and impose them on society with admirable speed and efficiency. It is an educated class – in its heroic period even more so than in the epoch of consolidating its position. The bourgeoisie is accustomed to organisational work, initiative, calculated risk and organisation. Various groups of the creative and professional intelligentsia with legal, literary, journalistic and technical culture flock to it ... *Consequently, the bourgeoisie perfectly articulates the principles of the new order, and propagates and disseminates revolutionary ideas in accordance with its vision of the aims and limits of the revolution. It is also a great reservoir of staff for the revolutionary apparatus of power; it organises the conquered terrain and it is difficult to question this role* [emphasis mine – G.K.].
> BASZKIEWICZ, 1981: 150

The author of *Wolność. Równość. Własność* then develops this important theme in the context of the consolidation of hegemony and the pacification of the popular movement threatening the bourgeoisie on the "left":

---

32   As he points out, "In the long cycle of bourgeois change there finally comes a stage when the bourgeoisie begins to lose speed, to give up its revolutionary readiness, to defend every – and thus also the semi-feudal – form of exploitation, to arrange its relations comfortably with the still vigorous forces of the *ancien regime*. Into this vacuum, by its very nature, *the revolutionary hegemony of the people* [emphasis mine – G.K.] tries to enter. It turns out, however, that this is a hellishly complicated task" (Baszkiewicz, 1981: 155).

> The bourgeoisie has a way of winning over ambitious and talented popular activists. By exercising its rule ... [on a basis broader than that of the former ruling class], it gives many people the chance to rise. The bourgeoisie, creating a new apparatus of power, is able to win over with jobs and careers even a part of the former elite, its natural enemies, and even more so its potential rivals from the people. *The ability to attract and absorb elites from the popular classes, to conform them, to locate them within the bourgeois system – this is the bourgeoisie's great asset for consolidating its hegemony* [emphasis mine – G.K.].
>
> BASZKIEWICZ, 1981: 150–151

Reflecting on the mutual relations of the bourgeoisie and the masses in the context of revolutionary hegemony, Baszkiewicz suggests that although "the masses play a colossal role in the bourgeois revolution as a battering ram crushing the resistance of the former ruling classes", it is much more difficult for them "to emancipate themselves from the political tutelage of the bourgeoisie, to consolidate their own revolutionary hegemony and to pursue their own goals" (Baszkiewicz, 1981: 156).

Another important observation of Baszkiewicz is that a particularly good "terrain for realising the hegemony of the bourgeoisie ... is national unity and independence" (Baszkiewicz, 1981: 148). At times this could mean raising the issue of the independence of "the national economy threatened by the expansion of foreign capital" (Baszkiewicz, 1981: 148). As he states, "The propertied classes, in accordance with their actual position, *have long played the role of the ensign of the national cause, and they are able to bring together a great variety of social forces for common action under this banner* [emphasis mine – G.K.]" (Baszkiewicz, 1981: 148).

This provides a good introduction to the discussion of another feature that may indicate the bourgeois character of the revolution – the "external aspect". In this context, Baszkiewicz in particular draws attention to the fact that

> the connection of the bourgeois revolution with *the national problem* [emphasis J.B.] ... becomes more and more important as capitalism and the bourgeois nations develop. The political emancipation of the nation is a fundamental postulate of bourgeois democracy ... Well, *the national problem is often related to the external aspect of the revolution. It is sometimes faced with the task of liberating the nation from foreign power ... or from colonial rule...* [emphasis mine – G.K.].
>
> BASZKIEWICZ, 1981: 39

Concretising this point, the author of *Wolność. Równość. Własność* pays particular attention to three issues. Firstly, he notes that the countries of Central and Eastern Europe "entering the path of capitalist development (or those advanced in it like Germany or Italy) reveal a close relationship of social, political and national revival. Here, ways are sought simultaneously for the overthrow of feudalism (or its still strong relics) in favour of democracy (or, at least, for a liberal-constitutional system) and for national unity and independence" (Baszkiewicz, 1981: 231–234). Secondly, Baszkiewicz stresses that the necessary conditions for the aforementioned "national unity", to which the bourgeois revolution contributes, also include "the liberation of the national economy from the domination of foreign capital" (Baszkiewicz, 1981: 236). Finally, and thirdly, using the example of Giuseppe Garibaldi and the "Redshirts" during the Italian Risorgimento, the author of the essay explains how, in his opinion, the "national idea" and its instrumental use by the liberal bourgeoisie can negatively influence the realisation of radical and popular demands:

> Garibaldi, the conqueror of Sicily and Naples, did not fulfil Engels' hopes that he would turn out to be as great a politician as a general. After his victory, he gave way to a Piedmontese government that erased the social reforms in the South. The ease with which the Garibaldi "Redshirts" allowed themselves to be disarmed, both ideologically and militarily, attests to the weakness of Italian radicalism. *The infatuation of the Radicals with the national idea, skilfully appropriated by the Savoy dynasty and the Liberals attached to it, was also at work here* [emphasis mine -G.K.].
> BASZKIEWICZ, 1981: 104–105

7

Another feature of the bourgeois revolutions in Jan Baszkiewicz's model is the presence of "the (political) staffs" and, in particular, their "intellectual character". In *Wolność. Równość. Własność* the author explains that:

> The dynamic outbursts would not have turned into revolutions had it not been for the action of the *political staffs* [emphasis mine – G.K.]. Their role in arousing and orienting revolutionary consciousness is enormous. The boundaries between them and revolutionary power are fluid, but *the staffs function also before the revolution gains power* [emphasis mine – G.K.] (and it is known that not all of them do), often as the nucleus

of the revolutionary government. *The revolutionary staffs begin to form already before the revolution* [emphasis mine – G.K.], which of course does not mean that they have revolutionary consciousness from the start. At the threshold of the whole cycle of bourgeois transformations *they try to define an alternative to the status quo, but as a rule they opt for evolutionary, peaceful changes, in cooperation with those in power, who are to be persuaded, rather than forced, to reform* [emphasis mine – G.K.]. Only at a certain point does this reformist project transform into a revolutionary one.

BASZKIEWICZ, 1981: 158

It seems, however, that under certain conditions this description can also be applied to non-bourgeois revolutions. This is probably why Baszkiewicz tries to make the concept more precise, adding that:

At the threshold of the cycle of bourgeois revolutions, a powerful impulse for the formation of revolutionary political staffs is the phenomenon which Crane Brinton described effectively as the *"desertion of the elites"*. [emphasis mine – G.K.]. Previously, intellectuals, outstanding writers and publicists, artistic talents and people of the liberal professions had long and loyally served the feudal social system. This is normal as the creative intelligentsia used to revolve in the orbit of the established order. However, *in a revolutionary situation, or even slightly before it, the intellectual elite deserts* [emphasis mine – G.K.].

BASZKIEWICZ, 1981: 158

The above passage, apart from introducing the concept of the "desertion of the elites", signals another important feature of the so-called "staffs" in bourgeois revolutions, which is the large role played in them by the intelligentsia. Baszkiewicz points out that the "leadership organs of the revolution" are not, as one might think, composed of "bankers, industrialists and merchants" alone. On the contrary, the role of the "classical commercial, financial and industrial bourgeoisie" in these bodies is "rather modest, sometimes even strikingly insignificant" (Baszkiewicz, 1981: 161). The author of *Wolność. Równość. Własność* notes in this context that attempts were made to explain this with the aid of the universal, humanist and democratic message of the revolution:

the revolution, as it were, "sends" to its staffs people of talent, intelligence and knowledge, and not bankers or factory owners who would give it a narrow class, bourgeois stamp. ... *There is, in fact, no contradiction between*

> *the claim that the French Revolution was a historic triumph of the bourgeoisie and the observation that it is the intelligentsia elite that appears as the main protagonist of this drama. The bourgeois intelligentsia is bound by a thousand threads to the bourgeoisie; these threads are ideological, cultural, political, personal, and economic ... The intelligentsia can therefore loyally and effectively, although perhaps not always in full awareness of the consequences, represent the aspirations of the bourgeoisie in the course of the revolution* [emphasis mine – G.K.]. It can do this all the better because, after all, it is precisely the intelligentsia which possesses a particular political, rhetorical, journalistic and legal culture, and these are qualities necessary in the revolutionary process. Without them it is difficult to formulate a revolutionary project, rally great social forces around it, and above all carry it out thus rebuilding the political system and social institutions.
> BASZKIEWICZ, 1981: 162–163

Yet another feature of bourgeois revolutions is, according to Baszkiewicz, the announcement, and realisation in practice, of the idea of "completing" the revolution, whether in its entirety or in its particular aspects. In this context, he mentions two areas of revolutionary activity in particular: the destruction of symbols of the old regime and their replacement with new ones reflecting the spirit of the revolutionary (or post-revolutionary) times, and changes in education. With regard to the first of these points, the author of *Wolność. Równość. Własność* points out that

> cases of iconoclasm are not always a manifestation of spontaneous and uncontrolled movements; on the contrary, they can be a premeditated action of the new, bourgeois power. It is worth remembering that these church statues and royal monuments, toppled by the Dutch or French Revolution, were proud and intrusive symbols of the old order, which brought people endless suffering, oppression and humiliation. Is it any wonder that efforts were made to take revenge and brutally obliterate its visible traces?
> BASZKIEWICZ, 1981: 267–268

Then, using the example of the French Revolution, Baszkiewicz presents the activity as constructive rather than destructive and consisting of the revolutionaries' efforts to fill public space (both physical and discursive) as much as possible with symbols of the new order: "Even city planning is to be a tribute to revolutionary and republican virtues, hence the resolution of the Paris Commune [1789–1795] to remake the streets and squares of the city and the districts' quarrels over the fair distribution of the great heroes of antiquity" (Baszkiewicz, 1981: 273–274).

And as far as education is concerned, the author of *Wolność. Równość. Własność* observes that, in revolutionary times, perhaps more than in more peaceful periods of history, "Politics also enters widely into the classroom", and he goes on to explain that

> new revolutionary dogmas are inserted into the old catechism, traditional disputes between "Romans" and "Carthaginians" become saturated with politics. The pupils smash miniature Bastilles with small cannons and playing with soap bubbles is a lesson on the fate of conspiracies against the Republic (at first they seem alluring, they shimmer with beautiful colours, they grow but they always burst without leaving a trace in the end).
> BASZKIEWICZ, 1981: 274

The passage clearly raises the question of propaganda in its broadest sense and its role in bourgeois revolutions. In several places in *Wolność. Równość. Własność*, Jan Baszkiewicz signals this problem quite clearly. For example, he calls the American Revolution a "war of quills with the English" (Baszkiewicz, 1981: 177), singling out in this context especially Thomas Paine's pamphlet *Common Sense* (Paine, 1986), which, in Baszkiewicz's opinion, "changed the course of events" of that conflict and is "the best example of the power of the pen in shaping revolutionary moods" (Baszkiewicz, 1981: 177). Elsewhere, Baszkiewicz refers to the events in France in 1848: "Tocqueville considered the porter of his house to be a 'born socialist' because he was a drunkard who constantly beat his wife: *one can judge by this what 'propaganda of fear' the tabloid anti-communist polemics developed* [emphasis mine – G.K.]" (Baszkiewicz, 1981: 87). Finally, the author of *Wolność. Równość. Własność* points to the coexistence of at least two parallel historiographies of each bourgeois revolution: "Aside from the readily read literature with a counter-revolutionary tinge … there is thus an almost official version, a republican 'vulgate' of the history of the revolution of 1789 …: patriotic, unifying, seeking to heal the antagonisms of the internal revolutionary front and conservative" (Baszkiewicz, 1981: 12).

An element on the border of the concept of "completing" the revolution and revolutionary propaganda, which Baszkiewicz also draws attention to in his essay, is the return "to the sources" (alternatively: "to the roots", or possibly to a "better past"). Also, in this case, the author of *Wolność. Równość. Własność* uses the example of the French Revolution:

Many bourgeois politicians started in 1789 with the intention of correcting abuses rather than rebuilding the world. However, only two years later, [Jean-Paul] Rabaut Saint-Étienne would write that, although the revolution was only meant to reform the abuses, "since everything in this country was abusive, the result is that everything has been changed". But even Rabaut thought that this *complete regeneration of the Nation was only a return to "original purity", to natural institutions that last, even if they are violated* [emphasis mine – G.K.], "like rivers flowing underground they appear again after a length and a few miles".

BASZKIEWICZ, 1981: 207

The above passage is Baszkiewicz's introduction to the following attempt at generalisation:

revolutionary millenarism is not ... the sole property of ardent and exalted activists; it permeates mass consciousness, especially where the peasant component is strong in the revolution [emphasis mine – G.K.]. The belief in the closure of history by a definitive return to the Promised Land accompanies the German peasant war, the radical currents of the Latin American revolution, and we find it still in the peasant movements of the fifth Spanish revolution ... [François Noël] Babeuf expressed a very widespread state of consciousness when he compared the revolution to a magnificent, but requiring great valour, flight from Egypt, the home of slavery, to the land of Canaan.

BASZKIEWICZ, 1981: 210–211

Baszkiewicz cites a number of other examples of this kind of "millenarism"[33] and then explains that "The historical argumentation, conservatively tinged, is mixed ... with legal and natural, prospective and universal arguments. The return to the times of Edward the Confessor is just a myth, a myth in the Sorellian sense, working on people's imagination" (Baszkiewicz, 1981: 212–213). Interestingly, according to Baszkiewicz, a myth like this often manifested itself in what he calls the "global project" that, as he claims, "was already well known to the mature, forward-looking bourgeois revolutions. Admittedly, there is also

---

33   For example: "Richard Overton will say that this ancient Anglo-Saxon system, which needs to be restored, is simply 'consistent with reason and universal justice'; Gerrard Winstanley, that it is consistent with the precepts of 'God, Christ and Scripture'" (Baszkiewicz, 1981: 212–213).

a certain conservative accent in the belief that its realisation will mean *the end of history* [emphasis mine – G.K.]" (Baszkiewicz, 1981: 214).

Going further, the author of *Wolność. Równość. Własność* links revolutionary fantasies with the issue of "completion" in the symbolic sphere:

> The belief in a perpetual "Christmas on Earth", and therefore accent of conservative utopianism in the revolutionary project, when it turns to the future, goes hand in hand with the trait of radical utopianism when it looks to the past. It consists in an ardent desire to abolish the inhuman and irrational past, in the belief that one can, as the French say, *faire table rase*, sweep everything off the table and start from ground zero a new history of human society. [Pierre-Joseph] Proudhon, who by no means carried Jacobinism in his heart, said mischievously but perspicaciously that "he treats the past not as an issue, but as an enemy".
>
> BASZKIEWICZ, 1981: 214

But perhaps the example that best illustrates the subtle connections between the category of "global change" supposed to mean a "return to the Promised Land" and "completion" of the revolution and revolutionary propaganda in Baszkiewicz's essay, is the one contained in the passage devoted (once again) to the French Revolution:

> The proclamation of the Republic in September 1792 raised hopes of global change. The idea of a break in continuity was eloquently expressed in the introduction, from the autumn of 1793, of a republican calendar. Its co-author, [Philippe] Fabre d'Églantine, would say in the Convention: "We could no longer count the times in which we were oppressed by kings as years of life". And the chief creator of the calendar, mathematician and member of parliament Gilbert Romme will declare "Here time opens a new book of history [...] It will carve the annals of a reborn France with a new and powerful chisel" ... [Louis de] Saint-Just will state in turn: "In an age of innovation, everything that is not completely new is disastrous" ... It is not enough now for the revolutionaries to destroy all the relics of royalism; the Convention is debating changes in geographical names, its Committee of Public Enlightenment is considering "rebranding" all communes and renaming the country "Les Gaules".
>
> BASZKIEWICZ, 1981: 218

8

Finally, there remain three issues, discussed quite succinctly by Baszkiewicz, concerning bourgeois revolutions, which I recognise as features present in his model. First, using the example of the French Revolution, the author of *Wolność. Równość. Własność* analyses what he calls the "system of institutional terror,"[34] listing its four components. The first three are executions, mass arrests and mass confiscations. What seems particularly interesting from the point of view of the model of bourgeois revolutions, however, is the fourth element:

> a whole sphere of *economic terror* [emphasis mine – G.K.]: taxes, requisitions and compulsory loans, sometimes without any statutory basis; forcing commercial transactions on terms far removed from market *terms of trade*; maintaining the value of paper money by confiscating precious metals and jewellery. Some ... went even further, ordering the compulsory exchange of gold for paper assignats [a form of fiat money in late 18th century France – G.K.].
> BASZKIEWICZ, 1981: 262–263

Such a specific, purely economic form of terror, taking into account Lenin's comment cited by Baszkiewicz, who claimed that "economic domination is everything to the bourgeoisie, and the form of political domination is of very little importance" (Lenin, 1964b: 53) can, I believe, be considered the historically most durable counterpart of Marx's "bourgeois manner" on the ground of revolutionary violence.

Secondly, in *Wolność. Równość. Własność,* Baszkiewicz also raises the issue of the role of religion and the clergy in bourgeois revolutions. Thus, we read there that:

> It is a common misconception that the problem of religion played a major role only in the early revolutions (the Great Peasants' War, the Dutch

---

34 Of course, Baszkiewicz's reflections on revolutionary terror *in general* are much more elaborate, starting with basic definitions and typologies: "Among the problems of revolutionary violence, the question of terror is the most intricate. Revolutionary terror seeks to destroy the positions of the counter-revolution in such a way as to cast terror on all enemies. However, it appears in various forms. It can be a popular, spontaneous and anarchic terror, both on an individual level (individual popular self-judgements) and on a mass level (massacres of the type of the Paris prison murders of September 1792). ... However, of greatest importance is terror as a system of government set in motion by the revolutionary authorities" (Baszkiewicz, 1981: 253–254).

and English revolutions) when the challenge to feudalism began with a frontal attack on clerical feudalism. It is true that these early revolutions brought about an incredible flare-up of religious conflict, and breaking the social dominance of the ruling Church (Catholic or Anglican) was one of the main revolutionary demands. But the protest against Church rule will also be voiced – albeit with less radicalism – by the American Revolution. The conflict with the Church, as the support of the old order, will appear (sometimes in a very sharp form) in the French, Spanish, Latin American, Italian and also Russian revolutionary cycles (in the latter due to the special role of the Orthodox Church in the system of tsarist despotism). There was a peculiar mix of ideas of freedom of belief and various fanaticisms (Calvinist, Puritan, but also "de-Christianisation" in 1793). The bourgeois tendencies towards anticlericalism and Machiavellian attempts to exploit the war against the Church as a diversion in the class struggle, as well as the conviction of the bourgeoisie that religion is a pillar of the social order, as it reconciles the underprivileged with their earthly lot, were all intertwined. *The whole tangle of these intricate conflicts left its mark on almost all the bourgeois revolutions; the exceptions (e.g. the February Revolution of 1848 in France) are very few and far between* [emphasis mine – G.K.].

BASZKIEWICZ, 1981: 230–231

Elsewhere in the book, in turn, Baszkiewicz argues that *"the influence of the clergy* [emphasis mine – G.K.] and the primitive nature of rural life will create in the countryside [Spanish in the mid-19th century – G.K.] a serious *reserve for reaction* [emphasis mine – G.K.]" (Baszkiewicz, 1981: 91).

Finally, in his essay, Jan Baszkiewicz does not limit himself to showing only "large social structures" as the "motor forces of revolution":

such a force ... *are also individuals whose history has elevated to the role of leaders ... In fact, their role is enormous* [emphasis mine – G.K.]. They are necessary for the revolution because the loose party structures and individualism inherent in the bourgeoisie require that leaders ensure the cohesion of political orientations and governmental teams. Leaders are also needed by the great social forces. In the midst of revolutionary confusion, the bourgeoisie needs a "strong man", a guarantor of order, a bulwark against anarchy: William of Orange [the Silent], [Oliver] Cromwell, [George] Washington, [Marie Joseph de] La Fayette, [Louis-Eugene] Cavaignac, [Camillo] Cavour, [Venustiano] Carranza, ... [Thomas] Jefferson, [Maximilien] Robespierre, [Louis] Blanc, [Giuseppe] Garibaldi,

[Emiliano] Zapata ... *Some of the heroes of the revolutionary drama are surrounded by an almost charismatic cult, sometimes spontaneous, sometimes skilfully directed* [emphasis mine – G.K.]. "In the revolution", wrote [François-René de] Chateaubriand "a name means more than an army".
BASZKIEWICZ, 1981: 174

In this context, the author of *Wolność. Równość. Własność* is particularly interested in the aforementioned "cult of revolutionary leaders", especially in, as he puts it, the cases that are not so obvious:

here is La Fayette, of whom Napoleon Bonaparte used to say *"ce niais"*, "that fool" – and he was probably not really exaggerating, here is Robespierre, outwardly completely unimpressive, with a badly pitched voice, a typical provincial lawyer, here is Washington, whose qualities – reason, moderation, modesty, balance – are so hardly "charismatic". How is it that they rise to the rank of charismatic leaders for shorter or longer periods? Let us note first of all *that their cult is an instrument of party politics* [emphasis mine – G.K.]. This does not mean that it has to be obtrusive in its application.
BASZKIEWICZ, 1981: 182

Baszkiewicz then goes on to specify: *"the three examples chosen thus show the party entanglements of the cult of the leader* [emphasis mine – G.K.]. La Fayette's prestige is needed by moderates and liberals, the popularity of Robespierre by the radical democrats and the cult of Washington by the Federalists, advocates of the US system as it was in 1787" (Baszkiewicz, 1981: 184).

CHAPTER 3

The Polish Systemic Transformation as a Bourgeois Revolution in Tadeusz Kowalik's Selected Works

1

Tadeusz Kowalik had been interested in the topic of systemic changes long before the collapse of real socialism,[1] with the events of 1989 only, seemingly, intensifying and deepening his investigations.[2] Studies of the literature unambiguously indicate that Kowalik's theory of economic systems and his views on the Polish systemic transformation found their fullest expression in *Systemy gospodarcze* of 2005 (Kowalik, 2005a) and *Polska transformacja* published in 2009 (Kowalik, 2009b).[3] It is the content of these books, especially the second (in its slightly modified English version, published in 2012 and titled *From Solidarity to Sellout* (Kowalik, 2012a)),[4] which is particularly devoted to the

---

1 His early reflections on this matter can already be found in his work from the 1950s. See, for example, (Kowalik, 2013f).
2 In this context, it is worth recalling especially Kowalik's theoretical disputes in the first half of the 1990s. Apart from the already signalled polemic with Maurice Glasman (Glasman, 1994; Kowalik, 1994), the most important is also the one with the views of Zygmunt Bauman (Bauman, 1994; Kowalik, 1996a), János Kornai (Kowalik, 1992b) and Andrzej Walicki (Kowalik, 1997b; Walicki, 1997).
3 Kowalik himself must have regarded these two books as, at least to some extent, the culmination of his work on the issues to which they were devoted. He distinguished them in this way, for example, in a text from 2012, where we read: "The author of this paper ... [in] the book *Systemy gospodarcze* singled out countries with the most profiled systems and discussed in separate chapters the systems of: United States, Germany, Japan and Sweden. In the most extensive part, as well as in a separate book [*Polska transformacja*], both the systemic features of the Polish socio-economic order and the road to it are discussed. Although reference is made to ... books on the differentiation of capitalism, no ... classification is made to the Polish system, contenting oneself with the thesis that the model for the Polish transformation was the Anglo-Saxon model" (Kowalik, 2012c: 571).
4 It is worth noting that the differences between the Polish edition of *Polska transformacja* and its English translation of three years later, the full title of which is: *From Solidarity to Sellout. The Restoration of Capitalism in Poland*, concern, above all, the adjustment of the translation to the needs of English readers less familiar with Polish affairs. The most important structural differences between the two books are the complete absence in the English edition of Chapter 15 ("Systemic Sources of the Present Crisis") and the omission of the Polish-only part of the work entitled "Effects and Defects of the Polish Transformation" (preceding the first part and containing only one chapter), which resulted in moving the first chapter to

changes of the 1980s and 1990s, that my reconstruction in this chapter will be based on most.⁵

Let us begin this reconstruction by pointing out that, in Tadeusz Kowalik's works, there are essentially no descriptions of class conflicts in Poland during the period of the Polish People's Republic. This is, I believe, an element of a more general tendency: in the texts of the author of *From Solidarity to Sellout*, in the context of real socialism, references to social classes, in general, are almost absent. When writing about that system, if he even refers to its social structure, Kowalik usually limits himself to mentioning Milovan Djilas's concept of the party-communist bureaucracy as a *new class*.⁶

A possible explanation can be found in the following fragment of a text from 2001 (already quoted in chapter one), in which Kowalik notes that

> The novelty of the situation in Poland [in the 1980s] is that the labour movement did not confront a stronger, better-organized force. A fully fledged capitalist revolution took place under conditions where a *bourgeois class and its organized representation were non-existent* [emphasis mine – G.K.]. Thus the *new rulers were anticipating the future by creating the foundations of a new system favourable to the middle-class-to-be* [emphasis mine – G.K.].
> KOWALIK, 2001b: 224⁷

It is therefore likely that Kowalik did not write about social classes (in particular about the bourgeoisie) in reference to real socialism, because he did not

---

the first part in the English version. I am grateful to the translator of the book, Ms Eliza Lewandowska, for her valuable information on the creation of the English edition of *Polska transformacja*.

5 At this point, one organising remark is required: in further considerations, for obvious reasons, I will not take into account works from before the thesis of the "epigonic bourgeois revolution" in Poland was put forward by Kowalik in 1996, because I cannot treat views that were expressed prior its formulation as justifying the thesis.

6 For example as follows: "The Yugoslav dissident, Milovan Djilas, called … [the bureaucracy] a 'new class'. Two leading Polish dissidents, Jacek Kuroń and Karol Modzelewski, evaluated it similarly (and it cost them several years in prison)" (Kowalik, 2002e: 616). Tadeusz Kowalik is obviously referring to (Djilas, 1957). It is worth noting here that even when Kowalik used the concept of class, he did not define it in any way.

7 In *From Solidarity to Sellout*, on the other hand, in a passage that will be discussed in more detail later in the chapter, we read that, at the turn of the 1980s and 1990s in Poland, "there was yet no distinct capitalist class in existence, the political authorities acted in the name of an 'imaginary' middle class that was supposed to create the foundations of the liberal-democratic order" (Kowalik, 2012a: 293).

consider it legitimate in the context of that specific socio-economic system.[8] What is more, such an interpretation seems to be justified on the grounds of some theoretical views of the author of *From Solidarity to Sellout*.

Although Tadeusz Kowalik allowed for various solutions as to the nature of real socialism, especially interpretations falling into the categories of a "mixed system", a "transitional system" or even "state capitalism,"[9] in the works on systemic transformation taken into account here, he did not present his views on this issue in a coherent and unambiguous manner, focusing at most on the presence of a "bureaucracy" in this system, as a distinguishing feature and – at the same time – an obstacle on the way to "democratic socialism."[10] However,

---

8   Let us add that we also do not find many other notions closely related to the category of class, like *exploitation*, in Tadeusz Kowalik's works on the restoration of capitalism in Poland. The connection between the two was perhaps most succinctly expressed by Geoffrey de St. Croix: "Class ... is the collective social expression of the fact of exploitation" (Ste. Croix, 1981: 43).

9   Tadeusz Kowalik developed this view fully in perhaps only one essay: *Państwo dobrobytu – druga fala* [Welfare State: A Second Wave] from 2004 (Kowalik, 2004b). He wrote there that "in its socio-economic content, communism or sovietism was a specific, mono-party-state *substitute for market capitalism* [emphasis T.K.]. *It was a kind of state capitalism* [emphasis mine – G.K.]. The basic function of communism (sovietism) was the industrial modernisation of backward countries, carried out by draconian means. *The strongest argument in favour of ... treating Sovietism as state capitalism is the exceptionally smooth transition to free-market capitalism, the ease with which the former party nomenklatura, especially the part of it most involved in the economy, was converted into a business nomenklatura* [emphasis mine – G.K.]. The ease with which communist parties transformed into social democratic ones, with strong neoliberal tendencies, was striking" (Kowalik, 2004b: 69).

10 Thus, we read in Kowalik, for example, that "Many socialists, Trotskyites, and social democrats have denied that this formation ever had any socialist character, going so far as to say that this was distorted or degenerated socialism. For a long time, however, it seemed that under favorable circumstances the system would *evolve in the direction of democratic socialism* [emphasis mine – G.K.]. And the main obstacles to be overcome – according to the proponents of this theory – were not some imminent errors existing in the doctrine, but the obstinacy of the *structured bureaucracy defending its own interests* [emphasis mine – G.K.]" (Kowalik, 2012a: 16). Elsewhere, he claims that *"The party-state bureaucracy* [emphasis mine – G.K.] created to meet the needs of imposed industrialisation [after 1945] did not give way anymore. It was incapable of reforming the system, and it was also incapable of reforming itself. *Actually, that was the greatest cost of that transformation and modernisation* [emphasis mine – G.K.]. [Real socialism] ... was not socialism, but a communist substitute for capitalism, whatever it proclaimed about itself" (Kowalik et al., 2013: 651). Finally, from a text published in 2002 we learn that "even ... in those countries [of real socialism] which could record some progress in industrialisation, sometimes called imposed industrialisation, its costs were very high. *Probably the most important cost was the growth and petrification of the party and state bureaucracy, the formation of an all-embracing cadre nomenklatura which controlled almost all areas of social, political and economic life* [emphasis mine – G.K.]. ... It was this *bureaucracy* [emphasis

in at least several passages of his most important works on systemic transformation, Kowalik expresses his view on the direction of the causal relationship between the system of property rights in the economy (and the changes occurring in it) and the class social structure.

Thus, in *From Solidarity to Sellout* we read, for example, that "In economic writings ... [the] important and extensive *social functions of ownership transformations are overlooked, above all, as a factor of the new social stratification* [emphasis mine – G.K.]. And yet ownership co-defines and at times even determines many areas of public life" (Kowalik, 2012a: 181–182).[11] Elsewhere in the book its author even names this direction of influence:

> Economists say that ownership forms make up one of the main pillars (next to the market) and, in certain arrangements, the main pillar of every economic system. The foremost feature of a capitalist economy is considered to be "private ownership of, and private enterprise with the means of production". On this score, there is no difference between ... [any] neoclassical economist ... and the Marxist Oskar Lange. ... in Poland [however], interest in this especially conflict-generating and so to speak *"class-generating"* [emphasis mine – G.K.] domain is much smaller than, for example, in allocation and market issues.
>
> KOWALIK, 2012a: 173

---

[11] T.K.] which prevented the necessary, sometimes commonly perceived and postulated reforms" (Kowalik, 2002e: 616). The contents of this and the previous footnote may indicate the influence on Tadeusz Kowalik of contacts with Trotskyist thinkers, e.g., with Isaac Deutscher, about Kowalik's meeting with whom Bellofiore, Karwowski and Toporowski (2014b: 2) write. However, this issue would require separate in-depth studies.
Similarly, in *Nierówni i równiejsi* [The Unequal and the More Equal] we read: "Among economists, even those who recognise property as an important system-forming factor, there is little awareness that *property and property relations form the basis of social stratification and that, at the same time, property transformations are transformations of the social structure* [emphasis mine – G.K.]" (Kowalik, 2002a: 67). To examine to what extent such an approach to the problem fits, for example, into the categories of the Marxist understanding of social relations is beyond the scope of my book. At this point I will only signal that doubts in this respect seem to be justified. For example, Zbigniew M. Kowalewski points out that "The thesis that in every (antagonistic) mode of production the basic relation of production is the relation of exploitation is inseparable from the thesis of the primacy of production relations over productive forces. The opposite thesis, i.e., that of the primacy of the productive forces, *inevitably destroys the notion of relations of production and replaces it with the notion of legal forms of property, and makes Marxism 'a kind of evolutionism in its materialist version tinged with technological determinism'* [emphasis mine – G.K.]" (Kowalewski, 2020: 412–413).

Kowalik's position, in which social structure is the effect of legal and institutional changes occurring in society, and not their cause, is not limited to the narrowly understood problem of ownership. In *Systemy gospodarcze* we can read, for example, that

> the shock therapy, aimed mainly at stabilising the economy, became a tool for creating a new, capitalist social structure. This did not take place according to textbook canons of organic capital formation through hard work, increasing productivity, puritanical savings and accumulation of surplus [emphasis T.K.].
>
> KOWALIK, 2005a: 299[12]

Therefore, according to Kowalik, it is property relations, but also events like "shock therapy" that shape the social structure and, as is implicit and obvious here, in this framework cause conflicts. One of the crucial consequences of the above statement is that Kowalik perceives social conflict as primarily the *result* of the systemic transformation in Poland: "*The result of transformation* [emphasis mine – G.K.] was to create a system pregnant with *social conflict* [emphasis mine – G.K.], conflicts softened initially by the social acceptance of 'shock therapy' and then by fast economic growth" (Kowalik, 2001a: 39).[13]

It is no coincidence, then, that the few references made by Kowalik to any class struggle in Poland refer almost exclusively to the 1990s. For example, in *From Solidarity to Sellout* he writes that it was in the years 1990–1993 when "[t]he backbone of the working class was broken" (Kowalik, 2012a: 140), and elsewhere in the book he refers to the views of Jacek Tittenbrun, expressed in his four-volume work *Z deszczu pod rynnę* [From the Rain to the Gutter] (Tittenbrun, 2007):

> Tittenbrun ... points out the significant difference between the conditions and methods of privatization in state-owned enterprises in industry and services and the privatization of the state farms [in the 1990s]. In cities,

---

12   Interestingly, this is a view that Kowalik held even before he formulated his thesis on the epigonic bourgeois revolution in Poland. For example, in a short polemic in 1995 with Jeffrey Sachs by Kowalik and Mieczysław Kabaj, we read that "Numerous analyses indicate that the rapid creation of a market economy and rapid privatization [in Poland after 1989] caused considerable stratification – in other words, rapid enrichment of the few and impoverishment of many" (Kabaj & Kowalik, 1995: 8).

13   This is not to go into the extent to which Kowalik identified these "social conflicts" with class conflicts.

an authentic struggle of the workers took place over the forms, conditions, and pace of privatization. The people were aware of their rights, organized, and well oriented in the situation of the country and the company. *There were many manifestations of "class" struggle – as Tittenbrun rightly calls it – between capital and labor* [emphasis mine – G.K.]. Often this had a positive effect on the form and pace of ownership changes.

KOWALIK, 2012a: 231–232[14]

And yet, incidentally and indirectly, Kowalik also refers to the existence of social classes in the Polish People's Republic. One such reference is made by the author of *From Solidarity to Sellout* to something which, again drawing on the thought of Jacek Tittenbrun, he describes as "the specific character of the Polish social conditions":

---

14   The explicit issue of class struggle in Poland after 1989 returns in Kowalik's work in only one more context – the danger of its occurrence in an unspecified future: "The new phenomenon of mass demonstrations by peasants early in 1999 were the first indications of joint worker-peasant action. *A potential threat for the entire socio-economic order, a threat of rebellion, or at least destabilizing class struggles* [emphasis mine – G.K.] stem from the fact that the *systemic transformations, including ownership transformations, are being carried out* against *the will of the two basic social classes – workers and peasants* [emphasis mine – G.K.]" (Kowalik, 2001b: 246). This is, by the way, not the only passage in which Kowalik expresses his fear of the manifestations of class conflict in the form of popular protests. In the middle of the first decade of the 21st century, he warned, for example, that "the elimination of trade unions [in Poland] may threaten *wild, uncontrolled mass protests* [emphasis mine – G.K.], conditioned by the lack of an organised dialogue partner" (Kowalik, 2005a: 328). In this context, however, another of the paradoxes in Tadeusz Kowalik's views is revealed. In addition to warning of the "threat of destabilizing class struggles", Kowalik – in an interview given in 2004 – argues that "without organized social movements within individual countries, there are poor prospects of moving away from the policies that have been imposed on the world by America. ... What is needed are social movements on a national scale and their international interaction" (Kowalik & Wielgosz, 2004: C), and further, in the context of Poland, he adds that "Probably *only a social revolt, mass demonstrations, strikes could force the power elites to change course* [to the one desired by Kowalik; emphasis mine – G.K.]" (Kowalik & Wielgosz, 2004: C). Meanwhile, another interview, this time from 2010, reads, "The government is also an expression of social pressures. If there aren't any, then the government is part of the political-business arrangement. Not only when it directly gives orders to private business and has close ties with it. The general atmosphere is that corporations and the mass media tend to make governments the exponents of the richest classes or strata. *If they act differently, it is only under the influence of social pressure* [emphasis mine – G.K.]" (Kowalik & Leszkowska, 2010), and then that "Naomi Klein is very right when she says that only a social explosion can open the media more to social problems" (Kowalik & Leszkowska, 2010).

> One of the features distinguishing Poland from other countries of the former socialist bloc was the *much higher degree of articulation of classes, which were not only aware of their own interests, but were also able to exact them effectively* [emphasis mine – G.K.]. The autonomy of enterprises, the large role of the trade unions, *the sense of strength of the working class supported by a rich tradition of class struggle* [emphasis mine – G.K.] – these factors did not exist in such intensity and in such a combination in the neighboring countries.
>
> TITTENBRUN, 2007 [Vol. 4]: 11; quoted in KOWALIK, 2012a: 213.

Although in the passage quoted above, Tittenbrun (and Kowalik after him) describes the realities of the 1990s, it seems obvious that the phenomena to which he refers, for example when he mentions the "rich tradition of class struggle", did not appear as a result of the systemic transformation, but were also present in preceding decades.

However, when Kowalik presents the realities of the Polish People's Republic independently and refers to them directly, he clearly changes the terminology – classes and their possible conflicts are replaced by "interaction of various social groups":

> One of the failures of "real socialism" was that top-down regulation met with much resistance in society and generally proved to be inapplicable. *Much of the social energy was wasted on circumventing the authorities, and on defensive reactions, which could include: boycotts, ignoring the orders of the authorities, corruption, theft, escaping into the shadow economy, etc.* [emphasis mine – G.K.]. The system was becoming increasingly uncontrollable. ... And vice versa. *The formation of the new system was the result of multicoloured social reactions to the authorities' actions and the interaction of various social groups* [emphasis mine – G.K.].
>
> KOWALIK, 2005a: 286

This quotation is very important for two reasons. Firstly, it turns out that contrary to the oft-expressed belief it was the systemic transformation's new social structure that led to the occurrence of class conflicts on a full scale in Poland, in his works on the Polish transformation of 1989, Kowalik was not able to ignore the social conflicts shaping this transformation. Instead, in describing tensions of this kind, he did not use the term "class struggle". Secondly, it is worth noticing that Kowalik reversed the cause-effect relation: the emergence of a new system is, in the above fragment, an *effect* of "social reactions to the authorities' actions" or "interactions of various social groups", and not their cause. This constitutes, as we shall see later, only one of many paradoxes present in the views of the author of *From Solidarity to Sellout*.

Meanwhile, Kowalik goes even further, in at least one work in some way linking the "veiled" issue of social conflicts in the Polish People's Republic with the statement I quoted earlier, that at the turn of the 1980s and 1990s "the new rulers were anticipating the future by creating the foundations of a new system favourable to the middle-class-to-be" (Kowalik, 2001b: 224), and thus explaining, as it were, the social sources of the second circumstance mentioned. Discussing the content of one of Henryk Słabek's books (Słabek, 2004), Kowalik states that, in his opinion, this author presented an interesting explanation for the collapse of real socialism in Poland, consisting in the tendency for "self-destruction" within the "establishment broadly understood as such". In *From Solidarity to Sellout*, he quotes the following passage from Słabek's work:

> The system collapsed because for various reasons, also understandable ones, it was abandoned (betrayed?) by its initial beneficiaries and sentries. *For people of the economic nomenklatura of the Party and – though probably on a smaller scale – of the party apparatchiks, with the passing of time the system would become a straightjacket that was becoming less and less comfortable as incomes rose* [emphasis mine – G.K.]. [...] The managers, and particularly the economic elites were drawn to solutions patterned after the West, in the hope for a future secured for themselves and their families after becoming independent of the political authorities, which could erase the career of a director at any moment, and *after acquiring and multiplying appropriate assets* [emphasis mine – G.K.].
>
> SŁABEK, 2004: 384–385; quoted in KOWALIK, 2012a: 49–50

Kowalik's main objection to this line of argumentation is that, in his opinion, "complicity" in this matter should also be attributed to the Solidarity opposition. Writing about some of the "opposition activists who had found financial support in the rapidly developing private sector", Kowalik states explicitly: *"Not only the old official nomenklatura, but also these new groups turned in the direction of the state sector for enfranchisement* [emphasis mine – G.K.]. In the material economic base, conditions were developing for the *common interests of both groups* [emphasis mine – G.K.], 'above divisions' of a purely political nature" (Kowalik, 2012a: 43). Elsewhere, the author of *From Solidarity to Sellout* points to one practical example of such an already crystallised "common interest", set in the circumstances of 1989: "In the course of the Round Table negotiations, unlike at the political 'table' where two opposing parties were seeking a compromise, *the economic 'table' talks were conducted by economists who had evidently more in common than what they might disagree about* [emphasis mine – G.K.] (Kowalik, 2012a: 60).[15]

Trying to summarise the considerations that have been presented so far, we may risk putting forward a working hypothesis that Tadeusz Kowalik's reconstructed views give rise to a kind of cycle in which property relations first form a social structure, but then the tensions and conflicts arising between the classes forming this structure, or simply the changing consciousness and interests of certain social groups, lead finally to the formation of new property relations, which in turn cause new tensions and conflicts, etc.

Of particular importance for me, however, are the passages on the changes that occurred in the consciousness of the nomenklatura and the Solidarity intelligentsia, the references to "creating the foundations of a new system favourable to the middle-class-to-be" and to shock therapy as "a tool for creating a new, capitalist social structure" (and thus the embodiment of these changes in consciousness). Together, they constitute, I believe, premises for the recognition that, in Tadeusz Kowalik's works on the transformation of 1989, there are not only suggestions as to the existence of certain class-based tensions in the reality of the 1980s in Poland (not named as such, but nevertheless sufficiently explicit), but also "significant transformations in the class basis of the system" and, as a result, "a change in class rule".

A manifestation of the "tensions and contradictions in the functioning of the socio-economic system" according to Baszkiewicz's model is, however, also a "chronic crisis" besides the "class struggle" already discussed in this section. In Tadeusz Kowalik's work, we can find numerous references to economic stagnation, an issue very closely related to just such a crisis[16] that was, in his opinion, largely responsible for the collapse of real socialism or, as he put it

---

15 Elsewhere in the book, Kowalik refers to the same processes taking place in the Polish People's Republic (and in other Eastern Bloc countries) using Włodzimierz Brus's conceptual instrumentarium: "The increasingly bold reforms in the countries of Central Europe, especially in Hungary and Poland, mostly consisted of greater borrowing of systemic institutions from capitalism. While this did not adequately improve economic efficiency, it did serve to level out systemic differences. *Brus called this 'the progressing indeterminacy of socialism'* [emphasis mine – G.K.]" (Kowalik, 2012a: 28). The latter term, as Kowalik himself points out, even appears in the title of one of Brus's works (Brus, 1992).

16 Some authors even refer to stagnation as an *endless crisis*: "Stagnation ... produces all sorts of social and political crises …. For the vast majority of the population – excluding the big winners at the top – it feels like an *endless crisis* [emphasis mine – G.K.]" (Foster & McChesney, 2012: vii).

elsewhere borrowing a term from Włodzimierz Brus, "the breakdown of the monocentric order" (Kowalik, 2013b: 212).[17]

Thus, beyond general statements such as that real socialism "lost in the rivalry with capitalism because of its deeply rooted systemic defects" (Kowalik, 2012a: 254),[18] the author of *From Solidarity to Sellout* pointed precisely to the

---

17 In the passage in which he introduces this term, Kowalik also argues that this kind of collapse was a contingent predecessor to change: "The great events of 1989 seem to testify that the Brus position was spectacularly confirmed. After all, it was not only in Poland, but also in the entire Soviet bloc that the *monocentric order first broke down, a pluralistic political system was created, and only in the wake of this breakdown was deep, fundamental change to the economic systems initiated* [emphasis mine – G.K.]" (Kowalik, 2013b: 212). This statement, however, seems to be to some extent in contradiction with others, in which Kowalik argued that systemic changes (however limited and, in his opinion, ineffective) took place in Poland gradually throughout the 1980s. This is also largely the meaning of: "The economic reform carried out at the beginning of martial law meant, in theory, a quite fundamental reduction of directive planning in favour of steering the economy by means of such economic instruments as prices, wages, interest rate, credit. ... Moreover, *in the second half of the 1980s, the process of 'self-enfranchisement of the nomenklatura', above all of the party economic cadres, began to intensify. This process involved the transfer of the state production apparatus into private hands* [emphasis T.K.]" (Kowalik, 2002e: 617–618). Finally, Kowalik perhaps somewhat weakens the claim of the necessity of the "breakdown of the monocentric order" for "fundamental systemic changes in economies" when he writes: "I believe that the collapse of communism was inevitable. However, *it is possible to imagine many variants of this collapse, both in terms of time, pace and forms of transformation* [emphasis mine – G.K.]" (Kowalik, 2004b: 70).

18 The passage from which this sentence is taken reveals yet another of the possible paradoxes in Tadeusz Kowalik's views. We read there that "the system which is now history in Europe [real socialism] has obviously failed in economic terms. It lost in the rivalry with capitalism because of its deeply rooted systemic defects. This truth became indisputable at the turn of the 1980s. Market socialism, or at least [socialism] recognized as such in the versions we are familiar with (Yugoslav), had to lose as well. Even those who believe (and I am one of them) that this theoretical model has never been tried out anywhere, do not suggest it can be implemented in the foreseeable future. The spectacular breakdown of real socialism, together with the decentralized Yugoslav version, calls for caution in suggesting comprehensive system[ic] proposals" (Kowalik, 2012a: 254). Kowalik thus seems to regard the transition to capitalism as an objective historical necessity, which historiography (at least Marxist historiography) usually associated with *progress*. However, in other works Kowalik will refer to the same process as *social regress*: "the opinion that the expansion of the private sector meant a *social regress* [emphasis mine – G.K.] in Poland seems justified. The expansion of the range of goods on the consumer market and the ascendancy of some workers to owner-occupiers do not offset the decisive deterioration of working conditions and the dehumanisation of labour relations. They often signify primitive, nineteenth-century exploitation. Thus, in every respect – freedom, equality, participation – there is a denial of social justice" (Kowalik, 2002a: 74). There are, however, some clues as to how the author of *From Solidarity to Sellout* reconciled the two views. Perhaps the most important of these is contained in an interview Kowalik gave in

stagnation at the root of the transformations of the late 1980s in at least several works:

> Thus, even if one assumes that the final collapse of the communist system in Central and Eastern Europe was due to the great military duel between the two superpowers, the United States and the USSR, it was *the stagnation of the communist economies and, against this background, the growing dissatisfaction* [emphasis T.K.] of society that was the basic cause of America's success.
>
> KOWALIK, 2002e: 616–617[19]

2005 (Kowalik & Sierakowski, 2005). There he stated: "I define capitalism as a megasystem within which there are distinct variations. I attach great importance to this, because the differences are not trivial. *I believe that capitalism is a historically transitional formation. For today, however, my critical perspective on capitalism actually goes little beyond the Austrian-German-Swedish mix. These are patterns that have already managed to take shape in the contemporary world and are most sufficient for me as a horizon of change that I consider real and desirable* [emphasis mine – G.K.]. I do not object if I am described as a socialist, although neither today nor in the foreseeable future, for example, twenty years, *would I be inclined to propose a socialist prescription, that is, a system fundamentally different from capitalism. Why? I believe that communism contained certain elements borrowed from socialism and revised them negatively. This applies above all to property, but also to planning* [emphasis mine – G.K.]. On the other hand, *the Scandinavian countries, some among the East Asian countries, have taught us to socialise private property to such an extent that it somehow makes it possible to reconcile individual and social interests* [emphasis mine – G.K.]. Of course, if we conceive of property as a bundle of rights, divisible among various sub-entities, and not as a legal title to property. ... *I am not inclined to proclaim socialism as a fundamentally different system, because I do not know of a model that is at the same time democratic, just and efficient* [emphasis mine – G.K.]. Yes, I am in favour of workers' self-government. I think this is a huge, very important area [for action]. ... The Nobel laureate James Meade spoke of an infinite number of possible combinations of forms of ownership, organisation, remuneration. *It is necessary to keep looking for combinations of forms of ownership, forms of socialisation of private property, in a word, different forms of owner democracy, parliamentary democracy, and so on* [emphasis mine – G.K.]" (Kowalik & Sierakowski, 2005: 207–208).

19 In this respect, too, Kowalik distributed the emphasis of his argumentation differently in different works. In fact, in a text written two years later, we read that "the recourse ... to external forces from outside the nomenklatura led to the defeat of the [communist system] reformers ([Imre] Nagy, [Nikita] Khrushchev, [Alexander] Dubček. And finally the similar defeat of [Wojciech] Jaruzelski and [Mikhail] Gorbachev led to the collapse of the system. *This was favoured by the external environment – especially Reagan's Cold War military confrontation, who declared war on the communist 'evil empire'* [emphasis mine – G.K.]" (Kowalik, 2004b: 70).

And in another text, Kowalik wrote:

> *What proved fundamental for the fate of real socialism was the increasingly evident economic stagnation, which became all the more acute as the results of the IT revolution became more apparent* [emphasis mine – G.K]. And the extremely bureaucratic system proved incapable of even absorbing its results. If it succeeded, it was only in military technology, but at an exorbitant cost.
>
> KOWALIK, 2006a: 136

Finally, we find some clarification of the above thought in *Systemy gospodarcze*, where Kowalik states that real socialism

> suffered most from "production for production's sake", i.e. the production of an ever larger production apparatus, heavy industry, etc., which very slowly translated (if at all) into an increase in consumption or, more generally, into social development. One can say that the costs of functioning (maintenance) of that system consumed the lion's share of human and material resources.
>
> KOWALIK, 2005a: 25[20]

2

Although the work of the author of *From Solidarity to Sellout* contains some statements which can be regarded as references to the manifestations of a revolutionary situation in Poland at the end of the 1980s, Kowalik mostly takes a rather ambiguous stand. A good example is the issue of the "reformist impotence" of the pre-transformation authorities in the face of the crisis. On the one hand, in his synthesis of the development of the socio-economic situation of the Polish People's Republic since the end of the 1970s, which he presents in *Systemy gospodarcze*, after describing the attempts at reform undertaken by the authorities and their effects, Kowalik states that "With the liberalisation of the 1980s and *the disintegration of the apparatus of power* [emphasis mine – G.K.], the economy became less and less controllable ... *On the part of the authorities there was a growing conviction that without the legalisation of*

---

20 In another work, seemingly the same thought Kowalik expressed briefly: "real socialism was devoid of *internal incentives for development* [emphasis mine – G.K.] and therefore was bound to collapse" (Kowalik, 2004b: 69).

independent trade unions and social support, further economic reforms could not bring about any fundamental improvement [emphasis mine – G.K.]" (Kowalik, 2005a: 293).[21] On the other hand, in the same work, we read that

> the Polish authorities attempted to "outrun the crisis". In December 1988, the government of Mieczysław Rakowski led the Sejm to pass the *Ustawa o działalności gospodarczej* [Act on Economic Activity] and the *Ustawa o działalności gospodarczej z udziałem podmiotów zagranicznych* [Act on Economic Activity with the Participation of Foreign Entities]. *Both were a breakthrough in the authorities' approach and thinking* [emphasis mine – G.K.] ... [or] as the *Rzeczpospolita* daily put it, "a completely new page in the development of economic relations in our country". ... The composition of the government was also an absolute novelty. People like Mieczysław Wilczek, already known as a businessman, was appointed Minister of the Economy and Deputy Prime Minister and the business-oriented Ireneusz Sekuła Minister of the Economy and Deputy Prime Minister ... Both ostentatiously proclaimed free market slogans. *In the summer of 1989, Mieczysław Rakowski's government released food prices and the Minister of Finance announced a stabilisation programme, negotiated with the IMF* [International Monetary Fund]*, which envisaged, among other things, the imminent transformation of state enterprises into State Treasury sole shareholder companies, intended as an initial step towards privatisation* [emphasis mine – G.K.].
>
> KOWALIK, 2005a: 293–294[22]

---

21   Similarly, and probably even more decisively, in the passage quoted earlier: "The party-state bureaucracy created to meet the needs of imposed industrialisation [after 1945] did not give way anymore. *It was incapable of reforming the system, and it was also incapable of reforming itself* [emphasis mine – G.K.]" (Kowalik et al., 2013: 651).

22   In a similar way one can probably interpret Kowalik's statement, quoted above, that "The strongest argument in favour of ... treating Sovietism as state capitalism is the *exceptionally smooth transition to free-market capitalism, the ease with which the former party nomenklatura, especially the part of it most involved in the economy, was converted into a business nomenklatura* [emphasis mine – G.K.]" (Kowalik, 2004b: 69). On the other hand, the same article states that "The rejected industrialisation and the military and police defence ... of the [communist] system in a hostile environment, led to the emergence of a *hierarchical, rigid power structure increasingly incapable of rational action, even of absorbing foreign innovations* [emphasis mine – G.K.]. ... In Poland, both the opposition and the decisive centres of power [finally] reached agreement at the Round Table. The condition for this readiness to reach an agreement, however, was ... the *political power weakened by martial law, which finally lost its sense of mission to modernise the country* [emphasis mine – G.K.] (Kowalik, 2004b: 69–70).

What in particular draws attention in the above is that the same communists (metaphorically rather than literally) who had earlier made attempts to reform the old system, which Kowalik had assessed negatively, are responsible for the majority of the fundamental transformations of the economy towards capitalism.

Not entirely satisfactory, from the point of view of seeking possible references to the revolutionary situation, are also Kowalik's statements on economic inequality in the last years of the Polish People's Republic. In the polemic which he undertook with Dariusz Rosati, the author of *From Solidarity to Sellout* points out that:

> In the second half of the 1990s ... many publications ... showed that *Polish income disparities at that time* [i.e. during the years of real socialism] *were greater than the disparities in the Scandinavian countries, Japan, and India, and were more or less at the level of the Federal Republic of Germany, Belgium, and the Netherlands* [emphasis mine – G.K.]. And so the causes of poor efficiency and the "disintegration" of the system of real socialism did not lie in excessive pressure ... to ensure social justice.
>
> KOWALIK, 2012a: 97

And in one of the chapters from a monograph entitled *Nierówni i równiejsi* we read that

> contrary to propaganda, past and present, *the countries of real socialism cannot be described as simply more egalitarian than capitalist ones. In any case, this does not apply to income disparities in the* PRL. *Numerous studies show that during the years of real socialism, income and wage differentials remained at a level characteristic of the more egalitarian capitalist countries of Western Europe* [emphasis mine – G.K.]. ... Already prior to 1989 Poland was closer to the middle of the levels of inequality in the countries of Western Europe. They were definitely greater than in Scandinavian countries, as well as Belgium and (West) Germany, reaching the level of the Netherlands. ... Among the communist countries, only Czechoslovakia had indicators similar to Finland, the most egalitarian Scandinavian country.
>
> KOWALIK, 2002a: 58–59[23]

---

23 And in 2010, Kowalik added in this context with indignation that "In the Czech Republic, Slovenia, Hungary ... as well as Slovakia, income inequalities (as measured by the Gini index) still today do not exceed those that Poland had before 1989!" (Kowalik & Dryszel,

The problem with considering the quoted statements as referring to a revolutionary situation (in Baszkiewicz's terms) is that, although they point to economic inequalities in the Polish People's Republic, they do not in any way address the dynamics of this phenomenon; in particular they do not answer whether, in the years immediately preceding the revolution of 1989, there was an *increase* in income and wage disparities.

Moreover, due to the lack of any significant references to the social crisis, political crisis, financial bankruptcy of the state or the increase in activity of the masses in the final period of existence of the Polish People's Republic in the works of Kowalik I have taken into account,[24] one can risk a claim that the only manifestation of the revolutionary situation fully consistent with Baszkiewicz's model is Kowalik's reference to the "disintegration of the apparatus of power". In *Systemy gospodarcze,* he states that "the 1980s were a period of *decomposition of power structures* [emphasis mine – G.K.] and processes of 'commercialization' of a considerable part of the nomenklatura, who intuitively sensed the twilight of the old order" (Kowalik, 2005a: 352).[25]

However, while explaining his attitude to real socialism in *From Solidarity to Sellout,* Tadeusz Kowalik also presents the following reflection on this system:

2010: 38). Interestingly, in an interview from 2005 Kowalik drew attention to a completely different dimension of social inequality with which Polish society entered the period of transformation: "It is not true that the communist nomenklatura entered the new system with sizeable resources that could have been multiplied. *They were rich not in resources, but … in information* [emphasis mine – G.K.]. I noticed many times that it was those from the economic nomenklatura and not the political apparatchiks that made the quick gains. Because they knew the people, the mechanisms, etc." (Kowalik & Sierakowski, 2005: 201).

24   In his reflections on the end of real socialism in Poland, Tadeusz Kowalik focused on – in addition to the issues already discussed, such as stagnation – completely different causes: "A number of factors contributed to the peaceful collapse of communism. In Poland, both the opposition and the decisive centres of power were ready to come to an agreement at the Round Table. A prerequisite for this readiness to agree was, on the one hand, the strong position of the Catholic Church, which supported the Solidarity movement weakened by martial law, and, on the other, the political power also weakened by martial law. … I would also not underestimate the role of the usual tactical mistakes made by Jaruzelski and Gorbachev. Both of them did not want the final demontage of the system, or at any rate not at that moment, but they miscalculated" (Kowalik, 2004b: 70). Kowalik's acknowledgement that it was precisely this combination of circumstances that was behind the Polish transformation remains, I believe, in close connection with, as I have already explained, his use of the term "revolution from above" in the first half of the 1990s, which is not inconsistent with the thesis of the "epigonic bourgeois revolution".

25   We also read on the decomposition – this time of "systems of power" – in Kowalik's review of the book by Henryk Słabek (Kowalik, 2006a: 142).

> The fact that such a system could last for seventy years ... bespeaks its longevity, albeit its existence was based on the strength of an open and secret machine of repression. But repression itself is not enough to maintain power. The process leading to the downfall of socialism revealed that the machinery of repression becomes powerless *if societies in their mass reject the existing system* [emphasis mine – G.K.].
> KOWALIK, 2012a: 26

Thus, in the quoted fragment, Kowalik refers to one of the essential elements of the model "revolutionary consciousness", i.e. he presents a thesis that society, Polish society in this case, rejected the old system (real socialism).[26] However, he does not try to prove this thesis either for the general public or for entire social groups but gives quite convincing examples concerning politically influential individuals. For example, when reporting on the political and economic discussions at the Round Table talks, Kowalik refers to a statement by Władysław Baka, who voiced the need to build "a system of operation of the economy based on monetary-market economy logic, *which must replace entirely the administrative-command economy logic* [emphasis mine – G.K.]" (Borodziej & Garlicki, 2004: 24; quoted in Kowalik, 2012a: 61). The author of *From Solidarity to Sellout* then juxtaposes this with the view of another participant, Witold Trzeciakowski, according to whom:

> The collapse of Polish economy, its immense indebtedness, the impoverishment of the people, the rising inflation leading to economic chaos and the contamination of the natural environment – these are the results of the existing system's order. *This order must be rejected* [emphasis mine – G.K.].
> BORODZIEJ & GARLICKI, 2004: 26; quoted in KOWALIK, 2012a: 62

It is unlikely that statements so openly negating the possibility of reforming socialism and emphasising the necessity of its rejection were the expression of a sudden and unreflective change of views. They must have been preceded by an evolution in thinking about systemic solutions in Poland, of which Kowalik seemed to be aware. Thus in *From Solidarity to Sellout* we read, for example, that "With the introduction of martial law in 1981, the very possibility of effectively reforming real socialism was questioned more and more

---

26 I will not here go into Kowalik's rather controversial formulation of the problem, from which it could follow that real socialism was rejected by *entire* societies rather than just specific social groups.

often" although with a caveat that "Most critics still took it for granted that the ossified system would continue (in stagnation) for a long time to come" (Kowalik, 2012a: 175). Elsewhere in the book, Kowalik makes the above opinion more precise in relation to opposition circles:

> The conditions of martial law and its repercussions in subsequent years were instrumental in making the illegal S.[olidarity] primarily an antisystem movement, adverse to the government and the system. *Even activists who had been moderate in the past now had doubts about the feasibility of the reform of really existing socialism, or even of its cautious liberalization or the admittance of social pluralism* [emphasis mine – G.K.].
> KOWALIK, 2012a: 35

Meanwhile, as the political situation developed (also, or perhaps above all, in the Soviet Union), views as radical as those of Stefan Kurowski, quoted by Kowalik in the context of three Polish attempts to adapt socialism to the free market in the 1980s, were articulated with increasing frequency:

> And so there will be no fourth attempt at [economic] reform. *There will be a change of the system. The central planning system must perish, so that no stone is left unturned. In its place another system will be built.* [...] *This system is market capitalism* [emphasis mine – G.K.] – a pluralist economy of many entities, in other words a society managing its affairs.
> JANCZAK [Kurowski], 1986 : 60; quoted in KOWALIK, 2012a: 176

However, perhaps the most significant opinion quoted or commented on by the author of *From Solidarity to Sellout* was the one by Jacek Kuroń (according to Kowalik, one of the most important figures in Polish politics at that time) at the very beginning of the 1990s, showing how the main architects of the events of 1989 justified the necessity of carrying out "shock therapy" with reformist impossibilism:

> Since no one succeeds with a planned economy and manual steering [...] then all the more is it impossible to implement the idea that it can be further steered, taking on additionally the burden of its planned transformation into a free-market economy.
> KUROŃ, 1991: 10, 17–18; quoted in KOWALIK, 2012a: 114–115

In his work, however, Kowalik does not limit himself to numerous quotes on how, in the second half of the 1980s, successive opposition activists lost confidence in the possibility of reforming real socialism. He also briefly discusses, referring in particular to the views of Ira Katznelson and Andrzej Walicki, the ideological evolution of the Solidarity intelligentsia closely connected with this "loss of faith".

The first of the above-mentioned authors was, according to Kowalik, very surprised in May 1987 by "the radically changed attitude: the rejection by the Solidarity opposition of the 'Self-Governing Republic' program in favor of conservative liberalism, which people began calling neoliberalism" (Kowalik, 2012a: 40). Andrzej Walicki, on returning to Poland after six years of absence in the spring of 1987 had a similar impression. As Kowalik quotes,

> When I came to Poland in May 1987 [...] the Polish intellectual scene turned out to be different than I had expected. The liberals were no longer treated as oddballs, unimportant lunatics or, at best, a handful of crazy intellectuals, propagating in a provocative way ideas that were maybe interesting, but that did not fit the country's reality. They became the most dynamic intellectual group, located in the best strategic point, pushing aside other groups to defensive positions. Proponents, or at least sympathizers of liberal ideas were visible nearly everywhere and greatly contributed to the change in the general intellectual climate. [...] Obviously, this process was the result of the new political circumstances, created by the general amnesty for political prisoners of September 1986, the pragmatic implementation of the policy of the communist authorities and finally [...] of the increasingly perceptible influence of the reform actions of Gorbachev.
> WALICKI, 2000: 37–38; quoted in KOWALIK, 2012a: 41

Importantly, Kowalik also noticed the same tendency in the communist elite:

> The process of implementing market elements into the economy led, at the same time, to the "commercialization" of the attitudes of the ruling elites and their loss of faith in the superiority of socialism, thereby to the erosion of any modernization mission. As soon as the most farsighted of the communist reformers began to realize that they would not be able to carry through more profound changes solely with the Party apparatus and state administration, they had to appeal to social groups beyond the party nomenklatura, which led to a change in the power status and finally to the collapse of the entire system.
> KOWALIK, 2012a: 28

The final effect of both politically conflicted sides' evolution in this common direction can be considered, in the light of Kowalik's work, the formation of

> *an understanding above divisions* [emphasis mine – G.K.] ... The faith in the inevitability of something in the way of primitive capital accumulation as an inseparable part of the transition to a market economy was then an integral part of the *imagination of the political and economic elites* [emphasis mine – G.K.].
> KOWALIK, 2012a: 96

The issue of the "imagination of the political and economic elites", undoubtedly falling within the broadly conceived category of "revolutionary consciousness", will return repeatedly in Kowalik's work. Elsewhere in *From Solidarity to Sellout* we read, for example, that "the Big Bang (or shock therapy, as the Balcerowicz Plan was sometimes called) was not necessary. It revealed *a neophyte faith that the main decision makers and their advisors had in the free market* [emphasis mine – G.K.]" (Kowalik, 2012a: 106). And in *Nierówni i równiejsi*, Kowalik points out that "the 'economic imagination' of the new power elite was shaped in the 1980s, i.e. at the peak of the success of the conservative-liberal (counter-)revolution carried out by Ronald Reagan and Margaret Thatcher in the United States of America and Great Britain" (Kowalik, 2002d: 12).

Reflections on this issue lead the author of *From Solidarity to Sellout* to also discuss the emotional character of the "elites' imagination":

> both in Poland and in many other countries, ... *emotions ... prevailed* [emphasis mine – G.K.], effectively influenced by the atmosphere of an easy victory of the political ... "spirit of the times" shaped by the ideas of Margaret Thatcher and Ronald Reagan. Because, at that time, it was their ideas that were on the offensive and social democratic ideas in retreat, although in 1989 Reagan was already retired, and Thatcher only a year later (at the end of 1990) spectacularly lost her job as prime minister. ... *The victors ... were those* [ideas] *that were in line with the spirit (or rather the global trend) of the times. For the choices of a particular social order are choices based on values, and these do not yield to the criteria of truth and falsehood. Hence the great role played by psychological motives in their choice* [emphasis mine – G.K.].
> KOWALIK, 2013b: 221

The above quote indicates that Tadeusz Kowalik, partly parallel to all the other considerations I have mentioned so far in this chapter, also sought the reasons for the shape of the Polish systemic transformation in the "way of thinking" ("atmosphere", "spirit of the times", "ideas" or "psychological motives"). He, therefore, did not look to objective social and economic factors like class conflicts or economic stagnation but in what takes place exclusively in the sphere of "values" that "are not subject to the criteria of truth and falsehood."[27]

This passage, however, cannot be regarded as definitively conclusive. Elsewhere, albeit briefly, the author of *From Solidarity to Sellout* allows for a more materialistic interpretation of the evolving consciousness of selected social groups in the Polish People's Republic during the 1980s. I am referring here to the appearance of the category of *interest* in his analysis. Critically reviewing Słabek's book, Kowalik quotes his question: whether "the 'communist' elites set fire to their own home?", to cite, not without approval, the following response by this author:

> They consistently acted to their own advantage, in accordance with their own, albeit changing interests. The interest was changing and so they also made haste to reorient themselves to fit the image of these new times they had undoubtedly dreamt about.
>
> SŁABEK, 2004: 400; quoted in KOWALIK, 2012a: 51

3

From Tadeusz Kowalik's *Systemy gospodarcze* we learn that:

> Many factors influence the choice of system and manner of systemic change. *When the authorities begin the process of change with a particular theoretical concept and practical approach, the power elite's "economic imagination" plays a huge role, consisting of both knowledge and persistent myths* [emphasis T.K.].
>
> KOWALIK, 2005a: 291

---

[27] It should be noted, however, that Kowalik himself happened to confront these two approaches (although he did not attempt to resolve the problems arising from a confrontation of this kind). Thus, for example, he wrote that "the shape and directions ... of [economic] policy depend not only on the often false, as [John Maynard] Keynes emphasised, perceptions of the ruling elite, but also *on the pressure of various social groups. It is they who break the authorities' rather natural tendency towards opportunism and impossibilism* [emphasis mine – G.K.]" (Kowalik, 2002d: 48).

The passage makes clear how fluid the line is between what can be considered a reference to revolutionary consciousness (here represented by the "elites' imagination") and what can constitute a "revolutionary project" ("the authorities begin the process of change with a particular theoretical concept and practical approach").

In the works by Kowalik devoted to the Polish transformation, the revolutionary project, that is the "ideas of social forces about the aims, tasks and limits of revolution" in Poland already appears quite clearly in the second half of the 1980s, above all in the authorities' concepts and decisions (heralding, in a way, the "revolution from above"), but also in the views of some representatives of the opposition. Moreover, as we shall see, the closer we get to 1989, the more crystallised this project becomes.

Let us start with the government. In *Systemy gospodarcze*, Kowalik points out that, already in the first year of martial law,

> an economic reform was implemented that meant a quite fundamental reduction of directive planning in favour of steering the economy with economic instruments (prices, wages, interest rate, credit, etc.). The reform was based on assumptions similar to the New Economic Mechanism implemented in Hungary since 1968, which was initially quite widely praised for its effective improvement of efficiency.
> KOWALIK, 2005a: 292[28]

It is still not a project for a drastic break with socialism, but only a rather moderate movement towards capitalism though, as Kowalik shows, already five years later, in 1987, the first important taboo, the issue of privatisation, was broken as it, probably for the first time in decades, appeared

> in a document coming from a government organ. The *Tezy w sprawie II etapu reformy gospodarczej* [Theses Concerning the Second Stage of Economic Reform], published in April by the Committee for Economic Reform, spoke of pluralism and the necessity of equal treatment of various ownership forms. A possibility was also included for the transformation of state-owned enterprises into State Treasury companies that would be supervised by commercial banks under the principle of capital shares.
> KOWALIK, 2012a: 177

---

28 For more on reforming the economy of the PRL and, in particular, the attitude of Polish economists to this issue, see (Tanewski, 2014).

Kowalik provides a brief explanation of this both rapid and far-reaching evolution:

> in the second half of the 1980s ... [t]he government was growing convinced that without the legislation of independent trade unions and social support, further economic reforms could not bring about any fundamental improvement. The anti-reformist wing of the ruling party had lost the Soviet Union's potential support where Mikhail Gorbachev was pursuing "glasnost" and "perestroika" (openness and reconstruction), clearly signalling that the time of protection for the rulers in the satellite countries was over.
> KOWALIK, 2005a: 293

These circumstances, Kowalik goes on to explain, prompted the authorities attempt to preempt the crisis:

> In December 1988, the government of Mieczysław Rakowski led the Sejm to pass the *Ustawa o działalności gospodarczej* [Act on Economic Activity] and the *Ustawa o działalności gospodarczej z udziałem podmiotów zagranicznych* [Act on Economic Activity with the Participation of Foreign Entities]. Both were a breakthrough in the authorities' approach and thinking ... [or] as the *Rzeczpospolita* daily put it, "a completely new page in the development of economic relations in our country". There was package of laws being prepared that would regulate economic life in a new way in areas like ownership of means of production, taxation, price and wage formation, credit and foreign trade. They were to supplement the principle of freedom and equality (in the treatment of economic entities and forms of ownership) with that of competition.
> KOWALIK, 2005a: 292–294

The content of the above-mentioned laws was probably most accurately summarised in January 1989 by Mieczysław Wilczek, their co-author, the then Deputy Prime Minister in Mieczysław Rakowski's government. Kowalik quotes Wilczek, via Waldemar Kuczyński, who states directly: "[as a government] we are definitely heading towards a market economy. We, political and state authorities, now know *there is no intermediate state between a market economy and a centrally controlled economy. All these were hybrids which did not work on the global scale* [emphasis mine – G.K.]" (Kuczyński, 1996: 281;

quoted in Kowalik, 2005a: 293).[29] According to the author of *From Solidarity to Sellout*, only a month later, during the Round Table talks, another Deputy Prime Minister, Ireneusz Sekuła's main message was "We have already begun the implementation of radical market reforms. Help us" (Kowalik, 2012a: 63).

On the other hand, as far as the *Solidarność* side is concerned, the earliest "revolution in the economy" projects are discussed in Kowalik's comment on "some of the opposition activists who had found financial support in the rapidly developing private sector", which, according to the author of *From Solidarity to Sellout*, "gave rise to economic societies" (Kowalik, 2012a: 43). Kowalik points out that:

> Already on January 1, 1989, one declaration, "Minimum zmian" [Minimum of Changes] was published by Economic Action, associating several regional economic societies. This minimum was quite substantial, as it included repealing rationing of production factors and liberating prices of production and consumption goods, and even of some public services, setting the interest rate at the market level, withdrawal of the state from the banking system, and many changes in the organization of the economy. And all this was to be done at once – "within half a year". As can be seen, in early 1989 there were already manifestations of views anticipating the shock therapy that was put forward more than half a year later by Jeffrey Sachs and Stanisław Gomułka.
>
> KOWALIK, 2012a: 43

As reported by Tadeusz Kowalik, Economic Action's position was obviously quite extreme for the conditions of the time (although these were changing very quickly, as we shall see later). However, it is an important point of reference, as it reflects well the character of one of the two main concepts of systemic transformation then functioning in Poland. Kowalik, discussing the Round Table talks, summarises both as follows:

> The first is the implementation of an economy based on cooperative, social-democratic principles that encourage a mixed economy, with considerable employee participation and a full-employment policy. This

---

29 In another work, Kowalik quotes a much more blunt statement by Wilczek when he writes that "[Prime Minister] Mieczysław Rakowski … does not seem to have realised to whom he entrusted power over the economy. *It was his 'law that finished off this bloody socialism',* boasted former minister Mieczysław Wilczek [emphasis mine – G.K.]" (Kowalik, 2009a: 11).

would bring the planned social order closer to the Austrian and Swedish models. The second is based on privatization in the form of joint stock companies, opened to global competition, the development of the stock exchange, and the desire to cooperate with the International Monetary Fund, combined with acceptance of what was then called the Washington Consensus along with its well-known conditionality principle (providing assistance under certain conditions).

KOWALIK, 2012a: 68–69

What is extremely important is that both concepts constitute the framework of the programme of transition from real socialism to capitalism. Thus, in Kowalik's view, already at the beginning of 1989, both sides of the political conflict were in agreement on this issue. In *From Solidarity to Sellout,* the author presents quite a few arguments in support of this interpretation.

Reporting on the position taken during the Round Table talks by the already mentioned Deputy Prime Minister Sekuła, Kowalik quotes what he calls Sekuła's "three fundamental slogans": liberty, equality, competition (sic!), while, as he explains, they all referred, in an extremely laissez-faire spirit, only to "economic entities" (Kowalik, 2012a: 64). Kowalik then recalls Sekuła's (and the entire government's) idea for fixing the economy: "the fastest possible introduction of a market economy wherever this is possible and as quickly as this is possible" (Kowalik, 2012a: 64). What is particularly striking is that, according to Kowalik, the implementation of Sekuła's project was to mean the establishment of a new economic order "as quickly as possible, not later than by the end of 1991" (Kowalik, 2012a: 66). It was therefore undoubtedly not only a vision of specific changes that should take place in the economy but also a timetable for putting this vision into practice (in this case taking the form of de facto "shock therapy").[30]

Tadeusz Kowalik also refers to *Solidarność* representatives' negotiation stance. In the statements he quoted (e.g. by Cezary Józefiak, Jan Mujżel and Janusz Beksiak), particular attention is drawn to the criticism of the government for insufficient radicalism in the proposed changes. As Kowalik summarises:

---

30 Kowalik frames this with a surprising comment: "Did this magic date signify a 'leap' into the new order, which would contradict the principle of evolution proclaimed in the [Round Table] [A]greements? *This question cannot be answered explicitly* [emphasis mine – G.K.]" (Kowalik, 2012a: 66).

> The discussion led to the crystallization of a concept of far-reaching free enterprise in the economy and its privatization. *Was this already the embarkation on the path to capitalism? The declarations of Minister Wilczek and Janusz Beksiak leave no doubt that in their opinion, and most probably also that of Cezary Józefiak, this was the only realistic solution* [emphasis mine – G.K.].
> KOWALIK, 2012a: 65

And referring more generally to the *Solidarność* economic programme in the spring of 1989, the author of *From Solidarity to Sellout* notes that,

> Solidarność had been advocating [in the months prior to June 1989 – G.K.] a self-governing market economy with a mixed ownership structure, winning over the existing power establishment to this programme. It went into the elections with a similar electoral programme. As far as the most systemic issues are concerned, it states that "We will work for the creation of a new economic order *based on the market and independent enterprises operating under market conditions* [emphasis mine – G.K.]".
> KOWALIK, 2002e: 620[31]

Thus, the Round Table talks, as one may think, only strengthened and accentuated the consensus on the desired economic system, which, in the light of Kowalik's work, prevailed among the main political forces at least since the beginning of 1989, and had consistently consolidated throughout the first half of that year. We find a passage in *From Solidarity to Sellout* that summarises this interpretation well:

> During the Round Table negotiations of 1989 ... not only the general concept of the new order, but also several other important provisions managed to gain the acceptance of both parties to these talks. First of all, there was acceptance of the cardinal demand for a "constitutional guarantee of the durability of a pluralist ownership structure". ... And so privatization was not treated as something marginal, since ... postulates were put forward to reduce the then huge budgetary deficit with resources derived mainly "from the sale and lease of components of state assets: apartments, land, shops, production facilities and ownership

---

31 The sentence quoted by Kowalik in this passage comes from: ("Komitet Obywatelski", 1989: 5–6).

stakes (shares and the like)". ... It was even agreed that by 1991 (which is exactly when this happened), the Stock Exchange would be established, which naturally assumed the existence of a significant number of private firms. *In terms of a program, a whole "new economic order" was on the agenda, although implemented by the evolutionary method* [emphasis mine – G.K.].

KOWALIK, 2012a: 187–188[32]

---

[32] The sentences quoted by Kowalik in this passage come from: ("Statut", 1981: 14). In another text, Kowalik discusses in more detail this "new order's" principles: "Here are six basic features intended to characterise this order: [1] *The development of self-government and worker participation.* [2] *Free formation of the ownership structure.* [3] *Development of market relations and competition.* [4] *The dismantling of the remnants of the command-and-control system and the reduction of central planning to the shaping of state economic policy, implemented with economic tools.* [5] *Uniform financial policy towards enterprises.* [6] *Subordination of the mechanisms of selection of managerial staff in enterprises to the criterion of professional competence* [emphasis T.K.]. An agreement was also reached on the establishment of a nationwide representation of employee councils and the creation of a National Property Fund, although both negotiating parties had a different view of their competencies and location in the power structure" (Kowalik, 2002e: 618–619). In the same work, we can also find theoretical reflections on the essence of the Round Table Agreements: "To this day, there are different assessments of the 'New Economic Order' outlined in the Agreements: whether it would be truly new or only a radically reformed previous order. ... However, even according to the old opposition of 'real socialism' and capitalism as two systems, *there is no doubt that the Agreements outlined the contours of the most radical systemic reform to date* [emphasis mine – G.K.]. ... In designing the radical reform, it was not resolved very clearly what this 'new economic order' was ultimately to be. It is likely, however, that for the majority of negotiators, the models most desirable and most familiar in Poland at the time were such varieties of *market economies* [emphasis mine – G.K.] as existed in West Germany, Austria or Sweden. Was it therefore a 'new economic order'? *The answer to this question depends on the definition* [emphasis mine – G.K.]. One can assume that the 'mega-systems' of both socialism and capitalism consist of multiple systems (orders). And drawing all the consequences from the demand for privatisation and marketisation, up to the creation of a capital market (stock exchange), one can probably assume that, together with the political changes in the Agreements, *a general framework for an 'open society'* [in Dahrendorf's sense] *was created* [emphasis mine – G.K.]. This framework left the space open enough that it did not close the way for further exploration precisely by the method of dialogue and agreements" (Kowalik, 2002e: 618–620). It is worth drawing attention at this point to the theme of workers' self-government, recurring regularly in Tadeusz Kowalik's works (among others, in the previously quoted fragment of an interview given by Kowalik, where, as we have seen, it was uttered: "Yes, I am in favour of workers' self-government" (Kowalik & Sierakowski, 2005: 207)). A discussion of this issue is beyond the capacity of this book, so I will limit myself to stating that such self-governance undoubtedly constituted an important element not only in Kowalik's political economy but also in his biography (see, for example, (Kowalik et al., 2013: 628 et seq.)).

In another work, Kowalik even writes in this context that "the differences of opinion [between the participants of the Round Table talks] consisted mainly in the fact that the government side clearly did not want to make more concrete commitments in the area of ownership transformation" (Kowalik, 2002e: 619). It is, therefore, not surprising that in the months that elapsed between the development of the Agreements and the final adoption by Tadeusz Mazowiecki's new government of the concepts that ultimately made up the Balcerowicz Plan, there was only a crystallisation, or sharpening, of the program of breaking with real socialism and the rapid transformation to capitalism, on both sides of the political scene. Kowalik points to several important indicators showing that this process was indeed on-going.

Let us begin with a description of the evolution of the government's position, starting with *Założenia programu gospodarczego na lata 1989–1992* [Assumptions of the Economic Programme for 1989–1992] ("Założenia programu", 1989) published in July 1989 in *Rzeczpospolita*, as reported by Kowalik:

> Rakowski's team had already postulated the general commercialization of state-owned enterprises, treating this as an introduction to privatization, far-reaching market economy, radical reduction of the quantity of money in the economy, and a profound restructuring of enterprises, combined with bankruptcies and unemployment. The author of one of the first histories of this period [Krystyna Bolesta-Kukułka] would evaluate the content matter of this document as "nearly entirely concurrent in the basic aims and methods with the program later implemented as the Balcerowicz Plan". ... This is the view shared to this day by the main architect of this document, former finance minister Andrzej Wróblewski, who publicly said that he was happy that Balcerowicz implemented his plan.
>
> KOWALIK, 2012a: 86[33]

This is not the only fragment from *From Solidarity to Sellout* in which the author presents Wróblewski's position as symptomatic. Describing the project for the reform of the Polish economy developed by George Soros in the spring of 1989 (and consistently referring to it as the "Big Bang"), Kowalik refers to the correspondence on this matter between Soros and Wróblewski, citing, among others,

---

33   The quote by Kowalik in this excerpt is from (Bolesta-Kukułka, 1992: 141). In a 2010 interview, Kowalik even credits Wróblewski with claiming that the latter "is happy that Leszek Balcerowicz has put his programme into practice" (Kowalik & Dryszel, 2010: 39).

> [an] extensive, three-page letter [from Wróblewski to Soros] of May 23, 1989, ... devoted nearly entirely to the character and manner of establishing ... the capital market, pegging the zloty to the ecu, ... converting debt into shares in state enterprises and the sale thereof, and the powers of the Paris Club. He did not, however, touch on the issue of the Big Bang with regard to prices, subsidies, and unemployment together with its social safety net. *Could it be that a member of the formally "communist" government accepted in advance such a radically shocking proposal? As we shall see, such a speculation is not too distant from the somewhat later documents of the ministry* [emphasis mine – G.K.].
>
> KOWALIK, 2012a: 92

Finally, of Kowalik's numerous examples of how the programme of revolutionary economic change in Poland was shaped on the government side, the one concerning Dariusz Rosati undoubtedly stands out. The author of *From Solidarity to Sellout* recalls that the then advisor to Prime Minister Rakowski was

> One of the extreme proponents of a free-market economy. ... Shortly before the parliamentary election [June 4, 1989], he outlined a concept that was concurrent not only with the forthcoming Balcerowicz Plan, but also with the more radical proposals of Beksiak's group. He postulated "liberated prices and – please use bold type here [he requested – T.K.] – liberated wages, and also: lowering tax burdens", fluid [sic!] interest rates balancing supply and demand, a capital market, currency convertibility, foreign competition, and opening up to privatization. The market transformations were to last one to two years.
>
> KOWALIK, 2012a: 93–94

On the other hand, Kowalik devotes a lot of space to how the opposition's economic plans and concepts evolved. The description of the attitude of *Solidarność* circles to the Jeffrey Sachs (and David Lipton) plan since the spring of 1989 is particularly emblematic. Undoubtedly, one of Kowalik's most important comments notes the change that occurred in the character of Sachs's proposal within the space of a few weeks as it changed from a programme of cautious stabilisation to a "leap" into the market. According to the author of *From Solidarity to Sellout* "[it] bespeaks its political character and not the alleged economic necessity of selecting the shock therapy, as would be declared afterward" (Kowalik, 2012a: 101).

However, from the point of view of searching in the work of Kowalik for a revolutionary project, his focus on Sachs's plan as being in fact consistent with the Rakowski government's very well-publicised proposals turns out to be more important. Kowalik also notes that the plan received widespread recognition from the opposition elite and names Aleksander Paszyński and Marek Dąbrowski among the supporters of the "jump into the market":

> The only economists who from the beginning publicly backed Sachs's program were Aleksander Paszyński and Marek Dąbrowski. Dąbrowski explained his support in a ... desperate way ... Though he conceded that the patient may not survive this "major surgery" (the people may revolt), he asked nonetheless, "Is there any other therapy that offers better chances for survival?"
>
> KOWALIK, 2012a: 102

Another *Solidarność* supporter of the "leap" who also drew up his own, quite concrete proposals, was Stanisław Gomułka. Kowalik quotes a fragment of his *Guardian* article from mid-August 1989:

> Poland needs the competitiveness to service the debt, and it needs the unemployment to create competitive labour markets to produce greater labour mobility, work discipline and the control of wage inflation. The Polish economy clearly requires a surgical operation to remove the outdated and inefficient industries. A similar operation in [Great] Britain in the early 1980s led initially to much higher unemployment and to an improvement only later. The interesting question is whether a Solidarity-led government will be capable of conceiving and implementing such a Thatcherite policy.
>
> GOMUŁKA, 1989: 5; quoted in KOWALIK, 2012a: 86–87[34]

Finally, the author of *From Solidarity to Sellout* cites another important circumstance in this context:

> On the commission of ... Bronisław Geremek, Beksiak's group [cooperating with Sachs for some time as Economic Rescue Team – G.K.] prepared and published a report that proposed total withdrawal of the state from

---

34 The quote has been corrected according to the original. Kowalik, while writing *Polska transformacja*, was not yet aware that Gomułka's article, just a few days after its publication, had already been translated into Polish by Jerzy Osiatyński as *Polskiej gospodarce potrzeba wstrząsu* and distributed among the MPs of the Obywatelski Klub Parlamentarny [Civic Parliamentary Club, OKP]. See (Kowalik, 2010b: 465).

> the economy; a market economy was to come into being spontaneously. There were to be no price regulations and no building of a new system by the state (constructionism). This merely confirmed the extreme, uncompromising laissez-faire policy disclosed by Beksiak at the Round Table. At any rate, the signatures under the report, of Jan Winiecki and Stefan Kurowski ... spoke for themselves.
>
> KOWALIK, 2012a: 117

In the light of the above quotes from Kowalik's works, one may risk a claim that it was thanks to the unanimity prevailing among the parties of the political dispute in Poland in the winter, spring and summer of 1989 that a revolutionary project was born, which was finally implemented in the form of the Balcerowicz Plan. The author of *From Solidarity to Sellout* cites, as he puts it, "the only comprehensive public presentation" of this Plan (Kowalik, 2012a: 121), i.e. a brochure supplement to *Rzeczpospolita* of 12th October 1989, commissioned by the Ministry of Finance and entitled *Założenia i kierunki polityki gospodarczej* [Assumptions and Directions of Economic Policy] ("Założenia i kierunki", 1989).[35] As Kowalik claims, the basic premise of the programme is summarised in this publication:

---

35 Kowalik succinctly, and at the same time comprehensively, presented the history of the creation of the successive documents collectively referred to as the Balcerowicz Plan in an interview from 2010: "At the time of his appointment, Balcerowicz himself had no plan, other than a general belief that a free market economy was the most efficient. So, faced with an imminent trip to Washington for the annual session of the IMF and the World Bank, he commissioned Sachs and Lipton to outline an economic programme. He went to Washington with a text heavily reworked by Stanisław Gomułka (who was becoming Balcerowicz's chief advisor) and colleagues. On the basis of this English-language text, Balcerowicz's then deputy, Marek Dąbrowski, wrote a more extensive outline of the programme, which was published in early October by *Rzeczpospolita*. It was a list of intentions rather than a programme of action. The fullest and most systematic exposition of the assumptions of the Balcerowicz plan was contained in a letter of intent, signed by Balcerowicz and NBP [National Bank of Poland] President Władysław Baka, but written, according to IMF custom, by the Fund's experts. The letter was negotiated with the Polish authorities. ... Of course, this text was never published or translated in Poland. After that, there were only internal studies running in two directions: the budget for the following year and the programme, broken down into a dozen or so bills, ten of which were hurriedly passed by parliament in the last days of December '89. And then there was Balcerowicz's parliamentary speech about a successful life instead of a pretended one. No wonder, then, that polemics and criticism of the final version of the Balcerowicz plan appeared when it was 'over' and the plan was implemented" (Kowalik & Dryszel, 2010: 40).

> The Polish economy requires essential systemic changes. Their goal is to build a market system similar to the one existing in the highly developed countries. This has to take place quickly, by means of radical measures, in order to shorten as much as possible the interim period so arduous for the people. This path has been chosen also following the bad experiences of the superficial reforms in the 1990s. […] No ad hoc measures can change the situation. *Only a bold turn suited to the historical challenge Poland is facing will enable it to come out of the civilizational collapse, to build an order that meets the social expectations* [emphasis T.K.].
>
> "Założenia i kierunki", 1989; quoted in KOWALIK, 2012a: 120

Kowalik's commentary on the quoted text was:

> On the one hand, S.[olidarność] activists accentuated the break with the economic policies of the previous authorities, and on the other, many authors pointed out the similarity of the program (or at least this version of it) with the earlier one, presented by the former government to the IMF for negotiation. … *In general, there is a striking similarity between the concepts of the old and new administration, which simply resulted from the adoption of the general schemes proposed by the IMF* [emphasis mine – G.K.].
>
> KOWALIK, 2012a: 121–122

In so much as the Balcerowicz Plan is treated as a manifestation of a revolutionary project, attention must also be paid to Tadeusz Kowalik's suspicions that the drastic difference between the values assumed in this Plan and the actual basic macroeconomic indicators for the Polish economy may have resulted not so much from an "overshoot" as from the project authors' concealed real intentions that were later simply put into practice, particularly in the form of very high unemployment. In this context, the author of *From Solidarity to Sellout* recalls that

> until entry in the EU, the average unemployment rate [in Poland] was about 16 percent. What was most painful and alarming was that *this took place in accordance with the vision of the main architects of the new order* [emphasis mine – G.K.] … [i.e.] the projection of the main economic indicators for the years 1990–2000, drawn up in the Department

of Economic Analyses of the Ministry of Finance.[36] ... *The equivalence of predicted unemployment and actual unemployment in the year 2000 seems to be important in that it rules out the treatment of this development as an accidental result of unforeseen circumstances, in contrast to the imagination and aims of the ruling elites* [emphasis mine – G.K.].

KOWALIK, 2012: 276–278[37]

---

36   Perhaps even more categorically, Kowalik made the same point in a 2010 interview, in which we read that in Poland in the 1990s we had "planned and executed unemployment, which outrages me. When I came across an article that included a table of unemployment from an expert report by the Ministry of Finance – 16% and that was for the whole decade up to 2000 – the discovery shocked me. I have been involved in the politics of many governments, and countries, but I have never encountered a government that planned for such high unemployment for so many years. You could be wrong, you could understate, you could lie, but to plan for 16% unemployment? That was nowhere to be found. So the question is: did those who planned such unemployment realise that the scourge of unemployment must translate into the scourge of poverty, into a whole system of pathologies? Here I do not have clarity" (Kowalik & Leszkowska, 2010).

37   This is another important paradox in the work of Kowalik. Only a dozen or so pages further on, he writes about the same problems in a completely different tone: "Poland happened to be the first to take the plunge into the unknown [i.e. systemic transformation – G.K.]. *Hence it was easy to 'overshoot', to apply excessively strong measures, to amass them in a very short time* [emphasis mine – G.K.]. In my opinion, the authorities should rather be blamed for their inability to at least partly withdraw from this stance so as to diminish social distress" (Kowalik, 2012a: 305). Similarly, in *Systemy gospodarcze* we read that "*Because of high inflation, it was difficult to avoid an adaptive recession with rates close to those projected by the government when it prepared the programme* [the Balcerowicz Plan; emphasis mine – G.K.]. It seems, however, that the government overlooked the fact that, although the inflation triggered by the freeing of food prices was high (in October it was over 50%), it was already falling rapidly at the end of 1989 (to 23 and 18%) and, most importantly, it was inflation that at the end of 1989 eliminated the surplus of 'empty' money, which the authorities also failed to notice. *The discrepancy between projection and implementation was thus mainly due to the government's and experts' misreading of the rapidly changing situation and to shortcomings in the art of forecasting* [emphasis mine – G.K.]" (Kowalik, 2005a: 298). Apart from the contradiction in the interpretation of the events described, what draws attention in the passages quoted is the forbearance with which Kowalik refers to the Plan and its creators. However, there are more statements like this – surprising in view of the rather common perception of Kowalik as one of the harshest Polish critics of the Balcerowicz Plan. Probably the most positive statement about this reform package was made by Kowalik in a text from 2002, when he wrote that "The Balcerowicz Plan actually consisted of two different programmes: *a stabilisation programme* and a *systemic change programme* [emphasis T.K.]. The first one was to consist mainly of measures restoring market equilibrium, especially reducing inflation. ... *The expected and positive effect* [of the introduction of the Plan; emphasis mine – G.K.] was an *almost immediate equilibrium on the commodity market* [emphasis T.K.]. The drastic increase in prices and the contraction of real savings meant that shop shelves filled up immediately, and with it the nuisance of queuing and the 'black market' disappeared.

What is more, according to Kowalik's work, Stanisław Gomułka, one of the mentioned "main architects of the new order", openly admitted that high and long-lasting unemployment was within the Plan's aims and assumptions. In *From Solidarity to Sellout* we read that:

> Defense of the strategy of the implementation of the Balcerowicz Plan was taken up by Stanisław Gomułka, advisor and co-author of it. He outlined his reasoning in the two ... texts, where he dwelt on several selected issues. ... *He considered the charge that there was a wide discrepancy between the assumptions of the stabilization program and its execution misplaced, given that, as early as August 1989, he himself was in favor of a Thatcher-style shock operation, openly speaking of the high social costs* [emphasis mine – G.K.]. The same view was shared by a "significant portion of the Balcerowicz group".
>
> KOWALIK, 2012a: 146–147[38]

In Kowalik's account, Gomułka seems to claim that his postulate quoted earlier in this chapter and summarised as "Poland ... needs unemployment", was put into practice in the form of the Balcerowicz Plan with full premeditation. Another significant excerpt is from Kowalik's Foreword to the first volume of Stanisław Gomułka's documents. The author of *From Solidarity to Sellout* juxtaposes Sachs's "rash encouragement to jump into the market, [combined] with an idyllic belief that after just a few months everyone would be better off" with Gomułka's "more factual, dry 'plan' that promised no idylls" (Kowalik, 2010a: 18–19). According to Kowalik, Gomułka, presenting his proposals at a meeting of the OKP parliamentary club, claimed that "if we want to avoid the South American syndrome, we have to decide on a *shock involving far-reaching sacrifices* [emphasis mine – G.K.]" (Kowalik, 2010a: 18–19). Importantly, Kowalik claimed that "this argumentation found its way into the new authorities' thinking", quoting Bronisław Geremek:

> *A positive but unexpected* [emphasis mine – G.K.] effect was that *export companies, mainly state-owned, quickly switched from eastern to western markets* [emphasis T.K.]. The increase in exports to the West compensated for the decline in exports to the COMECON countries. Thirdly, *the budget was balanced* [emphasis T.K.] (and in the first year even achieved a certain surplus). *Other benefits resulting from the tightening of corporate budget constraints were to become apparent in the longer term* [emphasis mine – G.K.]" (Kowalik, 2002e: 621). The fact that this is from a textbook may have significantly influenced this particular passage's content.

38   The text referred to by Kowalik is (Gomułka, 1994).

> Not even for a moment did I have [...] a shadow of a doubt that it [the Balcerowicz Plan – T.K.] would require serious sacrifices from the entire society [...]. But without sacrifices, and serious sacrifices at that, we had no chance of overcoming the distance that separated us from the threshold enabling the integration processes to begin.
> GEREMEK & ŻAKOWSKI, 1990: 364–365; quoted in KOWALIK, 2010a: 19[39]

4

As I have explained in chapter one, the year 1989, and especially its second half, is, in Tadeusz Kowalik's reflections on the "epigonic bourgeois revolution", the moment in recent Polish history when, in his opinion, a revolution of this kind most probably took place. In particular, I think it is worthwhile to draw attention to one event described by Kowalik from that breakthrough year, which can be regarded as a kind of catalyst or spark – a watershed moment meaning a "crossing of the Rubicon" of the Polish bourgeois revolution, or at least its fundamental acceleration, i.e. as its detonator.

The author of *From Solidarity to Sellout*, reporting on the course of talks on the economy during the Round Table and at the meetings of the *Komisja Porozumiewawcza* [Consultation Committee] established on the basis of its provisions, points to the consensus formed on "freeing prices". While in February 1989, according to Kowalik, Deputy Prime Minister Kazimierz Olesiak had to persuade the opposition to accept this solution, "At a meeting of the Committee, Olesiak no longer had to convince anybody about the operation of liberating prices itself; he even had to explain why this had not been done earlier" (Kowalik, 2012a: 70).

However, although agreement was reached on the general idea, this did not prevent, according to Kowalik's account, a serious political conflict centred on the extent of salary indexation: "The liberation of food prices came into force

---

39   In another work, Kowalik commented on this statement as follows: "Writing 'in the heat of the moment' ... Geremek was convinced that the Balcerowicz Plan would cause a temporary 'impoverishment of all social groups', that it involved serious sacrifices 'from the whole society'. I am not familiar with Geremek's later views on ... the 'revolution in incomes' [which took place in Poland after 1989 – G.K.], *creating a highly polarised society, blatantly counter to these 'serious sacrifices' from 'all social groups' of 'the whole society'* [emphasis mine – G.K.]" (Kowalik, 2002e: 627). Kowalik's extensive commentary on the book by Żakowski and Geremek can be found in (Kowalik, 1991a).

on August 1 [1989] and was accompanied by heated disputes. The day before the Sejm had passed a law, imposed by the S.[olidarność] caucus, on full price indexation to offset the effects of introducing a free-market system" (Kowalik, 2012a: 70–71). As the author of *From Solidarity to Sellout* quotes Władysław Baka, this law became Mieczysław Rakowski's government's "nail in the coffin" and, as a consequence, sort of opened the way to the realisation of the "shock therapy" plans (as we have seen of both sides of the political conflict). Baka, quoted by Kowalik, had already predicted that, before the decision to introduce market prices came into effect,

> there will be an immense inflow of "empty money" and deepening of the already glaring wage disproportions, destruction and breaking up of the market till the end, intensification of inflation, etc. Without any doubt, no government will be able to exercise its power any longer, having this law "on its shoulders". It is obvious that in the thinking of the architects of this law, that is, the leadership of "Solidarity", its passing is to play the role of "a nail in the coffin" for the government created by the coalition hitherto in power [i.e. Rakowski's government – G.K.].
> BAKA, 2007: 258; quoted in KOWALIK, 2012a: 71

If there is a single event from 1989 that, in the light of Kowalik's work, would be crucial for the further "revolutionary" course of events, which would constitute a point, a seeming "outburst" beyond which there would be no return and which would therefore, to some extent, fulfil the function of a "revolutionary detonator", I consider the most serious suggestion for such an event to be the above-described marketisation of food prices with full indexation of salaries from 1st August of that year.

But what was to be such an "outburst" in 1989 in Poland? In Tadeusz Kowalik's works one can, it seems, find statements containing hints in this respect. In *From Solidarity to Sellout* we read that,

> When analyzing the great leap from real socialism to capitalism, we cannot overlook the historical context of this event. This was not only a period of ordinary technocratic transformation of one system of economy into another (described as the natural succession of the free market after the disintegration of the command-distributive system), but something much more important. There were also intense changes in the social structure, *of which the most important was the radical shift of part of the wealth from the poor to the rich, shoving aside certain social groups and*

> *elevating others* [emphasis mine – G.K.]. There was shock, disappointment, and paralysis for the former, but thriving prosperity for the latter.
> KOWALIK, 2012a: 105

Apart from the already discussed changes in the social structure, in the above fragment, what attracts attention is the "radical shift of part of the wealth from the poor to the rich", which in his other works, Kowalik, quoting Czesław Bywalec (1995), will consistently refer to as the "revolution in incomes". In another place in *From Solidarity to Sellout*, Kowalik explains that,

> As a result of the recession and extraordinary expansion of the new private sector, in 1990 to 1993 there occurred "a true revolution in incomes". These are the words of Czesław Bywalec, who presented the altered share of the individual population groups in the general incomes of the population ... incomes of wage earners fell to a level only several percent above one-quarter of the total income of the population. ... Only the incomes of the "profit earners" grew rapidly – their share rose by two and a half-fold! *This was an unprecedented shift in the income (and social) structure in peaceful conditions* [emphasis mine – G.K.].
> KOWALIK, 2012a: 139–140

This "shifting income (and property) from the poor to the rich" was also accompanied, as Kowalik argues further, by

> making about three million workers redundant with small chance of finding work, and concealing the dimensions of lowered employment among disability pensioners and earlier retirees (from 1.5 to 2 million) [which] also meant lower prestige of work, a worse position of the workers, and the deterioration of workplace hygiene and safety. The backbone of the working class was broken, the trade union movement was weakened, and for many years offering work for low wages was sanctioned.
> KOWALIK, 2012a: 140[40]

---

40 Similarly in *Nierówni i równiejsi*, where Kowalik quotes Jacek Kurczewski: "Poland once again finds itself in its original state, when property titles have to be distributed among the participants in the social game [...] In the war over power, property and wealth, everyone is really involved, although the chances were not equal at the start, and this inequality reveals itself at every turn – with a sense of injustice on the one hand and arrogance on the other" (Kurczewski, 1995: 12; quoted in Kowalik, 2002a: 63). Kowalik comments: "It is clear that *this war over property and wealth* [emphasis T.K.] is being fought in

Finally, in *From Solidarity to Sellout*, its author mentions yet another dimension of the changes taking place at that time:

> Small privatization, that is, the sale (or lease) of state pharmacies, shops, or small manufacturing enterprises, was also carried out very quickly. As a result of both of these changes, *within a short time the number of registered private firms rose from over 800,000 to over one and a half million*. ... A middle class *of a particularly backward character was emerging* [emphasis mine – G.K.].
>
> KOWALIK, 2012a: 138–139[41]

A picture of changes as far-reaching as they are violent, taking place over an extremely short time, emerges from these descriptions. It seems that in the context of our reflections on the revolutionary "outburst", there are two possible interpretations of the above argumentation. The first boils down to the recognition that, since the transformations described by Kowalik have a common cause in the Balcerowicz Plan,[42] its elaboration, passing into law and implementation meant a revolutionary "outburst" in Poland.[43] In the second, much broader, interpretation, the "outburst" of the bourgeois revolution would be, on the other hand, all the events and circumstances between 1989 and 1993[44] described in the passages quoted above, i.e. not only the Balcerowicz Plan

---

all post-communist countries, and its outcome is of vital importance for the shape of the new regime" (Kowalik, 2002a: 63).

41 In *Nierówni i równiejsi*, Kowalik described this growth as "turbulent", dated it to 1989–1993 and assessed the extent of the change as from 800,000 to 1.6 million (Kowalik, 2002a: 72).

42 Kowalik himself points to such a cause-and-effect relationship: "Admittedly, the Balcerowicz Plan did not contain a developed systemic concept. *However, it turned out to be a very important step on the unfortunate path of systemic transformation* [emphasis mine – G.K.]. The unprecedented-in-peacetime revolution in incomes that then occurred radically changed the social structure – it initiated the creation of a social order by means of primitive capital accumulation" (Kowalik, 2013h: 188).

43 This would also be in line with Kowalik's claims in the first half of the 1990s which I have already described, when he maintained that there was not so much an "epigonic bourgeois" as a "from above" revolution in Poland, and that it was the Balcerowicz Plan.

44 These exact caesuras are set out by the author of *From Solidarity to Sellout* for example in the following passage from a 2007 text: "In Poland, the transition from 'real socialism' to capitalism took place through shock therapy, sometimes referred to as the *Big Bang*. Between 1989 and 1993, there was both the collapse of 'real socialism' and an embarking on the path to a capitalist economy. A new social structure was formed, new economic rules were created, among which the market plays a dominant role" (Kowalik, 2007: 270).

itself but the entire process of the Polish restoration of capitalist social and economic relations. Let us add that these are not, as it seems, mutually exclusive interpretations.

However, the character of the Polish systemic transformation reported so far, and in particular the references to the pace of these transformations, clearly raise the issue of another feature of Baszkiewicz's model of revolution: "a rapid change in the state, breaking the continuity of the law and creating own legality". Kowalik expressed his conviction about the violent character of the Polish changes, as we have seen, many times. To the fragments already quoted, let us add only those mentioning the "*sudden* [emphasis mine – G.K.] and unexpected collapse of the communist system in Central and Eastern Europe" (Kowalik, 2005a: 64) or the fact that *"Within not even half a year* [emphasis mine – G.K.], Poland performed 'a leap to a market economy'" (Kowalik, 2012a: 55).

The author of *From Solidarity to Sellout* also referred to the pace of change introduction in the formal and legal sense, linking the issue of the "rapidity of change" with the problem of the "revolutionaries" "creating their own legality". Particularly noteworthy in this context is his account of how the Balcerowicz Plan was enacted into law:

> In late December 1989, the Sejm, in which parties and factions of the old system prevailed, nearly unanimously passed the legislation put forward by the government, allowing for the program to be implemented. For the first package, tabled in early December, *the government turned to the Sejm for express examination of sixteen bills, nine by the end of the year* [emphasis mine – G.K.]. And so, though the proposition submitted by Lech Wałęsa for endowing the government with extraordinary powers was rejected (even with certain distaste), *both the government and parliament acted as in an extraordinary situation. The Sejm appointed the Extraordinary Committee expressly and this inhuman pace was even defended by Aleksander Małachowski, who was otherwise critical of the government's measures* [emphasis mine – G.K.]. He said: "No normal government or Sejm should consent to such acceleration. But this is not a normal government. It has the great task of leading the country out from collapse and it must be helped in this". The decisive part of the package came into force on January 1, 1990. The form of presentation of the program and the haste in its ratification made it impossible for public opinion to absorb its significant part, and especially *the great leap of the operation* [emphasis mine – G.K.]. The final version was not and in these circumstances could

not have been discussed publicly, in the manner of decisions of great historical significance.

KOWALIK, 2012a: 131[45]

5

In *From Solidarity to Sellout*, Tadeusz Kowalik expresses the view that "all authorities ... tend to shut themselves off from the outside, unless *through the pressure of large social groups* [emphasis mine – G.K.] they are forced to listen and to take up dialogue" (Kowalik, 2012a: 130). This is, as one might think, a certain generalisation of his reflections in the context of the Polish revolution of 1989. For, as I showed in chapter one, Kowalik wrote that, similar to "the bourgeois revolutions of continental Europe" in which "workers played the key role" (Kowalik, 1997a: 49), also in Poland in the 1980s "the bourgeois, capitalist revolution was the work of ... a mass movement of wage workers" (Kowalik, 2005a: 358). Later, however, I explained that this was an unfortunate mental shortcut on Kowalik's part, as in other works he indicated that, in the period in question (1980–1992), two revolutions not one in fact took place in Poland, and that one can speak of the active causation of the popular classes only in the case of the first, which was a workers' revolution.

When we combine this with the possibility, not inconsistent with the thesis of the "epigonic bourgeois revolution", of considering the Polish transformation in terms of a revolution "from above" (where the "movement of the masses" is either completely superfluous or its pacification is even the primary goal), which was what Kowalik considered in the Polish context in the first half of the 1990s, it will not be surprising that, as is clear from many of his works, the restoration of capitalism in Poland required not so much the activity of the masses, but, on the contrary, their permissive *passivity*. This is how he writes about it in *Systemy gospodarcze*:

> Violent upheavals, and especially bloody revolutions, often bring about unexpected and unwanted results. *In Poland, however, the transfer of power took place peacefully, as a result of a compromise reached earlier. The workers were supported by the intelligentsia, which facilitated this compromise* [emphasis mine – G.K.] and should have ensured a greater predictability of the further course of events.
>
> KOWALIK, 2005a: 359

---

45 Kowalik quotes Małachowski's statement after (Kuczyński, 1992: 105–6).

Kowalik then fully develops the argument about the "tacit consent" of workers to the shape of change and the reasons for this passivity:

> how was it possible that a social movement like *Solidarność*, which so recently had ten million members, allowed for the realisation of a programme [the Balcerowicz Plan] that so severely hit the old system's real gravediggers [i.e. the workers – G.K.]. Many reasons contributed to this consent, firstly to active support, and later to [their] *tacit consent* [emphasis mine – G.K]. ... at the time Parliament adopted the Balcerowicz Plan and began to implement it, a significant part of society seemed to believe in the necessity of making drastic (albeit short-term) sacrifices in the name of a better future. The plan was not publicly discussed or negotiated with the trade unions, *which they often did not even ask for because, as it was understood, the authorities were "ours" – people proven as partners in battle and in prisons* [emphasis mine – G.K.]. Before it was realised that this better future was always receding, the trade union movement incurred a huge loss of social trust because of the protective umbrella over the authorities. *And yet, it was precisely this umbrella and the possibility of administering shock therapy to society without negotiations that determined the drastic nature of the programme* [emphasis mine – G.K.].
>
> KOWALIK, 2005a: 364[46]

In at least one text, Kowalik also indirectly points, as it seems, to a concrete example of this passivity in 1990, when the social effects of the implementation of the Balcerowicz Plan, which he describes extensively, were already becoming sufficiently tangible. The then minister in Tadeusz Mazowiecki's government, Jacek Kuroń recalled his visits to workplaces, quoted in *From Solidarity to Sellout*, which reveal that the implementation of the economic reform was accompanied by dissatisfaction, but not by hostility or rebellion:

> They all believed that Wałęsa will come soon and make everything all right. [...] None of these people, apart from school teenagers, understood

---

46 Interestingly, commenting on these events as they unfolded, Kowalik seemed to suggest that the described passivity of the broad masses was something that the political elite had hoped for: "the consensus [of political forces around the Balcerowicz Plan] was only implicit, *more calculated for the society's passivity than for its active role as a co-creator of the program* [emphasis mine – G.K.]" (Kowalik, 1991a: 7).

> a market economy, capitalism. *They only explained to me that [...] if I paid them more, everything would be all right* [emphasis mine – G.K.].
>
> KUROŃ, 1991: 110; quoted in KOWALIK, 2012a: 115

An attempt to explain this phenomenon can be found in the views of Juliusz Gardawski, whose research, as Kowalik explains, has led him

> to the conclusion that *"workers largely acquiesced to the social degradation of the class to which they belonged". The "myth of competition" was to take over the mentality not only of the elite, but also of the workers* [emphasis mine – G.K.]. And it was precisely this "deproletarianisation of working class" that meant that the reform elite did not have to negotiate systemic changes with trade unions.
>
> KOWALIK, 2009b: 118[47]

In Kowalik's view, "deproletarianisation" like this was another cause, apart from those mentioned earlier, of the passivity of the masses' during the Polish transformation. It could not be, however, in Kowalik's opinion, the relative weakness of the working class (as well as peasants) in confrontation (actual or potential) with other social groups. He states that "in 1989 the non-agricultural and non-manual private sector was still thin after all, it had no representation and *workers' organisations presented greater social power* [emphasis mine – G.K.]" (Kowalik, 2006a: 142).

The problem of the passivity of the popular classes obviously directs our attention towards other social groups which, in Tadeusz Kowalik's view, could

---

47 The excerpts quoted by Kowalik are from (Gardawski, 2009: 62–63). The above does not mean, however, that, according to Kowalik, "the takeover" of the workers' mentality by the "myth of competition" was tantamount to the spread of full acceptance of capitalist social relations among the representatives of this class. Elsewhere in *From Solidarity to Sellout*, we read, for example, that "In the mentality of the workers the prevalent belief, for years repeated by the [communist] authorities, was that ultimately the workplaces are public property and thus their property as well. Therefore, the closest thing to the implementation of their thus far vague and hazy rights [of the privatisation ideas considered at the time – G.K.] was the transformation of their firms into employee companies, which at that time was the most frequently employed form of de-statization of state firms. The myth of the 'Self-Governing Republic', formulated by the first S.[olidarność] Congress (1981), was merely expressed in different wording but drawn from the egalitarian doctrine of real socialism. Hence the frequent complaints of pundits and the journalists, economists and sociologists in their service. Włodzimierz Pańkow often spoke of the dilemma that the non-communist authorities were then facing: how to reconcile the liberal objectives of the government with the social-democratic attitude (or views) of the social base" (Kowalik, 2012a: 215).

have been an active actor (as Baszkiewicz puts it: "the class that plays a leading role during a revolution (or one of its phases) in relation to the other revolutionary classes") of the 1989 changes, that is, which could have exercised hegemony in that revolution. Kowalik does not use this term anywhere, so he also does not refer to the possible leading role of the bourgeoisie in the Polish transformation. However, it is possible to identify threads in his works which, at least to some extent, fit into such an interpretation.

In spite of the above-mentioned descriptions of certain classes' passivity, we can also find references to the activity, and "spontaneity", of broad social groups in the 1980s in Kowalik's works on the Polish transformation. Thus, in *Systemy gospodarcze*, we read that "systemic changes in Poland ... *still of a spontaneous rather than conscious character* [emphasis mine – G.K.], began earlier [than in other countries of the Eastern Bloc], almost a quarter of a century ago [i.e. around 1980 – G.K.]" (Kowalik, 2005a: 352). In *From Solidarity to Sellout* Kowalik specifies this: "In the second half of the 1980s, there was an eruption of *uncontrolled privatization of the economy from below* [emphasis mine – G.K.]. Just before the collapse of the previous system, the legal framework was furnished for this process" (Kowalik, 2012a: 203).[48]

Thus, as can be presumed, Kowalik signals in this characteristic way devoid of explicit references to class that, as Polish workers became more and more passive, the activity of the bourgeoisie *in spe* grew in the economic sense, i.e. in the area of social life which, for this class (even, as here, still *in statu nascendi*) is usually, as I explained in the previous chapter citing Lenin quoted by Baszkiewicz, the most important.

Tadeusz Kowalik expressed himself most clearly on this issue in one of the subchapters of *From Solidarity to Sellout*, in which he polemicised with the authors of the concept of *managerial capitalism* as a class explanation of the changes, allegedly specific for Central and Eastern Europe at the turn of the

---

48   Subsequently, Kowalik explains that "the players of the nomenklatura offshoot of privatization consisted of managers of state firms of various rank, government and party functionaries associated with them, along with their families. The process, commonly called 'enfranchisement of the nomenklatura', deserves attention because it was then that the phenomenon of corruptive privatization, or arranged clientelistic privatization, developed. This led me to formulate the warning, as early as 1988, against 'the threat of Panamization of the Polish economy'. The state sector shortly became a cash machine, which was made easier by the authorities through relevant legal regulations. ... *the number of private owners of firms doubled within just a few years* [emphasis mine – G.K.]. In the decided majority, these were persons outside the nomenklatura, which *brought financial (to a lesser extent social) advancement for hundreds of thousands, and together with families, well over a million people* [emphasis mine – G.K.]" (Kowalik, 2012a: 204–205).

1980s and 1990s. Kowalik begins this discussion by quoting from an article by Gil Eyal, Iván Szelényi and Eleanor Townsley (1997), in which they claim that

> The most *distinctive characteristic of post-communist social structure in East Central Europe* [in the second half of the 1990s – G.K.] *is the absence of a capitalist class* [emphasis mine – G.K.]. Private property rights are in place, markets in labor and capital exist, these economies are open to world markets, and they have strong relationships with international financial institutions. However, there is no organized group of major capitalists. [...] Indeed, the result of privatization in most of the region has been highly diffused property rights. This is the puzzle we seek to understand: what explains the distinctive class structure of the fledgling capitalist economies of East Central Europe? In the absence of a capitalist class, who has power?
> EYAL, SZELÉNYI & TOWNSLEY, 1997: 60; quoted in KOWALIK, 2012a: 291

As Kowalik reports, according to the authors of the concept of *managerial capitalism*, in Poland, the Czech Republic and Hungary – unlike in Western countries and especially the United States – the economically dominant social group and the political power elite belong to different classes. The collapse of communism in Central and Eastern Europe has allowed, as they put it, a "technocratic-managerial elite to assume leading positions in the economy", but

> [it] was not in a position to make a bid for political power. The key positions of political power were taken by humanistic intellectuals. They quickly organized a tight ruling group, or "politocracy", which only later formed an alliance with the new technocratic-managerial elite.
> EYAL, SZELÉNYI & TOWNSLEY, 1997: 67; quoted in KOWALIK, 2012a: 291

Kowalik – admitting that "[a]t the outset of Polish capitalism, there was, in fact, a distance between the technocratic-managerial group and what the authors call the politocracy" (Kowalik, 2012a: 292) – strongly dissociates himself from this thesis:

> a genetic differentiation of these two groups [technocratic-managerial elite and "politocracy" – G.K.], and especially defining the system with the help of one group, seems to be of little cognitive value. It obliterates the social aspects of this system, exaggerates the role of managerial professionalism, and underestimates the bureaucratic imprint of

the emerging system. *I do not see much sense in separating the role of the managerial group from other holders of power* [emphasis mine – G.K.]. Most probably, seeing in managers the *"dominant class"* [emphasis mine – G.K.] was based on the authors' belief that current and systemic economic policy is determined by a small number of important decisions influenced by this politically dominant group. Meanwhile, in the process of transformation, and especially privatization, the matter is much more complex. There are hundreds of thousands of decisions concerning personnel, credit, taxes, and customs (also deferring, for example, the execution of overdue credits, taxes, insurance premiums, customs duties, demolition of illegally erected buildings). All these constitute the *closely interconnected power apparatus, along with the administration and local self-government, with great and small businesses* [emphasis mine – G.K.]. These links are hidden and harder to research than the official lines of policies declared by the government or parliament. It also does not seem that the time sequence between the establishment of the "politocracy" and the moment of "concluding the alliance" with the technocratic-managerial staff would be of importance, as the authors write. This is especially so when the initially evident contradictions between the objectives of the authorities and the interests of this proto-technostructure turned out to be short-lived. ... *Since there was yet no distinct capitalist class in existence, the political authorities acted in the name of an "imaginary" middle class that was supposed to create the foundations of the liberal-democratic order* [emphasis mine – G.K.]. ... There is ... a large sphere of economic policy that is not transgressive. In three areas, the *declared objectives of the authorities are absolutely concurrent with the interests of the new proprietary class* [emphasis mine – G.K.]. These are lowering taxes for enterprises and for the affluent, efforts to downsize the welfare state, and further "flexibilization" of the labor market.

KOWALIK, 2012a: 292–293[49]

Thus, in Kowalik's work, we find not only an unambiguous statement that, in the process of Polish systemic transformation, a key role was played by one social group ("the dominant class"), which in itself can be regarded as akin to class "hegemony", but also that this group was constituted not by "managers"

---

49   It is worth noting in passing that Kowalik's statement that "the declared objectives of the authorities are absolutely concurrent with the interests of the new proprietary class" seems to harmonise well with the interpretation of the Polish transformations in the terms of "revolution from above".

separated from the bourgeoisie (as Eyal, Szelényi and Townsley postulated) but rather by "holders of power."⁵⁰ Moreover, Kowalik points to a "closely interconnected power apparatus, along with the administration and local self-government, with great and small businesses."⁵¹

All the groups listed in the above-mentioned sentences can be easily included, if not in the already existing bourgeoisie, then undoubtedly in the rapidly emerging bourgeoisie. This is suggested by Kowalik himself in accordance with his views on the "class-generating" role of systemic transformations, when, as I have already discussed, he writes that "Since there was yet no distinct capitalist class in existence, the political authorities acted in the name of an 'imaginary' middle class that was supposed to create the foundations of the liberal-democratic order" (Kowalik, 2012a: 293).⁵²

Arguments in favour of the existence of bourgeois hegemony in the 1989 revolution in Poland can also be found in Kowalik's characterisation of the individual key figures of Polish politics at the time:

> The very composition of the [last communist] government ... already came as a shock for many observers in Poland and abroad. Ireneusz

---

50   In the Polish edition, Kowalik used a slightly more expansive phrase here, the exact translation of which is "the broadly defined collective of holders of power and human and material capital" (Kowalik, 2009b: 216).

51   In the context of the "apparatus" referred to here, it is worth noting that the "power elite" is another term used by the author of *From Solidarity to Sellout*. In some of his work, Kowalik points out that it was the aspirations of this particular social group that revealed themselves in the events of 1989 in Poland: "the quartet headed by Mazowiecki [Mazowiecki, Balcerowicz, Kuczynski, Kuroń – G.K.] could not have played such a great role [in shaping the Polish transformation – G.K.] if it had not expressed the *aspirations of the majority of the widely understood power elite, i.e. the new and the old establishment* [emphasis mine – G.K.]" (Kowalik, 2005a: 307). Attention in this context is also drawn to the following passage from Henryk Słabek, quoted by Kowalik: "If they [the workers – T.K.] contributed to the overthrow of communism, it was [...] by the fact that they most effectively blocked the necessary reform of the economy (wages, prices, employment) in fact in the name of a deepened egalitarianism ('yes to socialism, no to its distortions'), and not because they chose the capitalist order as better ... *the heroes of the restoration, including of Polish capitalism, are – it seems – above all people of the economic-technical 'communist' elite* [emphasis mine – G.K.]" (Słabek, 2004: 399; quoted in Kowalik, 2006a: 141). Kowalik does not enter into a polemic with this view of Słabek.

52   Moreover, in *From Solidarity to Sellout*, Kowalik mentions once again the same social groups to describe them as "beneficiaries" of the systemic transformation: "Sociologists ... name as beneficiaries [of the transformation], next to managers and individual proprietors of fortunes, two other social groups: people of the political authority and state administration and the petit bourgeoisie, based on small business" (Kowalik, 2012a: 295).

> Sekuła, a *businessman* [emphasis mine – G.K.], was made deputy prime minister and Mieczysław Wilczek, a well-known and wealthy *entrepreneur* [emphasis mine – G.K.], by the standards of the time, became minister of industry. Advocates of radical reform also included another deputy prime minister, Kazimierz Olesiak, who quickly became known as a consistent proponent of freeing food prices and apparently of the free market in general, and also the minister of finance, Andrzej Wróblewski, earlier involved in talks with the International Monetary Fund concerning assistance for Poland. Thus composed, the government began to energetically move toward profound reforms.
> KOWALIK, 2012a: 57–58

Thus, in the formally still "socialist" Polish People's Republic, as early as in 1988 we could find a "businessman" and an "entrepreneur" in key national economic positions. More of Kowalik's remarks in this respect, pointing to a similar tendency on the part of *Solidarność*, can be found in his description of the sessions of the so-called "economy table" at the Round Table talks. For example, when presenting Witold Trzeciakowski, the opposition co-chair of that table, Kowalik describes him as: "an entrepreneur and manager" (Kowalik, 2012a: 61).

In the author of *From Solidarity to Sellout*'s work we can also find statements illustrating the relation of the transforming "dominating class", as Kowalik calls it, to the working class, and in particular the framing of the "limits of revolution" by the former. It is a question of protecting the liberal-bourgeois revolutionary programme against too radical a turn to the left (which, according to Kowalik, seemed real in view of the demonstration of the power of the working class in the revolution of 1980–1981), but most of all ensuring the fulfilment of the condition of "systemic reforms toward a free market, along with a labor market", which was to be guaranteed by, in the imagination of the "dominant class" reported by Kowalik, the "break[-]down [of] ... the reemerging, once nearly ten-million-strong, S.[solidarność] movement" (Kowalik, 2012a: 279).

Significantly, in Kowalik's accounts, the intelligentsia representing the revolutionary "avant-garde" consistently expressed views of this kind in a manner independent of the dynamically developing political situation (especially in 1989). An example in Kowalik's work of one of the early voices of this type is Mirosław Dzielski who, in January 1989, conditioned the success of Rakowski's government on "the breaking up of groups that represented 'social interests [...] by means of decisive political moves'. Naturally [for Kowalik – G.K.], in the circumstances of those days, this breaking up would mean that repressive, or possibly coercive, means were to be used" (Kowalik, 2012a: 44). There were also similar statements in the summer and autumn of that year, and not only, as the author of *From Solidarity to Sellout* emphasises, among "free-market conservatives" in the ranks of the anti-communist opposition:

> Understandably, such declared free-market conservatives as Stefan Kisielewski or Piotr Wierzbicki warned against S.[olidarność] as a trade union. Wierzbicki felt that "the unionist origin and character of Solidarity constituted its accursed stigma and fettered its wings when it tried to become the vanguard of reforms reaching the foundations of the current system". Yet similar lines of thought were expressed by former activists of S.[olidarność], for example, Andrzej Celiński, secretary of the National Commission of the legal S.[solidarność], who even before the formation of the government of Tadeusz Mazowiecki warned that "the factor blocking changes is turning out to be the strength of the working class of manufacturing industry, especially as it has its [parliamentary – T.K.] representations".
>
> KOWALIK, 2012a: 39[53]

However, the fears of the representatives of the "elites" cited above turned out to be unfounded because, as Kowalik shows, the working class was completely marginalised in the drafting of the revolutionary programme and in its practical implementation:

> Though it is true that the Round Table negotiations, relayed in detail by the media, showed a fundamental change of climate, they were also accompanied by the allegedly "conspiring" sideline meetings in Magdalenka, Wilanów, and in other government palaces, which suggested an elitist character of the agreements. The worker rank and file of S.[olidarność] *ended up in the role of passive observers* [emphasis mine – G.K.]. This was in sharp contrast to the atmosphere of openness and many public controversies that characterized the 1980–81 period. Indeed, by now *no one was turning to the workers themselves – the original cause of it all* [emphasis mine – G.K.].
>
> KOWALIK, 2012a: 36

---

53 The statements quoted by Kowalik are taken from, respectively, (Wierzbicki, 1989: 8) and (Celiński, 1989: 3).

6

Judging by his work, Tadeusz Kowalik had no doubts as to the role of the intelligentsia[54] in shaping the Polish transformation.[55] He also mentioned various aspects of this involvement, from the "support of workers" by the intelligentsia[56] to its disappearing "social sensitivity."[57] The author of *From Solidarity to Sellout* also agreed that as a result of the events of 1989, "central power" was taken over mainly by "humanistic intellectuals" (although with the caveat: "provided we can call professors of economics 'humanistic', which I am not too sure about" (Kowalik, 2012a: 201–202)). Finally, in his book Kowalik also explicitly states that the Round Table talks, "that were to change Poland in such a radical way" were embarked upon by "leading intellectuals" (Kowalik, 2012a: 45).

In Tadeusz Kowalik's works it is not difficult to find passages indicating that even before 1989 the Polish intelligentsia had, to a large extent, moved to pro-capitalist positions. This applies both to the part of the intelligentsia representing *Solidarność* as well as those connected with the apparatus of power. As regards the evolution of the former, Kowalik states that

> many facts indicate that this pivotal turn took place earlier [than 1989] and was well pronounced on both sides of the political scene already in 1987. It not only reached the circles of the *intelligentsia* [emphasis mine – G.K.] involved in the programmatic and conceptual work but also the

---

54 Although he also tended to use the term *intellectuals*, we will omit here the differences between these groups, especially since, as Piotr Kulas (2015) points out, "the majority of researchers agree ... that in Poland intellectuals are part of the intelligentsia" (p. 66).

55 As I mentioned in chapter one, this is a theme that appeared very early in Kowalik's reflections on the Polish transformation, preceding the formulation of the thesis of an "epigonic bourgeois revolution". For example, in the 1995 chapter we read that "In post-communist countries, it is the intelligentsia, with the aid of State power, which assumes the role of the future middle class and carries out systemic changes" (Kowalik, 1995: 105).

56 "In Poland ... the transfer of power took place peacefully, as a result of a compromise reached earlier. *The workers were supported by the intelligentsia* [emphasis mine – G.K.], which facilitated this compromise and should have ensured a greater predictability of the further course of events and provided the possibility of choosing from among the known alternatives" (Kowalik, 2005a: 359).

57 "[T]he perpetrators of these profound changes [in Poland] came from the *intelligentsia, from people who were sensitive to social problems* [emphasis mine – G.K.] ... Yet when the American model 'won', with few exceptions the social liberal intelligentsia became silent on these matters [the question of departure from the Round Table Agreements – G.K.], probably in the name of the newly defined solidarity with colleagues in the government. Even those who saw the dearth of democracy had a ready excuse for it" (Kowalik, 2012a: 105–106).

> changing social base [of Solidarność]. … The U.S. political scientist Ira Katznelson and his university collaborated for years with democratic opposition circles in Poland and other countries of Central Europe, supporting them in various ways. When, after years of absence, he once again arrived in our country (May 1987), he was struck by the radically changed attitude: the rejection by the Solidarity opposition of the "Self-Governing Republic" program in favor of conservative liberalism, which people began calling neoliberalism.
> KOWALIK, 2012a: 40[58]

The author of *From Solidarity to Sellout* then quotes Katznelson himself, who addresses the Polish opposition intelligentsia directly:

> You embraced liberalism with affection and commitment as an alternative not only to your region's party states but to the revisionist Marxism of the 1960s to which you once had subscribed. […] you rejected talk of a "middle way" between the capitalism of the West and the socialism of the East, the in-between location thought at present to constitute an illusion.
> KATZNELSON, 2006: 57; quoted in KOWALIK, 2012a: 40[59]

Summing up this thread in his considerations, Tadeusz Kowalik polemicises with Karol Modzelewski, according to whom a fundamental change in the attitude of the *Solidarność* intelligentsia took place only in 1989 when activists migrated to the organs of political and business power. According to Kowalik, however,

> in the second half of the 1980s it was not S.[olidarność], not the worker movement in general that made up the direct base of the oppositional elite, but what some called the "alternative civil society". It was composed not of the reactivated S.[olidarność] deprived of its intellectual "head,"[60] but mainly the part of it that had survived martial law and the years that

---

58 The second sentence in the quoted passage is from (Kowalik, 2009b: 30), as it was removed from *From Solidarity to Sellout*.
59 The quote has been corrected according to the original: (Katznelson, 1996: 40–41).
60 Kowalik's conviction, expressed here in passing, that it was intellectuals who were the "head" of Solidarity from the beginning of the movement is also confirmed in his other pronouncements. For example, in a 2005 interview he stated that "many of the leaders and advisors of Solidarity left the union [after 1989] and then moved on to power and party structures, intellectually weakening the organisation. *It was, so to speak, decapitated* [emphasis mine – G.K.]" (Kowalik & Zybała, 2005: 38). However, a more in-depth

followed. This was the rich publishing-cultural network, various new groups aspiring to the role of political parties (such as the nationalistic Confederation of Independent Poland, Young Poland), the semi-legal seminars and clubs (the "Flying University") that continued the work as the Society for Educational Courses of the 1970s.

KOWALIK, 2012a: 42

And slightly further on (only in the Polish edition of the book), Kowalik describes the analogous process of transformation of the intelligentsia close to the power apparatus to pro-capitalist positions in the following way:

At this point, for the sake of symmetry, elements of a *neoliberal turn similar to those in the circles of the opposition should be presented in the broadly understood circles of power, i.e. the main leaders of the ruling party and its intellectuals. This turn is very much in line with the compromise reached at the Round Table* [emphasis mine – G.K.].

KOWALIK, 2009b: 41

Apart from drawing attention to the intelligentsia's ideological evolution, Kowalik also describes other changes in the group's attitudes in the second half of the 1980s and, above all, the increasing inclination to act on the basis of their own, broadly understood *interest*. This was to be manifested in a vigorous drive for self-enfranchisement and the entry of representatives of the former opposition into the structures of power and administration.[61]

---

examination of this interesting thread in the thought of the author of *From Solidarity to Sellout* is beyond the scope of this book.

61   In this context, the author of *From Solidarity to Sellout* quotes with approval a statement by Jacek Kuroń, who, according to Kowalik, repeatedly "indicated that the pattern of self-appropriation of the new power elites ... [persisted] throughout the systemic changes" (Kowalik, 2009b: 219) and who claimed that "The first non-communist administration was formed in such a way that the closest colleagues of the prime minister searched for names of friends in their pocket diaries" (Kowalik, 2012a: 53). Further on, Kowalik gives the floor to Kuroń himself on this issue: "This method was continued for the subsequent months and years, when it was necessary to staff banks, companies, voivodeships, embassies and the state media. [...] The Polish middle class emerging from the first version of post-communist capitalism did not gain its positions through the market. For a great portion – or at any rate for those who acquired great fortunes – it was not the free market that turned out to be the most important, but pocket diaries. And so if this group is in fact defending anything, it is these pocket diaries – the connections, arrangements, quotas, government orders, limits, customs barriers, monopolies, thanks to which it gained its current position. This is the Polish drama" (Kuroń & Żakowski, 1997: 91–92; quoted in Kowalik, 2012a: 53–54).

When arguing with Henryk Słabek, who maintained that the issues of the nomenklatura's enfranchisement were "totally absent [in public discussions in Poland], because they are inconvenient for all political groups, although for different reasons in each case" (Słabek, 2004: 384; quoted in Kowalik, 2012a: 52), Kowalik states:

> one must not forget that the *whole galaxy of intellectuals from the opposition defended head on the process of enfranchisement of the nomenklatura* [emphasis mine – G.K.] as the simplest form of "buying yourself out", or as the best way of keeping capital inside the country.
> KOWALIK, 2012a: 52

However, what seems more important in this context is the explanation offered by the author of *From Solidarity to Sellout* in connection with "how was it possible that a social movement like *Solidarność*, which so recently had ten million members, allowed for the realisation of a programme [the Balcerowicz Plan] that so severely hit the old system's real gravediggers [i.e. the workers – G.K.]" (Kowalik, 2005a: 364).[62] Of the three legitimate, according to Kowalik, answers the following one is also given and refers directly to the intelligentsia "the mass exodus of *Solidarność* activists, *especially intellectuals* [emphasis mine – G.K.], to the apparatus of power and administration, strongly weakened the movement right at the moment' of its emergence from the underground" (Kowalik, 2005a: 364).[63] This statement, repeated many times by Kowalik, can, I believe, be regarded as characteristic of the "desertion of the elites" described by Baszkiewicz.

However, it was not only the intelligentsia that Kowalik criticised in the context of their responsibility for the shape of the Polish political and economic transformations. He in some way reverses the focus of this criticism in at least one text:

> [At the end of 1989] Wałęsa ... proposed granting the government extraordinary powers with practically unlimited scope of authority (which probably has no equivalent in the history of trade unions). These

---

62 In another text, Kowalik, having remarked on the "exodus of Solidarity activists", describes them as "during Martial Law, quite detached from the 'mass' of the membership" (Kowalik, 2002e: 625).

63 Kowalik wrote about it even more bluntly in *August – A Bourgeois Epigone Revolution*: "Solidarity experienced ... a huge exodus of its *intellectuals, who were drawn away by the prospect of power and money* [emphasis mine – G.K.]" (Kowalik, 1997a: 54).

were to include restructuring the economy, ownership, demonopolisation of the state and cooperative sectors, reforming the tax and accounting system, the functioning of banks and the structure of the state including local government. This proposal was tantamount to a total surrender of the trade union to authoritarian power. *Solidarity activists, who were often workers, accused the intelligentsia of betrayal. And what did the most important worker want to do to the workers?* [emphasis mine – G.K.].

KOWALIK, 2010a: 17[64]

Finally, I believe it would not be groundless to try to combine two themes identified in Kowalik's work: the lack of a bourgeoisie in the Polish People's Republic and the related increased significance of the intelligentsia in the transformation process. If this were the case, it would have to be acknowledged that Kowalik's considerations implicitly contain a suggestion that, in the Polish revolution, the intelligentsia was to some extent a substitute for the bourgeoisie[65] and thus, as if in place of the bourgeoisie, it also exercised a hegemonic role.

---

64 Kowalik's remark seems to be misguided insofar as it is based, firstly, on the generalisation of an individual to a whole social group and, secondly, on the assumption that the Lech Wałęsa of 1989, already for many years a "career" trade union leader and Nobel Prize winner, can still be described as a "worker".

65 Indeed, this would not be an isolated position in the literature. For example, Gavin Rae writes that "Given ... the absence of a genuine business class [before 1989], the Polish intelligentsia has stood in under the new capitalist order as a *surrogate bourgeoisie* [emphasis mine – G.K.]. Its role during the Communist era had already equipped this stratum and its offspring with the cultural capital required to fill the upper ranks of a reconstituted class society, transmitting its understanding of Western values and lifestyles to those below; now [during the transformation – G.K.] it began to acquire real capital as well" (Rae, 2020: 94). Moreover, it would undoubtedly be worth considering, though unfortunately not in this book, the attempt to juxtapose the problem so outlined in recent Polish history with Alexander Gerschenkron's concept of "substitutes" as presented in his seminal work *Economic Backwardness in Historical Perspective* (Gerschenkron, 1962). As Paul R. Gregory explains, Gerschenkron argued there that "relatively backward countries can create conditions for rapid growth by substituting for missing preconditions. *If there is no middle class to supply entrepreneurs, foreign entrepreneurs can be used* [emphasis mine – G.K.]. If a skilled labour force is lacking, capital-intensive machinery can be substituted. If domestic capital formation is deficient, state capital formation or foreign saving can be used in its place (Gregory, 1992: 65). I am very grateful to Professor Henryk Szlajfer for drawing my attention to Gerschenkron's concept and its possible application in the context discussed here.

As in the case of the activity of the popular masses, also the "external aspect" of the Polish revolution manifests itself in a most perverse way in Tadeusz Kowalik's works. While, as I have shown in the previous chapter, in Jan Baszkiewicz's model bourgeois revolutions are often closely linked with "the task of liberating the nation from foreign power or from colonial rule" or with the need to "liberate the national economy from the domination of foreign capital", Kowalik's account of the Polish transformation seems to describe the exact opposite: inspiration (or even pressure) from abroad played a very important role, perhaps not instigating the revolution but certainly affecting its form.

A general framework for considerations of this kind can be found in the passage from *Systemy gospodarcze*, where we read:

> Many factors influence the choice of system and modes of systemic change. ... The aspirations of the elite encounter constraints or favourable circumstances, such as the balance of internal forces, aid or *external pressures, which in turn depend on the degree of indebtedness of a given country, or the share of foreign capital in key branches of the economy* [emphasis mine – G.K.].
>
> KOWALIK, 2005a: 291

In another text, Kowalik – setting his considerations precisely in the context of the Polish transformation – adds to these strictly practical factors the rather ambiguous issue of the "geopolitical aura", which

> was conducive to the peaceful "Polish break-out" of the domination of the USSR, and thus to the burial of "real socialism", [but] *was not conducive to an independent transition to the new system* [emphasis mine – G.K.]. The ideological and political invasion of Reaganism and Thatcherism, and especially *the USA's imperial policy as the sole military-political superpower, proved to be destructive both for the trade unions and for the social democratic option* [emphasis mine – G.K.].
>
> KOWALIK, 2013b: 211–212

In practice, according to Tadeusz Kowalik's works, this factor was to play a very important role in the Polish revolution. However, in the context of the international conditions of the Polish transformation, Kowalik devoted most attention not so much to the "geopolitical aura" and its long-term effect, but rather to the *direct* external economic pressures stemming from Polish debt, primarily from the International Monetary Fund.[66]

The author of *From Solidarity to Sellout* explains that, at the beginning of June 1989, the Fund's experts set three conditions for aid provision to Poland, which were "[1] absolute reduction of domestic demand, [2] broad restructuring of the economy, including the methods of its operation, and [3] 'external balance', which would enable debt repayment" (Kowalik, 2012a: 71). According to Kowalik, the Fund's intervention at a key moment in Poland's transformation was not, however, limited to economic issues, but also consisted in exerting pressure on the staffing of government positions

> in the appeal for aid drawn up in the *Solidarność* Brussels office signed by Lech Wałęsa and Jacek Merkel and addressed to the authorities of Western countries a month after the elections, it was taken for granted that in return these countries would monitor both the progress in stabilising the economy and the systemic changes. In practice, this meant accepting such systemic changes that made up the Anglo-Saxon type of economic system. Their expression was the so-called Washington Consensus, embracing both international financial organisations and the American authorities. *In the basic programme assumption phase, external pressure was therefore not required. The situation changed only during Wałęsa's presidential campaign, which was directed against Balcerowicz's economic policy* [emphasis mine – G.K.]. The most generous formulation of Wałęsa's statement was that Balcerowicz should have a brother to rebuild what he would destroy first. However, a surprising thing happened: *after coming to power, Wałęsa kept Balcerowicz in his post. Most probably it was a gesture more or less forced by Washington and foreign capital* [emphasis mine – G.K.].
>
> KOWALIK, 2005a: 312–313[67]

---

66 This problem, according to Kowalik, did not only concern Poland, but also other countries undergoing transformation from real socialism to capitalism at the time. In *From Solidarity to Sellout*, Kowalik writes that "The basic pattern ... is also very similar in other countries considered to be leaders in reforms. Everywhere there was immense 'overshooting', and so there must have been some common source factors. These common premises can be found in the theoretical concept of the International Monetary Fund" (Kowalik, 2012a: 141).

67 The document referred to by Kowalik is (Wałęsa & Merkel, 1989).

Kowalik then points out that "There was a noteworthy, publicly recorded, demonstrative visit by the US ambassador, [Thomas] Simons, to Balcerowicz at a time when the entire government had already resigned" (Kowalik, 2002e: 628) and then recalls Stefan Kisielewski's comment on this event:

> After his first talks as President-elect, Wałęsa became frightened. He realised that Balcerowicz was supported by western banking and press factors, which, by the way, did not very well understand the Polish situation. Aware of the price [of the potential removal of Balcerowicz from the government – G.K.], Wałęsa decided on a compromise, which I do not much like, but which I can understand.
>
> KISIELEWSKI & GABRYEL, 1991: 6; quoted in KOWALIK, 2002e: 628

It is therefore not surprising that the "external factor" which, as Kowalik argues, had such a great influence on the Polish reality, was able to impose radicalism on the changes planned by the "revolutionaries". In this context, the author of *From Solidarity to Sellout* discusses the "sharpening" process, which, in his opinion, the Balcerowicz Plan underwent under the influence of the IMF at the conceptual stage. Kowalik quotes Waldemar Kuczyński, who claimed that even the version of the Plan that emerged as a result of the two-day negotiations with the Fund's experts on 27–28 October 1989 was

> [a] *very mild version of stabilization.* [...] *Basically it was not a shock operation concept* [emphasis mine – G.K.]. In December 1990 the retail prices were to be, according to this version, 572 percent higher than in December 1989, whereas in the final version of the program, that is, in the letter of intent to the IMF, this value was lowered to 95 percent. This shows *how much the stabilization program was made more severe in the course of work* [emphasis mine – G.K.], because it must have been known that a more radical stifling of inflation required drainage of a much greater quantity of money.
>
> KUCZYŃSKI, 1992: 98–99; quoted in KOWALIK, 2012a: 123[68]

---

[68]   In the context of the "sharpening" of the Balcerowicz Plan, it is worth noting Kowalik's implicit suggestion that the Polish revolution of 1989 was, to use Baszkiewicz's categories, a revolution running "along an ascending line". In *Wolność. Równość. Własność*, Jan Baszkiewicz explains that "every revolution has its own rhythm. It can develop along an *ascending line* [emphasis mine – G.K.], that is, radicalise and deepen social change. It can also follow a *descending line* [emphasis mine – G.K.], when the highest elevation of the wave occurs at the beginning, after which the revolutionary wave inexorably descends. The two revolutions in France, in 1789 and in 1848, are classic examples of 'upward' and

Kowalik comments: "Kuczyński leaves no doubt that the final implementation of a harsher plan was forced by the IMF" (Kowalik, 2012a: 123), and quotes another passage from that author's book as confirmation: "We were told this clearly many times, publicly and privately, that significant assistance from the West would be possible only after we came to terms with the International Monetary Fund" (Kuczyński, 1992: 100; quoted in Kowalik, 2012a: 123).[69]

However, the author of *From Solidarity to Sellout* sums up the whole of the above thread by stating that "the new Polish decision-makers agreed to such developments all too easily. Kuczyński stresses that there was a 'climate of goodwill' during the negotiations" (Kowalik, 2012a: 123). And in another text, Kowalik notes more generally that "in general the Polish ruling elite went further than the free-market wishes of the West. This is because this elite was strongly motivated by the desire to play a pioneering role. This role, or in fact a mission, was the result of an internal need and not external pressure" (Kowalik, 2002e: 628).

These statements signal, I believe, how Kowalik's particular attitude on this matter relates to his view that the Polish transformation was a *bad choice made by elites*. This is clear in the polemic with Juliusz Gardawski, which we find in *From Solidarity to Sellout*. Kowalik begins by saying that, for Gardawski, the direction in which the Polish transformation went was not "Mazowiecki's fundamental mistake", but an expression of sad necessity. Then he quotes a fragment of his adversary's work:

'*downward*' [emphasis mine – G.K.] development. However, this distinction should not be schematised. The English revolution or the great French revolution yes, they rise, but only up to a certain point. For the revolutionary process in France of 1789–99, the solstice came halfway: in July 1794" (Baszkiewicz, 1981: 24). The definitions above make one look at yet another of Kowalik's descriptions in a different way: "the chief of the IMF experts, Michael Bruno ... was visibly astonished that at a certain point *the Polish government unanimously chose the harshest variant of those presented by the IMF* [emphasis mine – G.K.]. Such was the decision of the shock advocates, in *their belief that the more radical the program the better it would serve to quickly install the new system* [emphasis mine – G.K.]" (Kowalik, 2012a: 123).

69   It is worth noting at this point that in the early 1990s Kowalik in passing presented yet another hypothesis based on the belief that it was an external factor that influenced the shape and pace of the Polish transformation: "'Solidarity' was completely unexpectedly elevated to power. So the political upheaval, as it were, came on its own and without much effort. Thus, there was psychologically an understandable social demand for the next systemic 'great leap'. *The idea of such a leap was brought by 'a young but very distinguished and already well-known professor of economics at Harvard University* [i.e., Jeffrey Sachs; emphasis mine – G.K.]'" (Kowalik, 1991a: 7).

> Poland's international creditors and global financial institutions were ready to help only if … [their] assistance would not be wasted. From their point of view, this could only be guaranteed by a decision to adopt the Washington consensus.
>
> GARDAWSKI, 2009: 62–63; quoted in KOWALIK, 2012a: 160

However, for Kowalik it is

> a surprising but very open admission that the form of transformation was determined by Poland's dependence on foreign capital (international creditors). And that … the *Solidarność* elite was the executor of this (in my opinion false) necessity. Gardawski is not worried about the fact that if that was the case, then the widely celebrated moment of regaining freedom on 4th June [1989] takes on a different meaning than that publicly expressed.
>
> KOWALIK, 2012a: 160; 2009b: 118[70]

The author of *From Solidarity to Sellout*, unlike Gardawski, believes that

> *The Polish authorities did not try to compensate for the unfavorable position of debtor by launching the pioneering character of Poland's undertaken changes* [emphasis mine – G.K.], or the power of the myth of Solidarity, still popular in the West. … the leaders governing the economy … appeared to proceed in the opposite direction. The great changes were to justify the particularly acute and painful character of the prescription. The S.[olidarność] elites who made the key decisions did not make them either in conditions of a threat to self-government, or any open imposition by the West of specific forms of a market economy. *They did not have to so much as wanted to* [emphasis mine – G.K.] take a "shortcut" to reach the Anglo-Saxon model, and there was plenty of evidence for this.
>
> KOWALIK, 2012a: 162

Finally, in Tadeusz Kowalik's deliberations, the issue of the way in which the "transformation elites" presented both the general vision of changes as well as detailed proposals of solutions to the rest of society appears several times. In other words, Kowalik refers to the broadly understood issue of propaganda.

---

70 Only the first sentence of the quoted passage was included in the English translation of the book.

The starting point here is Jacek Kuroń's belief, quoted by the author of *From Solidarity to Sellout*, that the programme of changes must either be preceded by a "psychological shock"[71] in society or that a programme of this kind should have a particular "political value". Karol Modzelewski, quoted by Kowalik, claimed that Sachs "charmed" Kuroń by giving

> simple answers. This could be presented in an understandable way. Jacek could do that. [...] Back in 1981 [...] Jacek Kuroń wrote that the sacrifices required to overcome the crisis will not be accepted by the people unless it is under the influence of a *psychological shock* [emphasis mine – G.K.]. [...] Such a government was created and it adopted a liberal concept, also as a psychological shock.
>
> "Podziały", 1991: 5–6; quoted in KOWALIK, 2012a: 102

The above, according to Tadeusz Kowalik, was confirmed by the dialogue between Ryszard Bugaj and Kuroń that developed following Jeffrey Sachs' speech at the OKP parliamentary club meeting at the end of August 1989. The author of *From Solidarity to Sellout* quotes Kuroń's recollection that

> Rysiek [Ryszard Bugaj] said, "What nonsense this guy is saying!" And I replied: "I don't know much about that stuff [...] but listening I know that this scheme has political value. [...] The program can be economically better or worse. But it must have *political value, that is to say, you present such a program to the people, and they understand what you have said and will support it. If you obtain this support and can maintain it, you can do the strangest things* [emphasis mine – G.K.]".
>
> "Podziały", 1991: 4; quoted in KOWALIK, 2012a: 102

The statement that even a "worse" programme of change, i.e. one which was less convenient from the point of view of the majority of the society, could be implemented if it was simple enough for people to understand (which at the same time Kuroń considered to be a sufficient condition for supporting a project like this), was undoubtedly significant and reflected the essence of propaganda.

---

71   It is striking how well these words fit into the characteristics of the policies of many countries, including Poland during the systemic transformation period, referred to by Naomi Klein as the "shock doctrine" (Klein, 2007). Interestingly, Klein refers to Kowalik in this book as a "prominent Polish economist and former Solidarity member" (Klein, 2007: 193).

However, it can be deduced from Kowalik's considerations in *Systemy gospodarcze* that the "simplicity" of solutions like this turned out to be insufficient in the case of the Polish transformation since the first *Solidarność* governments had to resort to, as he puts it, "mystifying rhetoric":

> The neoliberal rhetoric of [Vaclav] Klaus legitimised his economic policy [in Czechoslovakia/Czech Republic] in the eyes of the West. The social-market rhetoric of Mazowiecki (and even Prime Minister [Hanna] Suchocka) legitimised Balcerowicz's neoliberal policy. It created a barrier to the absorption of the real content of the West German model. It mystified the breaking of social contracts, which Solidarność representatives in government were morally obliged to uphold.
>
> KOWALIK, 2005a: 365

The author of *From Solidarity to Sellout* also offers quite concrete examples of the application of "rhetorical mystification" in particular areas of economic life, one of which was privatisation:

> Janusz Lewandowski and Jan Szomburg wrote about the mass participation of citizens in property ownership, which *created an entirely illusory impression* [emphasis mine – G.K.] that this denoted a new form of socialization, more effective than state ownership. The program, it was said at the time, would consist of "handing over property" into the hands of all adult citizens, "democratization of ownership", and creation of "people's" or "democratic" capitalism. ... *In truth, the initiators of this program had clear objectives outlined from the beginning, but only some members of the new power elite admitted this openly* [emphasis mine – G.K.]. The idea was to consist of mass privatization that would indirectly lead to the rapid concentration of property in private hands. ... Conservative liberals (especially Lewandowski and Szomburg) were looking for a way to have speedy privatization that would at the same time be acceptable for the people.
>
> KOWALIK, 2012a: 209–210

Propaganda manifested itself, in the light of Tadeusz Kowalik's descriptions, not only in what was said or written during the Polish transformation, but also in what was passed over in silence. For example, while trying to address the question (which I have already quoted twice in the book): "how was it possible that a social movement like *Solidarność* ... allowed for the realisation of a programme [the Balcerowicz Plan] that so severely hit the old system's real gravediggers [i.e. the workers – G.K.]", Kowalik states, let us recall, that "This plan *was not publicly discussed* [emphasis mine – G.K.] or negotiated with the trade unions" (Kowalik, 2005a: 364).

However, perhaps because of Tadeusz Kowalik's particularly personal attitude to the *Solidarność* legacy, the most vivid description of the Polish "new elites'" propaganda can be found in the crucial article from 1996:

> A large, perhaps preponderant part of ... former [Solidarity] advisers and activists went into an opposing anti-working class ideological camp, *misrepresenting the history of Solidarity and even slandering it* [emphasis mine – G.K.]. The most insidious effect was the widespread presentation of the mass movement of 1980–81 as exclusively oriented to anti-communism, civil rights and national independence. *The working class character of its demands and the social content of the movement were systematically passed over in silence* [emphasis mine – G.K.]. (An American political scientist, studying changes in Poland over a twenty-year period, has remarked: "the word worker disappeared almost completely from the political vocabulary".) Sometimes maybe this is "only" unintended bias. What is worse, perhaps, is that a persistently repeated myth of a "Second Solidarity" is being created; it is simply presented as an irresponsible, populist opponent of market reforms.
> KOWALIK, 1997a: 54

Conclusion

1

As would transpire from my reconstruction in chapter two, Baszkiewicz's model may be said to treat a bourgeois revolution as taking place when[1] (i) the tensions and contradictions in the functioning of the socio-economic system, manifested in class struggle and chronic economic crisis and conditioned by the "reformist impotence of the old regime" lead to (ii) a revolutionary situation, consisting, broadly speaking, of a social crisis, a political crisis and the rise of the activity of popular classes. More specifically, it involves growing economic inequalities, the financial bankruptcy of the state, a crisis at the highest level of power or the various possible negative consequences of defeat in war.

Consequently, on the one hand, (iii) revolutionary consciousness (the conviction that the existing order is fundamentally wrong and must be rejected at all costs and, at the same time, that another reality is possible) begins to take shape in society, and on the other: the revolutionised masses can, although as in the case of revolutions "from above", they do not have to, undertake specific forms of (x) activity, in particular, in the case of the popular classes, the political mass strike. There also emerges, not necessarily but often, (viii) a revolutionary project: the great social forces' imaginations of the goals, tasks and limits of the revolution crystallise. As a result, some landmark, though not necessarily in itself momentous, event, (iv) a detonator, leads to (v) a revolutionary outburst. This causes, of course, in the case of victorious revolutions, (vii) significant transformations in the class basis of the system (class rule); for without this we are more likely to have a putsch or revolt. On the other hand, the political result of a revolutionary explosion is (vi) a rapid change in the state, breaking the continuity of the law, or at least a change in the ruling elite. All the above must, at the same time, lead to the establishment, in the area covered by the revolution,[2] of capitalism, or, in the minimum variant, constitute a serious step

---

1 The numbering introduced in chapter two is continued.
2 It is worth noting at this point that – although not applicable to the present work – there are interesting theoretical positions that argue the exact opposite. For example, Nygaard, in an already quoted passage, referring to the French Revolution, writes: "The ties between the French Revolution and capitalist development were indeed complex and contradictory. In an immediate sense capitalist development on a national scale in France was fettered by the very Revolution that provided the most important national political preconditions of its development. Within a purely national framework, the developments of the state during the French Revolution could only be said to be 'capitalist' in a modern, industrial sense in

in this direction. Without this, the revolution, even if it fulfils the conditions of the model summarised here, does not have a bourgeois character.

It is also likely that in a revolution of this kind the bourgeoisie will assume (ix) hegemony (a leading role, especially vis-à-vis other classes), while exploiting (xii) the question of national unity and independence, closely linked to the "external aspect" of liberating the country from foreign or colonial rule and, among other things, demonstrating its ability to attract and absorb elites from the popular classes (to conform them). This task will be made easier for the bourgeoisie as from its very ranks or, more precisely, from the intelligentsia, the (xi) revolutionary staffs – the "leadership organs of the revolution" – will emerge; the process that frequently will involve the "desertion of elites" from the camp of power to the revolutionaries. It is also possible that a (xiv) revolutionary leader (or leaders) will emerge, whose person will be surrounded by a kind of cult. A major role in the later phase of this kind of revolution is likely to be played by (xiii) the concept of "completion" (announcing the necessity of destroying the symbols of the old regime and replacing them with new ones and introducing far-reaching changes in education) as well as some generalisation of this, i.e., revolutionary propaganda. At least at some stage, we may also be dealing with (xv) revolutionary terror, including strictly economic terror. In all likelihood, religion and the clergy will also play a reactionary role with respect to the changes taking place (xvi).

Let us now try to summarise the findings in chapter three. I find in Tadeusz Kowalik's works, devoted to the Polish systemic transformation, references to the creation of "the foundations of a new system favourable to the middle-class-to-be" and to shock therapy as "a tool for creating a new, capitalist social structure". Taken together with Kowalik's descriptions of the Polish economy's stagnation in the 1980s, they provide a rationale for concluding that, in his work, there are not only indications of the existence of certain (i) class-based tensions in the realities of the 1980s in Poland, but also of the occurrence of

---

the very long run. But national states and societies cannot be seen as developing in a void, according to formally universal standards. They develop within concrete totalities of international contexts. The same turmoil that produced a delay in French industrial development also provided Britain with the crucial opportunity to cement its competitive advance on its main commercial rival, thereby giving impetus to the industrial revolution and the immense strengthening of that country's economic position during the 19th century. *Within an international framework the Revolution produced capitalist results without delay, even though these results were geographically displaced and, in an immediate sense, contradictory to the development of French national capitalism* [emphasis mine – G.K.]. Also, the French revolutionary centralization and rationalization of the state had enormously significant international effects on the developments of states in other parts of continental Europe" (Nygaard, 2007: 167).

(vii) "significant transformations in the class basis of the system" and "a change in class rule" at that time and place.

The author of *From Solidarity to Sellout* mentions (albeit rather ambiguously) the communist authorities' reformist impotence at the end of the 1980s and also refers to the level of economic inequality but makes no reference to its increase. Instead, he repeatedly expresses the view that the collapse of real socialism was inevitable citing, in this context, among other things, the "disintegration of the apparatus of power". All of this taken together can be regarded as in some way signalling (ii) a revolutionary situation. Moreover, in Kowalik's view, Polish society rejected real socialism. This was particularly true of the representatives of the "elites" (both from the camp of power and from the opposition), losing faith in the possibility of reforming the system and becoming more and more convinced that it was necessary to replace it with another, which can be regarded as the formation of (iii) revolutionary consciousness. As a consequence, an increasingly well-defined (viii) revolutionary project begins to emerge in these "elites", initially assuming the old system's far-reaching transformation and then its complete change.

I have also pointed to excerpts from Tadeusz Kowalik's work that can be seen as describing both (iv) the detonator of the 1989 revolution ("price liberalisation" in August 1989) and (v) the revolutionary outburst. The latter could be, depending on the adopted interpretation, either the elaboration, enactment and implementation of the Balcerowicz Plan or the whole sequence of events between 1989 and 1993. In a sense, this eruption is indicated by Kowalik's descriptions of (vi) the rapidity of change in the state, which is in fact present in most of his references to the Polish transformation. What is more, in the discussed works there are also suggestions that, during 1989, whilst the details of the Balcerowicz Plan were being finalised, which involved adopting increasingly restrictive versions of it, there might have been, as Jan Baszkiewicz put it, a revolution developing "along an ascending line" in Poland.

An important subject of the Polish transformation is, in Kowalik's view, the "dominant class", defined here as the "holders of power" that corresponds to the model (ix) hegemon of the revolution. Thus, the author of *From Solidarity to Sellout* describes certain manifestations of spontaneous social activity in the 1980s in Poland, above all in the context of the grassroots privatisation of the economy. In doing so, he refers extensively to the key role of the intelligentsia (from both sides of the political conflict) in the entire transformation process, thus fulfilling the function of the (xi) "revolutionary staff". Kowalik also mentions the exodus of Solidarity activists to the new power apparatus, which is closely related to this feature of bourgeois revolutions for Baszkiewicz. Several works by the author of *From Solidarity to Sellout* also briefly discuss the (xiii) propaganda surrounding the revolutionary change of 1989, while there is no reference to the issue of "completing the revolution", which forms part of the same feature in the model.

Finally, two features of Baszkiewicz's view of the bourgeois revolutions are revealed in a *perverse* way in my reconstruction of Tadeusz Kowalik's views. The first of these is the role of the (xii) "external aspect" as, in Kowalik's view, foreign entities, especially the International Monetary Fund, are strongly present in the Polish transformation. However, in this case, there is no question of liberation from their "protectorate" but, on the contrary, their active participation in shaping the new order is emphasised, including the imposition of solutions. Secondly, instead of (x) the activity of the popular masses in Poland, according to Kowalik, their passivity turned out to be crucial in deciding the final shape of the changes. And from the list of features described in chapter two, for which I did not find any significant counterparts in the reconstruction of Kowalik's views, were (xiv) the cult of the leader, (xv) economic terror and (xvi) the reactionary role of religion and the clergy.

As I signalled at the beginning of the book, my investigations, like everything in the field of the history of ideas and history in general, inevitably involve selection and interpretation. Selection reveals itself from the adoption of Jan Baszkiewicz's work as a point of reference, through the selection of works by Kowalik taken into account in the reconstruction of his views, to the choice of excerpts capable of signalling issues related to a hypothetical bourgeois revolution in Poland. What remains in the realm of interpretation is the recognition of Kowalik's arguments in other discussions as fully transferable to considerations of a bourgeois revolution. This includes the possibility of determining how many (or conversely how few) of these arguments and references are enough (or not enough) to conclude that every single feature of Baszkiewicz's model of revolution is present in Kowalik's work. The attempt to answer the question posed in the Introduction to the book – whether selected views of Tadeusz Kowalik on the Polish systemic transformation, after their reconstruction into a coherent argumentation, can be regarded as a possible justification for the thesis of an "epigonic bourgeois revolution" in Poland – must therefore be undertaken with full awareness of the limitations arising from the above.

Assuming, as I did in chapter two, that if any of the features of bourgeois revolutions in Jan Baszkiewicz's model has several different manifestations, it is sufficient to identify only one in order to ascertain its occurrence, it can therefore be considered that I have pointed out threads in Kowalik's work corresponding to eleven (including all the "basic") of the sixteen model features of bourgeois revolutions. Two others (both from the "additional" list) appear, as I explained earlier, in a "perverse" form. And what is lacking in Kowalik's work, are statements corresponding to three of Baszkiewicz's criteria (also exclusively from the list of "auxiliary" features). Given that eleven or even thirteen of the sixteen features are a clear majority and, given that among these eleven (or thirteen) there are all the "basic" model criteria, it seems that the juxtaposition of my reconstruction of Kowalik's views with the reference point has yielded a positive result.

However, if, as I argue, some of Tadeusz Kowalik's observations and comments on the Polish transformation, scattered in his numerous works, collectively and after reconstruction, make up a coherent argumentation supporting the thesis of an "epigonic bourgeois revolution" in Poland, the question arises as to why Kowalik never combined these elements himself.

2

Before attempting to answer the above question, it is worth noting that – despite seemingly having every predisposition to do so – Jan Baszkiewicz did not discuss the Polish transformation in terms of a bourgeois revolution either. Significantly, he did not mention the possibility of a "revolutionary" interpretation of 1989 (and subsequent years) either in those works in which he presented the factors influencing the progressive decomposition of the system of power in Eastern Europe at the time. Thus, in his book *Władza* [Power], published a decade after the beginning of the Polish transformation, we read that,

> The ineffective, corrupt and lazy party and government bureaucracy [in the USSR] was unable ... either to sap the energy needed to modernise the country or to halt the *processes of decomposition* [emphasis mine – G.K.]. The situation was different in the satellite countries, above all in Poland, Hungary and Czechoslovakia. Here, 1956 marked the beginning of the twilight of the communist gods, as a long process of *"de-ideologisation" of the communist parties and "de-totalisation" of the system of power began, marked by violent and bloody crises, suppression and regress. The collapse of the basic ideological project became apparent here much more clearly than in the USSR, and its utopianism began to be perceived much sooner* [emphasis mine – G.K.]. A certain relaxation of Moscow's pressure went hand in hand with *the growing pressure of local societies and the weakening of the totalitarian self-confidence of the ruling parties. The sense of national identity and of traditions, not susceptible to sovietisation* [emphasis mine – G.K.] and only suppressed by Stalin's tyranny was very much alive.
> BASZKIEWICZ, 1999: 165

And, furthermore, Baszkiewicz states that,

> As the *ideological (and economic) collapse* [emphasis mine – G.K.] deepened together with that of the system's political reserves, the authoritarian power's muscles atrophied. Phenomena appeared that were completely heretical from the point of view of the only correct doctrine, like *the readiness to reconcile socialism with the market* [emphasis mine – G.K.], tolerance for the activities of political opposition (however, a limited and capriciously variable one). Support for the faltering regimes of "real socialism" was to be brought about by controlled openings towards the West and improved relations with the Church. ... *The apparatus of power corresponded less and less to the criteria of not only totalitarian, but even authoritarian governments: disoriented, uncertain of the future, incapable of anything other than coping with current affairs according to routine* [emphasis mine – G.K.]. While still often sinning in arrogance, it felt more apprehension than comfort in governing.
> BASZKIEWICZ, 1999: 166

In the passages above, it is possible, I believe, to identify at least some of the elements of Baszkiewicz's model of bourgeois revolutions, described in detail in chapter two. Thus, we have here the reformist impotence of the old regime, the germination of a programme of fundamental change ("the readiness to reconcile socialism with the market"), and the emergence and growth of an awareness that such fundamental transformations in the functioning of the system simply had to take place, if only because of the economic crisis ("collapse"), mentioned by Baszkiewicz in passing. Finally, one can also see in the above quotations suggestions concerning the growing activity of the broad masses of society as well as those pointing to the "national aspect".

Baszkiewicz, however, does not mention the possibility of viewing the described events in terms of a bourgeois revolution. Perhaps this is because – despite the great inclusiveness of his views – he did not allow such an interpretation of the Polish events of 1989 for theoretical reasons.

It is also possible that for almost two decades separating the publication of *Wolność. Równość. Własność* and *Władza* quoted above, their author had already managed to abandon such an inclusiveness of his position. Finally, it cannot be ruled out that Baszkiewicz believed the bourgeois revolution had taken place in Poland much earlier than in the late 1980s and early 1990s. Indeed, in the 1982 interview quoted above, he claimed that "the revolutionary cycle closed [in Poland] between [Tadeusz] Kościuszko [i.e. the 1794 insurrection – G.K.] and the democratic republic established after 1918" (Baszkiewicz, Rykowski & Władyka, 1982: 1, 4).

So if, as I argue, neither Tadeusz Kowalik nor Jan Baszkiewicz have done so, perhaps there were some fundamental obstacles other than, of course, the rejection of such a possibility on a theoretical level, preventing the presentation of a coherent and exhaustive argumentation in favour of the thesis that a bourgeois revolution took place in Poland (or, more broadly, in Eastern Europe) in the late 1980s and early 1990s? The negative answer to this question, however, turns out to be immediate. For in the 1997 article by Colin Barker and Colin Mooers, which I have already cited several times, one not only finds the thesis that "The East European revolutions ... make sense as a species of 'bourgeois revolution'" (Barker & Mooers, 1997: 35)[3] but also an extensive argumentation in support of the proposal.

Thus, we have indications in the work of Barker and Mooers that the Eastern European revolutions of 1989–1991 were revolutions "from above" ("The ruling class was recomposed ... but its privileged position was never seriously threatened" (Barker & Mooers, 1997: 23)). The authors of the article mention stagnation ("economic stagnation [in the 1980s] made them [the rulers of Eastern Europe] dissatisfied with their material situation" (Barker & Mooers, 1997: 24)) and crisis threatening social outbursts ("Marketization [of the real socialist economies in the 1980s] also brought new symptoms of crisis, and the threat of social explosions" (Barker & Mooers, 1997: 22)). The detonator of revolution is also present in the text, it seems: "The impetus [for change] came in Poland in 1988 from two waves of strikes" (Barker & Mooers, 1997: 22–23),[4] and the popular masses – as in Kowalik's work – are passive rather than active in the events

---

3 Elsewhere in the article they write that "On occasion crises of capitalist reproduction produce revolutions that accomplish a shift 'sideways' from one path of capitalist accumulation to another. ... Such, we suggest, were the 1989 revolutions" (Barker & Mooers, 1997: 36). This is all the more surprising because, as I showed in the Introduction, another author writing in the tradition of "state capitalism", Neil Davidson, using exactly the same argument about "sideways" movement, justified his *opposition* to the application of the notion of bourgeois revolution to the transformation in Eastern Europe in the late 1980s and early 1990s (Davidson, 2012: 464). A precise tracing of the similarities and differences between Davidson's positions and those of Barker and Mooers is, however, beyond the scope of my book. Therefore, let us just add that the very term "sideways", used in this context by both Barker and Mooers and Davidson, comes from the work of Chris Harman, who wrote that "the transition from state capitalism to multinational capitalism is neither a step forward nor a step backward, but a step sideways" (Harman, 1990: 82; quoted in Davidson, 2015: 134).

4 Elsewhere in the text we read that: "In Poland, two waves of strikes in April and August 1988 finally impelled the regime and Solidarity towards talks" (Barker & Mooers, 1997: 27).

described ("The revolutions [in Eastern Europe] involved only limited popular mobilization"; "popular self-mobilization was not the basis of these revolutions" (Barker & Mooers, 1997: 18, 38)).[5] Finally, in the discussed work, we have the issue, also understood similarly in Kowalik's work, of the "external factor" ("With the IMF and a host of western advisers pressing them forward, the new governments disclosed a less-remarked feature of 'civil society': new disciplines on labour" (Barker & Mooers, 1997: 36)).

The article contains interesting reflections on the question of an emerging revolutionary consciousness on the side of both the ruling elite and the opposition. On the evolution of views within the former group, in Barker and Mooers we read the following:

> The formerly homogenized elements of the "one-party" system [in the 1980s] showed marked tendencies to separation into distinctive "interests". ... ideological unity in ruling circles diminished. In a context of deepening economic crisis, sectors of the elite could more openly consider a redesign of the old political model.
> BARKER & MOOERS, 1997: 33

And as far as the opposition side is concerned:

> By the end of the 1980s, the thinking of *Solidarity intellectuals* [emphasis mine – G.K.] had been so transformed that their ideas on the relationship between the market and the state were virtually indistinguishable from those of the Communist Party. For both party and opposition, transition to the market was seen as the only possible salvation for the Polish economy. By 1990, leading figures in the former workers' organization, Solidarity, were presiding over a "shock therapy" to Polish society that shoved unemployment up and living standards down.
> BARKER & MOOERS, 1997: 31

The reference to "Solidarity intellectuals" signals one of the more important themes in Barker and Mooers' article, which is the evolution that the Eastern

---

5 Elsewhere more broadly and explicitly: "The year of 1989 was characterized by an 'absence' [of]: any significant element of independent grass-roots institution-building. No strike committees or workers' councils emerged, no peasant committees, to enunciate specific class demands. Certainly, nothing appeared in 1989 comparable to the workers' councils and civic committees of the 1956 revolution in Hungary, or the inter-factory strike committees and the like of Solidarity's birth in Poland during 1980" (Barker & Mooers, 1997: 28).

European intelligentsia underwent in the 1980s and how this change contributed to the final shape of the transformation. In this context, the authors point to what Baszkiewicz referred to as the "intelligentsia staff of the revolution":

> Leadership came from the intelligentsia, their organizations and their ideas. Even in opposition, the intelligentsia in Eastern Europe enjoyed a political importance, and a sense of self-importance, unmatched by their western *confrères*.
> BARKER & MOOERS, 1997: 25

The question of the internally anti-democratic character of Solidarity after the imposition of martial law in Poland also does not escape Barker and Mooers' attention:

> [a] shift in social composition and rightward evolution all made Solidarity an increasingly suitable "partner" for accommodation with the party's reform wing. To play that part, one thing was required: Solidarity must contain any radical tendencies on its own side. This it was willing and able to do. The leadership under Wałęsa drew the teeth of [i.e. disarmed] the 1988 strike movements, and systematically excluded former "radicals" from decision-making during the Round Table process. Once the June [1989] elections were decided, a selected "Citizens Committee" chose all the Solidarity candidates without any open election procedures. It was something of a come-down from the direct democracy of August 1980.
> BARKER & MOOERS, 1997: 26[6]

Finally, there is even a suggestion, albeit a very abbreviated and borrowed one, of the epigonic nature of the events described in Barker and Mooers' article: "[Jürgen] Habermas, [James] Petras and others have pointed to the notable absence of 'new ideas' in 1989" (Barker & Mooers, 1997: 28).

---

6 A separate issue, which undoubtedly requires in-depth study, is why Tadeusz Kowalik not only does not properly refer to this "withering away" of democracy in Solidarność in his works but does not raise the issue of the lack of universal democratic legitimacy for the 1989 changes at all. Probably his only mention of this problem dates from the early 1990s, when he wrote: "The thesis of the absence of an alternative, especially when one criticises the radical 'overshoot' of the Balcerowicz Plan, can be challenged from yet another point of view. I argue that the content of the Plan depended on the procedure of its creation. Moreover, it is not difficult to show that, contrary to the frequently promoted belief, *there was a positive correlation between the degree of democratisation of this procedure and the economic rationality of the Plan* [emphasis mine – G.K.]" (Kowalik, 1991c: 42).

CONCLUSION   161

Thus, it is clear that in the 1990s, it was possible to attempt a deliberate justification of the thesis of a bourgeois revolution in communist Poland. In the content of Barker and Mooers' article, when juxtaposed with any point of reference, if only with Jan Baszkiewicz's model of bourgeois revolutions, a whole range of features of these revolutions immediately become apparent without the need, as in the case of Tadeusz Kowalik's work, for any reconstruction. We therefore inevitably return to the question of why Kowalik never undertook the task. An attempt to answer this question requires, I believe, a closer look at certain aspects of the author of the *From Solidarity to Sellout*'s intellectual evolution.

3

Let us begin by drawing attention to an article from 1997 in which Kowalik, calling for the restoration of Michał Kalecki's work to its proper place in discussions on the distribution of national income, identifies a fundamental barrier in this respect: i.e., the "academic or even socially academic" factor, consisting of "our economists' reluctance to deal with the problems of the 'class struggle'" (Kowalik, 2013a: 243). "This concept", or "class struggle" is, as Kowalik continues, "considered ... unscientific, banished from good company. And yet Kalecki, already in the very title of his last (posthumously published) study,[7] exposed the class struggle as the causal factor in the distribution of national income" (Kowalik, 2013a: 243).[8]

A few years later, in *Systemy gospodarcze*, the author presents what he calls "the simplest definition of capitalism":

It is a system in which profit is the primary motive for economic activity and the market and competition are the main mechanisms of coordination. The social basis of capitalism is the class division of society into owners of

---

7 Kowalik here refers to (Kalecki, 1971).
8 This call for the study of class struggles seems to contrast with the fears expressed by Kowalik in the same period (and discussed by me in chapter three) about the manifestation of these conflicts in social life. This does not change the fact that in the same year of 1997, in the already mentioned polemic with Andrzej Walicki around the Polish edition of his book (Walicki, 1996), Kowalik claimed that he still found Marxism a useful tool for the study and critique of capitalism. In doing so, he added that he was concerned "not to lose what Marx gave to the social sciences" (Kowalik, 1997b: 63). Kowalik's review, however, like Walicki's book itself, was primarily concerned with Marx's vision of communism and conception of freedom.

> *capital (the means of production) and wage-labourers, selling their labour power on a contractual basis* [emphasis T.K.]. This means that private ownership of the means of production, used in a capitalist mode, determines the nature of social relations and the dynamics of development. The activation of these means of production depends on the expected profit. Robert Heilbroner based the characterisation of capitalism on Marx's well-known formula: M-C-M' (money – commodity – money plus profit), which emphasises that the purpose of business is not the use-value of goods and services, but money. Commodities are only a means to this end. For the capitalist employer, the means are not only goods and services but also workers. Their fate depends on the owners of capital. Hence the fundamental inequality between employer and worker.
>
> KOWALIK, 2005a: 35[9]

And further on we read that,

> In the inter-war period, and in Germany even as early as the end of the 19th century, under Chancellor Otto Bismarck, *workers won rights that formed the basis of the welfare state* [emphasis mine – G.K.]. These were radically expanded and generalised in the first quarter of a century after the Second World War. ... The balance of social forces (in short, the equilibrium between capital and labour), which has prevailed since the creation and spread of the welfare state, has its origin in the links between the structure of production and the social structure. To describe these relationships, French economists and sociologists use the term Fordism. ... The unintended effect of such an organisation of production, based on the size of buildings, factory canteens and common rooms, and often also on factory housing estates, was to concentrate many workers in one place, creating conditions for their *self-organisation, organisation of rallies, demonstrations and strikes* [emphasis mine – G.K.]. Thus, it gave the workers collective strength, and facilitated the struggle for higher wages, and better working conditions. ... The move away from the production line to small teams after the Second World War became one of the factors that weakened all these formations. Before this happened, *the trade unions, supported mainly by the socialist and social-democratic parties,*

---

9 In a 2005 interview, Kowalik makes a similar but shorter statement on the same subject: "I actually do not feel the need to replace the Marxian definition of capitalism as a system based on wage labour and a capitalist enterprise aiming at profit maximisation" (Kowalik & Sierakowski, 2005: 207).

> *had forced various entitlements that further socialised capitalism. This was fostered by many other factors, among them the memory of the revolutionary wave after the First World War* [emphasis mine – G.K.].
>
> KOWALIK, 2005a: 41–42

Based only on the above excerpts from Kowalik's work, one might conclude that it was written by at least an author holding Marxist views, or simply a Marxist, who not only calls for scientific analyses of class struggle and defines capitalism in a Marxist manner, but who also argues that it was the class struggle that led to bourgeois governments giving concessions that resulted in the introduction of elements of the "welfare state" into the capitalist economies.

And yet, as I have shown in chapter three, in Tadeusz Kowalik's analyses of the Polish systemic transformation, class struggles are actually present to a very small degree, as is the analysis in terms of class in general. There are no reflections in these works – in particular in *From Solidarity to Sellout* – that could be considered an understanding of history in the spirit of historical materialism, nor are there any references to the labour theory of value, capital as a social relation, exploitation and so on.[10] The need to define capitalism still prompted Kowalik to draw on the concepts of Karl Marx and his successors in *Systemy gospodarcze*, but the passage quoted above on class struggle as the driving force behind socio-economic changes already contrasts drastically with another one directly concerned with the Polish transformations:

> Social agreements reached through negotiated compromise, as a method of building a new socio-economic order, were already a tried and tested path to social change in 1980. If [in the Polish transformation] the principle of *pacta sunt servanda* had been followed, if the agreements concluded at the Round Table and the specific agreement concluded with voters, who were presented with a similar programme outline had been respected, the new socio-economic system, formed after 1989, would have had to look completely different.
>
> KOWALIK, 2005a: 365

---

10 Interestingly, in the aforementioned works Kowalik also makes virtually no mention of what Solidarity was actually fighting for in Poland at the beginning of the 1980s, and any references he makes to the fact that it was a workers' revolution are, as shown earlier, either indirect or extremely perfunctory. This is in rather stark contrast to his work from the 1980s, for example, the contents of his paper "Planning and Freedom" (Kowalik, 1982). This is pointed out and discussed in detail in (Rae, 2024).

So, at this point in *Systemy gospodarcze*, according to Kowalik, it was no longer class struggle, no longer "self-organisation, organisation of rallies, demonstrations, strikes" by workers, but "respecting the agreement" by the representatives of, as he described them elsewhere, "the elite", deciding over the heads of the workers on the shape of change, that would guarantee an economic order more favourable to the working class.

This is, by the way, probably part of a more coherent vision of the Polish transformation. In *From Solidarity to Sellout*, Kowalik writes, for example, that

> Polish capitalism is characterized on the one side by massive unemployment, a large portion of people living in poverty, and high and constantly rising wage and income disparities. On the other side, there is a diverse group of those who hold wealth and power, with strong clientelist or corruption links among its members. *Both sides are the result of not so much uncontrolled market processes as deliberate activity (or inactivity, depending on the circumstances) of the state* [emphasis mine – G.K.].
> KOWALIK, 2012a: 289–290

Thus, not only are there no longer class struggles, but the classes themselves are replaced in their role as the agent of change in society and the economy by two other forces remaining in a dichotomous arrangement: the market ("uncontrolled market processes") and the state.

Moreover, as is clear from many of his works, at least from the 1990s onwards, Tadeusz Kowalik was a staunch opponent of the revolutionary method of social change. He repeatedly cites, for example, a statement by Joseph E. Stiglitz[11] according to whom "the Bolshevik approach to changing society – forced changes from a revolutionary vanguard – has failed time and time again. The shock therapy approach to reform was no more successful than the Cultural Revolution [in China – T.K.] and the Bolshevik Revolution" (Stiglitz, 2001: 30; quoted in Kowalik, 2012a: 18). In a text from 2003, Kowalik comments as follows:

> [Stiglitz's] equating shock therapy with the *two revolutions that have made an inglorious mark on human history* [emphasis mine – G.K.] is as much a disavowal of Washington's earlier prescription as it is a warning

---

11 For more on Kowalik's attitude to the views of this economist see, for example, (Kowalik, 2011b).

> to countries embarking on the path of systemic change not to copy this concept.
>
> KOWALIK, 2003: 227–228

The author of *From Solidarity to Sellout* goes on to explain that, in his view,

> The shock method can only produce a sick social structure, full of pathology, with destroyed social institutions in the Weberian sense, i.e. rules (norms) of behaviour, and of the formation of new ones. [In Poland after 1989] New deviations were superimposed on the old, post-communist behaviour.
>
> KOWALIK, 2003: 230

My two aforementioned observations, about the only marginal presence of Marxism in Tadeusz Kowalik's analyses of the Polish transformation and about his attitude to the revolutionary changes in society, are well connected by a passage in *Systemy gospodarcze* concerning what Kowalik calls "constructivist thought in the emergence of a new socio-economic order":

> When ... one looks ... [at the various economic] systems, it is not difficult to see that they were all created with a large dose of ... constructivism. ... Constructivist thought particularly clearly preceded the creation of the new system in West Germany. ... The German experience appears ... as a successful example of moderate constructivism, and not only in economic terms. *Post-war Germany proved that government-controlled, far-reaching systemic change is possible, which not only does not threaten freedom and democracy, but extends them* [emphasis mine – G.K.]. ... the rejection of total constructivism (communist and fascist) should not invalidate its benign form ... For it is clear that *the interaction between, on the one hand, the projects and actions of state authorities and, on the other, the aspirations and behaviour of social groups (the organisations representing them) cannot be a one-off thing, but a process of negotiation and agreement* [emphasis mine – G.K.].
>
> KOWALIK, 2005a: 287–289

Economic systems are thus shaped, according to Kowalik, to a large extent in a constructivist manner and not, for example, spontaneously, as a result primarily of class struggles and, for the author of *From Solidarity to Sellout*, this is a desirable situation. Therefore, I think we may risk the thesis that, in Tadeusz Kowalik's works, at least those written in the last decades of his activity, it is not revolution, but reform that is considered the appropriate method of undertaking political and economic change.

I already signalled in the first chapter that the problem of revolution appeared in Kowalik's work since the 1950s. And since at least the 1980s he devoted more and more attention to the theory and practice of *gradual change* in society and the economy. What comes to the fore here is undoubtedly, as an independent continuation of reflections undertaken earlier with Michał Kalecki (Kalecki & Kowalik, 1991),[12] a consideration of the possibility of a *crucial reform* of (real) socialism (Kowalik, 1989). Kowalik explains that he means "changes ... [that] can be called radical, because of their impact on the *functioning* [emphasis mine – G.K.] of the whole national economy or its core" (Kowalik, 1989: 23).[13] Years later, Kowalik summarised the evolution of his

---

12 A good discussion of the content of this work and its relevance can be found in (King, 2014) and (Dymski, 2014). It is worth noting the highly original interpretation of Michał Kalecki's thought presented by Kowalik in 2004. The author of *From Solidarity to Sellout* attempts to place Kalecki's achievements within the framework of the "comparative systems" paradigm: "Contrarily to a widely held conviction that Kalecki limited his interest to a general theory of capitalism, and at a later time also to a theory of the 'really existing socialism', *we find in his writings concepts of a variety of capitalist economies* [emphasis mine – G.K.]: fully-fledged capitalism; the regime of political business cycle; capitalism of full employment; and, finally, the *crucially reformed capitalism, or neo-capitalism* [emphasis mine – G.K.]. In his other works ... we also find references to intermediate systems and mixed economies. We may also trace a variety of socialist economies, or 'socialisms' (centrally planned; planned and self-managed; *crucially reformed* [emphasis mine – G.K.], etc.) ... What is important, is that in all these cases the key to his [Kalecki's] classifications lies in broadly understood socio-economic policies, in the role of the state and the scope and strength of participation of main social classes. *One could write a textbook of comparative economic systems based only on Kaleckian terminology* [emphasis mine – G.K.]" (Kowalik, 2004a: 49).

13 The coincidence of such a definition of a "crucial reform" with the explanations, referred to in the Introduction, of what a "revolution from above" is, seems particularly striking. Incidentally, Tadeusz Kowalik seems to have expressed his doubts about the effectiveness of implementing "reforms" of this kind only in *Systemy gospodarcze*. When he comments on Louis Putterman's and Joseph E. Stiglitz's critique of the concept of market socialism, we read that: "While criticising market socialism, Putterman, like Stiglitz, are as far as possible from an apology of capitalism as we know it. On the contrary, they seek to respond to the demands of socialists, both advocating *a radical reform of capitalism* [emphasis mine – G.K.]. Neither of them, however, considers *to what extent the reforms of capitalism are permanent and irrevocable, and this is perhaps the greatest weakness of their reformist position. The experience of the last quarter of a century is hardly optimistic here* [emphasis mine – G.K.]. The post-war capitalist world has experienced indicative planning policies, income equalisation through high taxes and large social transfers. However, these reforms *proved to be reversible* [emphasis mine – G.K.]. 'Free' markets have replaced indicative planning. For the last twenty years, there has been a rapid process of rising inequality

views on crucial reform as a desirable formula for introducing changes in the economy as follows:

> The general collapse of real socialism came as a great surprise to me. In the 1980s, I was arguing in favour of [a] *crucial reform of "real socialism"* [emphasis mine – G.K.] ... or for a "mixed socialist economy" ... But there were *no sufficient social forces* [emphasis mine – G.K.] and leadership, above all in the USSR, for an evolution of this kind. In the new situation, my main concern was to save what was good in the so-called "socialist welfare state" and to draw on the best European models.[14]

In the following years, this evolution led the author of *From Solidarity to Sellout* towards postulating systemic solutions (and ways of putting them into practice) similar to those for example in John K. Galbraith's *The Good Society: The Humane Agenda* (Galbraith, 1996). From *Systemy gospodarcze* we learn that this work

> belongs ... to a group of *realistic utopias* [emphasis mine – G.K.], that is, utopias which, in view of the already existing material conditions, resources, qualifications as well as the conceivable way of functioning, [convince us] that it would be possible to create a system ensuring a good society. *What stands in the way are the interests of influential groups, the prejudices of a public that can be manipulated, monopolistic constraints, including the power of the mass media, the vast majority of which are subordinate to large corporations* [emphasis mine – G.K.]. The concepts [of realistic utopias] of [James] Meade and [John K.] Galbraith, which supporters of hitherto known capitalism may consider maximalist and

---

in the leading capitalist countries. The welfare state is in the fire of criticism" (Kowalik, 2005a: 72). These reflections, however, do not seem to have influenced the revision of Kowalik's position on class struggle and revolution as undesirable methods of social change.

14 This excerpt is a proposed paragraph that was supposed to be added to the English translation of *Polska transformacja*, but which was ultimately not included in *From Solidarity to Sellout*. It was forwarded by Tadeusz Kowalik to the book's translator, Eliza Lewandowska, in a message (e-mail) dated 10th January 2011. As I did not find any similarly formulated declaration in Kowalik's published works, in this case, I decided to depart from the principle of basing the book exclusively on the published works of the author of *From Solidarity to Sellout*. I have removed the bibliographical references from the quotation. Also, I have left unchanged the sentence which in the (bilingual) original reads "I was arguing in favour of [a] crucial reform of 'real socialism' ... or for a 'mixed socialist economy'", although I have corrected the spelling. I am very grateful to Ms Eliza Lewandowska for making her correspondence with Tadeusz Kowalik available to me.

socialists – minimalist, are *worth returning to, as it seems that only these ideas can provide a starting point for further discussion of the shape of systemic transformation in post-communist Europe* [emphasis mine – G.K.] and reforms in the European Union.

KOWALIK, 2005a: 63–64

4

Although all the remarks proposed so far on Tadeusz Kowalik's intellectual evolution bring us closer to understanding why he never developed an argument supporting the concept of "epigonic bourgeois revolution" in Poland, they still require, I believe, some systematisation and generalisation.[15]

Studying the work of the author of *From Solidarity to Sellout* leads me to the thesis that, while for at least the first decade of his scholarly and publicist activity, Kowalik functioned within what is broadly understood as Marxism-Leninism,[16] from the turn of the 1950s and 1960s onwards, both

---

15   I undertake such a task in the full knowledge that any attempt to explain, categorise or caveat all of Tadeusz Kowalik's biography and work on such a general level means shifting further away from the rational reconstructions I have dealt with so far towards *Geistesgeschichte* on the "axis" of Rorty's (1984) practice of the history of ideas.

16   Here a good example is the previously cited text from 1957 (although revisionist themes are already present in it). Kowalik reveals his self-identification there very openly, referring to, for example, "we Marxists" (Kowalik, 2013f: 436). Kowalik's Marxism from the mid-1950s can also be seen well in one of his first articles, devoted to the early works of Ludwik Krzywicki. We read there, for example, that in the 1880s "Krzywicki had ... *no reformist illusions. He came close to a correct view of the reforms in capitalism, stating that the reforms were only half-measures that could not bring about a radical improvement in the working class's material conditions and that only the abolition of capitalism and the establishment of collective ownership of the means of production could fundamentally change the living standards of the working masses* [emphasis mine – G.K.]. ... Krzywicki was already at that time ... under the strong influence of Marxism, he assimilated Marxism and *knew how to use it in principle in his fight against bourgeois ideology, offering a correct analysis of positivism, of its apologetic social function* [emphasis mine – G.K.]" (Kowalik, 1955: 166–167). And further on in the same text, we read that for Kowalik "The important thing in Krzywicki is that he sees a revolutionary way of social development, and he fights against a shallow anti-Marxist evolutionism, which is the theoretical basis of reformism. But revolution, in Krzywicki's reasoning, arises not from the objective development of society, not from the contradiction between relations of production and productive forces, but is brought about by progressive social theories. These theories are, moreover, somehow completely detached from the social classes representing progress. *Krzywicki saw, as we have already pointed out, the economic basis of the class struggle of the proletariat against the bourgeoisie, but he had not yet grasped that this class struggle inevitably leads to revolution, that the*

CONCLUSION

in terms of the method and the content of his research, his gradual evolution towards revisionism[17] began, with some influences of Trotskyism[18] in the political dimension and, probably to a greater extent, of Kaleckianism[19] in the economic one (which, however, still, according to Kowalik himself, clearly placed him among the Marxists),[20] and then, more so in the 1980s,

---

social theory, which he advocates and which he opposes to positivism, is, in fact, a generalisation of the interests and aspirations of the proletariat and becomes a material power when it takes possession of the masses [emphasis mine – G.K.]" (Kowalik, 1955: 169). I am obviously quoting these particular passages from an article by the less than 30-year-old Kowalik also in order to draw attention to the views of its author on the issues I discussed in the previous section: Kowalik's attitude to the reform of capitalism ("reformist illusions", "reforms are only half-measures") and towards class struggle and revolution ("class struggle inevitably leads to revolution").

17   In an interview given in 2006, Kowalik states "My main ... [intellectual] origins is rather *revisionism* [emphasis mine – G.K.], for which I was expelled from the party after twenty years of membership [in 1968 – G.K.]" (Kowalik & Lubczyński, 2006: 345).
18   I mentioned this in chapter three.
19   Kowalik himself perhaps summed up Kalecki's influence on his intellectual development most fully in (Kowalik, 2013c). A good deal on this subject can also be found in (Kowalik et al., 2013). Incidentally, in the context of Kowalik's collaboration with Kalecki, the evolution of also those views of the former, which make up the thesis of the "epigonic bourgeois revolution" in Poland, becomes quite evident. As I showed in chapter one, in one of the papers devoted to the thesis, Kowalik writes that in Central and Eastern Europe in 1918–1919, "revolutions ... meant a *political* defeat for the workers, but not a *social* defeat [emphasis T.K.]. From the social point of view, they meant the creation of the foundations of the welfare state (e.g. in Poland the eight-hour working day and many other workers' rights)" (Kowalik, 2003: 226). However, a quarter of a century earlier, in an article written with Kalecki, Kowalik spoke about the same events in a noticeably different tone: "Except for the 8-hour working day and various kinds of social insurance gained by the working class in many countries, *capitalism during the 1920s operated in more or less the same way as before the war* [i.e. First World War; emphasis mine – G.K.]" (Kalecki & Kowalik, 1991: 471).
20   That his views from the 1960s Tadeusz Kowalik considered to be, clearly, Marxist, we learn, for example, from the following statement: "[At the beginning of the 1960s] I ended up at the Department of Economic Sciences [of the Polish Academy of Sciences], headed by Bronisław Minc. ... He was afraid of my writing, and I happened to be preoccupied with Rosa Luxemburg and her book *Accumulation of Capital*. He wanted me *to file a declaration that I was a Marxist. Although I was convinced that I was one ('a real one!'), I considered any such declaration derogatory* [emphasis mine – G.K.]" (Kowalik et al., 2013: 630–631). It is beyond the scope of my book, but undoubtedly worth considering, to take up the issue of the "depth" of Kowalik's Marxism, that is, whether, and if so to what extent, this world view – shaped, after all, in the specific times of the war, the immediate post-war period, and especially in the Stalinist era, during the studies started by Kowalik in 1951 at the Institute for Training Scientific Cadres (later: Institute of Social Sciences) at the Central Committee of the Polish United Workers' Party (Kowalik et al., 2013: 622) – was, in his

towards an increasing eclecticism with, it seems, elements of (classical) institutionalism.[21]

case, from the very beginning a very specific form of Marxism. This does not refer only to Kowalik, but also to many others (perhaps even, at least to some extent, to a "generational experience") whose views and attitudes were formed under similar conditions. A suggestion to this effect is probably hidden in Kozłowski's opinion that Kowalik's "post-war biography, marked by his presence in the party, Marxism, party schools, was consistent with the life path of many" (Kozłowski, 2014: 49). Magdalena Mikołajczyk (2015) writes similarly: "insightful observers and critical reviewers of the socio-political transformations [after 1989 in Poland] were (initially exclusively, later, apart from others, also) *representatives of one intellectual, political and, importantly, generational formation* [emphasis mine – G.K.]. [This includes] ... Zygmunt Bauman, Maria Hirszowicz, Tadeusz Kowalik, Andrzej Walicki, Karol Modzelewski. Even if it is now possible or was possible ... to identify their declared attitudes, their positioning within the ideological and political spectrum, they were not identical (with the accentuation that *they were social democratic or social liberal*). *They are united by several features: representation of an academic milieu, the perspective of an engaged and critical intellectual-humanist, past political involvement determining the necessity of referring to the left-wing socialist utopia, referring to own past experiences, analysis of Polish transformation processes against the background of globalisation and the crisis of capitalism* [emphasis mine – G.K.]" (p. 91). For more on the specifics of the Institute for Training Scientific Cadres and the milieu of its "aspirants" (*aspiranci*) see (Connelly, 1996). In this text, the author points out that "some of Poland's leading 'revisionist' and critical thinkers passed through the institute" and emphasises that the Institute's head Adam Schaff "used connections to gain his students access to forbidden literature beyond the IKKN. ... Tadeusz Kowalik was able to read the Polish émigré journal *Kultura*" (Connelly, 1996: 325, 335).

21 These themes are already very much evident in, for example, (Kowalik, 1989) and, to a somewhat lesser extent, in (Kowalik, 2013e). On the other hand, in "Oskar Lange odczytywany na nowo" [Oskar Lange Read Anew] (Kowalik, 2013g), Kowalik writes "Due to the nature and limitations of this text, I will refer not so much to purely theoretical studies as to what Lange would have called *institutional economics* [emphasis mine – G.K.]" (p. 560). The very occurrence of the intellectual evolution I am writing about here in Kowalik is of course not something unprecedented. As Paweł Kozłowski points out in an already quoted opinion, "[Kowalik's] post-war biography, marked by his presence in the party, Marxism, party schools, *was consistent with the life path of many* [emphasis mine – G.K.]" (Kozłowski, 2014: 49). However, I do not undertake a qualitative assessment of the nature of this evolution, in other words, whether it was *progress* or *regression*. I believe that neither of these two possibilities should be accepted or rejected a priori without in-depth research. For while the thesis of progress, supposed to be an expression of the "natural" intellectual development of any thinker with the passage of time, is perhaps the most intuitive one, the opposite claim does not seem to be without merit if only because of a number of important confirmations of the possibility of such a regression in the history of ideas. For example, in his introduction to the Polish edition of György Lukács's *History and Class Consciousness*, Marek Siemek (1988) writes of the work and its author as follows: "the entire Preface to the second edition would deserve a separate analytical-critical study, namely as a rare document of the author's misleading self-assessment in the presentation of his own development. For it would be possible to demonstrate that, theoretically and

This evolution in scholarly inquiry was, in my opinion, accompanied (without resolving the relationship between the two) by another one: the political. Initially, Tadeusz Kowalik generally identified himself with a quite progressive agenda, associated in particular with Edward Abramowski, Ludwik Krzywicki and the idea of co-operatives. Then quite briefly, perhaps only for a few years, he moved closer to Marxist-Leninist socialism. For a number of subsequent years, the author of *From Solidarity to Sellout* identified himself with the concept of, as he himself termed it, "democratic socialism" (involving, in its range of variants, a large degree of workers' self-government). Finally, in the last decades through the transformation, Kowalik seems to have taken a rather social-democratic or even social-liberal stance.[22]

Having thus moved over several decades from an orthodox and then revisionist Marxism to a much more moderate, social-democratic position,[23]

---

philosophically, Lukács's development from *History and Class Consciousness* to, say, *The Ontology of Social Being* signifies regression rather than progress – and above all precisely on those points which ... the author himself proudly indicates as significant steps forward in his evolution" (p. XXXVI).

22 An excellent source for Tadeusz Kowalik's self-assessment of his own intellectual and political evolution, which at the same time forms the basis for all the assertions in the paragraph above, is an interview he gave in 2004 (Kowalik et al., 2013). The only exception in this respect is the lack of explicit references to the perceived evolution towards social democracy or social liberalism. In this case, however, it is not difficult to find relevant passages in the works by Kowalik. In *Systemy gospodarcze*, written around the same time as the interview, for example, he writes approvingly about the evolution of European left-wing parties: "the different varieties of the socialist movement, very much alive over many decades, have left a strong imprint on the world. Weakened, however, by communism attempting to pass itself off as the only alternative to capitalism, and even by fascism, which also appeared under socialist slogans (as "national socialism"), it now plays a marginal role. The exceptions are the social-democratic parties that grew out of the socialist movement, which in many countries sometimes act as a strong opposition, and not infrequently govern alone or in coalition with others. However, *even those that have retained socialist rhetoric do not set themselves the task of creating an alternative system, but confine themselves to the desire to reform capitalism in the spirit of a socialist axiology formed by values such as equality, social justice, solidarity, participation, universal education, etc.* [emphasis mine – G.K.]" (Kowalik, 2005a: 34).

23 It is otherwise striking how similar Tadeusz Kowalik's evolution, as I have described it here, is to that of Ludwik Krzywicki, which Kowalik himself summarised in the late 1950s as: "Like ... [Karl] Kautsky, Krzywicki was an orthodox Marxist. And like ... Kautsky, he had also undergone a major social and worldview evolution. He went from a youthful-revolutionary attitude, from revolutionary Marxism, through orthodox Marxism, through abstractly revolutionary Marxism, to reformism, justified, however, not in a Bernsteinian but in a centrist-orthodox manner. In the last, declining phase of his life, Krzywicki's Marxism was diluted and forced in his work, but not to such an extent that his work of

Kowalik – which is perhaps, I believe, the most significant factor differentiating the above two approaches – accepted capitalism as the desired economic system, focusing in his subsequent works only on the selection of the optimal "variant" of this, as he called it, "megasystem."[24]

However, Kowalik's intellectual and political evolution has also resulted in the author of *From Solidarity to Sellout* abandoning most Marxist analytical tools. In this, I see the first important reason for his abandonment of attempts at an exhaustive justification of the Polish "epigonic bourgeois revolution" thesis (and at the same time, at least in part, the causal factor behind some of the paradoxical contents of his works as I have shown many times in the book).

Apart from the evolution resulting in the abandonment of Marxism, another possible answer to the question of why Kowalik seemed to quite consistently choose "realistic utopias" rather than inquiries in terms of "the

---

this period could be regarded as bourgeois reformist, falling outside the general current of socialist thought of the Marxian direction" (Kowalik, 1959: 374–375).

24 On the meaning of the term megasystem see especially (Kowalik, 2005a: 14 et seq.). Kowalik's adoption of the view of – at least at a certain point in history – the non-alternative nature of capitalism probably came quite early. In *From Solidarity to Sellout* he discusses his own *Uwagi do programu dostosowawczego* [Remarks on the Adjustment Programme] from 1989 (Herer, Kowalik & Sadowski, 1989). The authors of this document postulated, according to Kowalik's account, above all the necessity to avoid unemployment (at least high or rapidly increasing unemployment) during the system transformation, but they did not question the "transition to a market-type economy" itself (Kowalik, 2012a: 127–130). Elsewhere Kowalik writes "it would be hard to perceive the rapid expansion of the private sector of small enterprises in Poland as a sign of social progress. The 'firms' – in the beginning spreading out their wares on camp beds in street and bazaar stalls – did not produce many *true business individuals* [emphasis mine – G.K.], not to mention the illusory hope that *a middle class would ever be formed as the social basis of democracy and contemporary capitalism* [emphasis mine – G.K.]" (Kowalik, 2012a: 206). Finally, it is also impossible not to draw attention in this context to an excerpt from a 2005 interview, already cited in chapter three, in which Kowalik states: "*I believe that capitalism is a historically transitional formation. For today, however, my critical perspective on capitalism actually goes little beyond the Austrian-German-Swedish mix* [emphasis mine – G.K.]. These are patterns that have already managed to take shape in the contemporary world and are most sufficient for me as a horizon of change that I consider real and desirable. *I do not object if I am described as a socialist, although neither today nor in the foreseeable future, for example, twenty years, would I be inclined to propose a socialist prescription, that is, a system fundamentally different from capitalism* [emphasis mine – G.K.]. Why? *I believe that communism contained certain elements borrowed from socialism and revised them negatively* [emphasis mine – G.K.]. This applies above all to property, but also to planning. On the other hand, *the Scandinavian countries, some among the East Asian countries, have taught us to socialise private property to such an extent that it somehow makes it possible to reconcile individual and social interests* [emphasis mine – G.K.]" (Kowalik & Sierakowski, 2005: 207).

interests of influential groups" in his analyses of the Polish transformation (although closely related to it and, again, without deciding on the direction of the causality), is to take into account the influence of ideas of those he considered authorities on the views of the author of *From Solidarity to Sellout*. This refers not only to world-famous economists like John K. Galbraith, James Meade, John Maynard Keynes, already cited in this context,[25] but above all to those with whom he had the opportunity to work, or even just exchange reflections, both at earlier stages of his intellectual activity (Michał Kalecki, Oskar Lange)[26] and when the transformation processes were already underway (Włodzimierz Brus, Kazimierz Łaski).

What is particularly noteworthy here is the influence that reading *From Marx to the Market* by Brus and Łaski (1989) might have had on Kowalik's gradual abandonment of his support for any version of socialism, even the market kind. For, as Kowalik claims, its authors

> reveal their axiological assumptions. Although *they rejected socialism (also in its market version) as an alternative system to capitalism* [emphasis mine – G.K.], they did not renounce socialist values. They subjected economic policy tools that would favour full employment, mitigation of cyclicality and income spreads to consideration.
>
> KOWALIK, 2013b: 218

On the other hand, in a text dedicated to Brus, Kowalik wrote of *From Marx to the Market*: "I know of no better, fuller and deeper theoretical analysis of the Soviet economic system, its internal springs and brakes, and description of the evolutionary processes leading to its collapse" (Kowalik, 2013m: 598).

Finally, in a much earlier chapter of the monograph written in the very early 1990s, Kowalik points out that

---

25   To this list we should probably also add Karl Polanyi, not mentioned earlier in this book, about whom Kowalik wrote: "[In 1989] ... I had long been an enthusiast of the author of 'The Great Transformation' – Karl Polanyi" (Kowalik, 2002b: 20).

26   In this context, it would undoubtedly be particularly worthwhile to examine to what extent in Kowalik's work there exists a certain split between, on the one hand, the positions taken by Oskar Lange with regard to combining socialism with the market, with his – developed for most of his life – model of market socialism discussed by Kowalik himself on many occasions, for example in *Historia ekonomii w Polsce 1864–1950* [History of Economics in Poland 1864–1950] (Kowalik, 1992a: 233–268) and, on the other, Michał Kalecki, expressing serious doubts in this respect (on this subject see, e.g. (Toporowski, 1995)).

> it was the failures of the New Economic Mechanism in Hungary [introduced in 1968] and a similar Polish reform [of the 1980s] much more than the resistance of power structures to similar reforms in other communist countries that led to a far-reaching disintegration among reform economists. They divided into those who advocated market socialism (with, at most, minimal planning) and *those who publicly acknowledged the failure of the socialist experiment as a separate economic system* [emphasis mine – G.K.].
>
> KOWALIK, 1991b: 90–91

Kowalik, I believe, also includes himself in the latter group, in addition to Brus and Łaski. From the text quoted above, however, we also learn that

> neither planning nor intergroup agreements, or workers' self-government, remove the necessity of the market in modern highly developed economies. *Planning and the market are not mutually exclusive but complementary regulators of collective action* [emphasis mine – G.K.]. ... From the perspective of later experience and currently prevailing beliefs, one could say that *history has even more negatively verified the tendency to overlook or even neglect the market as the primary regulator of highly developed economies* [emphasis mine – G.K.]. Rather, today the concepts of a "partnership" of planning and the market as two equal regulators are rejected. *Even proponents of a certain type of planning emphasise that the commodity, market character of the national economy is a condition for its effectiveness* [emphasis mine. – G.K.].
>
> KOWALIK, 1991b: 90

This belief that the market is indispensable as a guarantor of the proper functioning of a developed economy is, I believe, symptomatic not only of Kowalik's split with Marxism and of his succumbing to the arguments of Brus and Łaski. It is perhaps also indicative of another problem with the works of the author of *From Solidarity to Sellout* concerning systemic transformation, that is the narrow economic approach to the analysed phenomena and the limitation, despite Kowalik's great interdisciplinary inclinations, of approaching the discussed issues above all in categories characteristic of economic sciences and with the use of terminology and methodology characteristic of them.

The narrow *allocative* understanding of the market, evident in Kowalik's work I have considered here, is particularly striking against the background of reflections by representatives of other social sciences, especially history or sociology. A fragment of a text by Ellen Meiksins Wood, devoted to the changing role of the market in the history of capitalism, may serve as an example:

> Material life and social reproduction in capitalism are universally mediated by the market, so that all individuals must in one way or another enter into market relations in order to gain access to the means of life; and *the dictates of the capitalist market – its imperatives of competition, accumulation, profit maximization, and increasing labor productivity – regulate not only all economic transactions but social relations in general* [emphasis mine – G.K.].
> MEIKSINS WOOD, 1994: 15

However, there is also a very interesting commentary in this Meiksins Wood article that I think sums up the problem signalled here exceptionally well as regards Kowalik's attitude to the role of the market in economic systems:

> I am convinced ... that *various political programs of the left – from social democratic demands for a more "social" market in the context of capitalism, to somewhat more radical theories of "market socialism" – are still in some ways based on illusions about the nature of the market as a sphere of opportunity and choice, and a failure to consider the full consequences of treating the market as an economic regulator* [emphasis mine – G.K.]. I still remember ... how idealistic democrats in Eastern Europe [before and during the transformation] responded to warnings about the market from the Western left ... When people warned that "the market" means not only supermarkets with lots of choice but mass unemployment and poverty, the reply would be, "'Yes, of course, but that's not what we mean by the market". *The idea was that you could pick and choose what you want from the self-regulating market* [emphasis mine – G.K.]. The market can act as a regulator of the economy just enough to guarantee some "rationality", some correspondence between what people want and what is produced. The market can act as a signal, a source of information, a form of communication between consumers and producers; and it can guarantee that useless or inefficient enterprises will shape up or fall. But we can dispense with its nastier side. ... It is difficult to explain in any other way the notion of "market socialism", or even the less utopian social democratic conception of the "social market", in which the market's ravages can be controlled by state regulation and an enhancement of social rights. I do not mean to say that the "social market" is no better than free market capitalism. Nor do I mean to suggest that certain institutions and practices

associated with the market could not be adapted to a socialist economy. *But it's no good refusing to confront the implications of the one irreducible condition without which the market cannot act as an economic discipline: the commodification of labor power – a condition which places the strictest limits on the "socialization" of the market and its capacity to assume a human face* [emphasis mine – G.K.].

MEIKSINS WOOD, 1994: 38–39

Perhaps, it would be possible then to demonstrate as part of an in-depth study that it was precisely an insufficient openness to the findings of other social sciences in analyses of the transformation which was one of the reasons for Kowalik not developing or sufficiently substantiating the thesis of an "epigonic bourgeois revolution" in Poland.

Finally, it is worth considering at this point whether all the above-described changes in Tadeusz Kowalik's views were not caused by his adoption at some point (whether consciously or not is a separate issue) of a more general philosophical standpoint of *voluntarism*,[27] "which reduces all [historical]

---

27 Gavin Rae, on the other hand, in essentially the same context, writes about Kowalik's *subjectivism*, convincingly arguing that such a position was adopted by Kowalik from Krzywicki and Lange (and indirectly from Austro-Marxism) (Rae, 2024). Such a take on the problem seems uncontradictory to the one presented here. It is only worth noting further at this point that Kowalik's voluntarism (or subjectivism) may be closely related to yet another philosophical position that can be attributed to Kowalik on the basis of his works on systemic transformation, namely *idealism*. For example, the author of *From Solidarity to Sellout* wrote with appreciation that "the most outstanding economist of the 20th century, John Maynard Keynes argued that *ideas rule the world* [emphasis mine – G.K.]" (Kowalik, 2007: 269). Elsewhere, we read: "in Poland, as well as in many other countries, a shock prescription *à la* Margaret Thatcher has been applied … Why? Because it was not so much factual arguments as emotions that prevailed, effectively influenced by the atmosphere of easy victory of political … 'spirit of the times', *shaped by the ideas of Margaret Thatcher and Ronald Reagan. Because, at the time, it was their ideas that were in the ascendancy, and social democratic ideas in retreat* [emphasis mine – G.K.]. … In order to avoid misunderstandings, I would like to clarify that it does not follow from the thesis on the *dominant role of ideas and emotions* [emphasis mine – G.K.] that both people in power and their advisers did not use factual arguments. All I am saying is that it is difficult to say whose arguments per se were stronger. Instead, the winning arguments were those that were in keeping with the spirit (or rather the worldly gusto) of the times. For the choices of a particular social order are choices based on values, and these do not yield to the criteria of truth and falsehood. Hence the great role played by psychological motives in their choice" (Kowalik, 2013b: 221). Also Paweł Kozłowski argues that Kowalik "[b]elonged among those who – like, for example, Friedrich von Hayek or J.M. Keynes, believed that ideas are the most important. *They are what make up our world of collective existence* [emphasis mine – G.K.]" (Kozłowski, 2013a: 255). However, I do not elaborate

phenomena to the *will* [emphasis mine – G.K.] and sees it as the ultimate principle of reality" (Prusek, 2014: 9).²⁸

Tadeusz Kowalik expressed these beliefs in perhaps the most unambiguous manner in one of the chapters of *Nierówni i równiejsi*, where he stated that, in his opinion, "*It is necessary to move away from the contemporary version of historical determinism* [emphasis mine – G.K.], from the doctrine of a single pattern and succumbing to a new mono-idea" (Kowalik, 2002a: 84), in order to emphasise later in the argument the key role of the *will* of those in power in shaping the social and economic order. Thus, we read there that:

---

on the issue of Tadeusz Kowalik's idealism for at least two reasons. Firstly, it is not, as it seems to me, a contentious or novel theme: idealism was, as we can see, admitted by Kowalik himself, and his thought is also described in such terms by other researchers. Secondly, pointing here to the voluntarism of the author of *From Solidarity to Sellout* has its precise aim, which is to support the thesis I put forward earlier about Kowalik's departure from Marxism. Since the attitude of some Marxists to at least some versions of idealism seems to be more favourable than to voluntarism – a position fundamentally contradictory to Marxist axiomatics – by the same token, Kowalik's idealism cannot serve as an indicator of his break with Marxism. A good example of a Marxist thinker presenting a rather ambiguous attitude towards idealism is probably György Lukács, who, according to Kevin Anderson (1992), "In the 1920s ... had seen Marx's dialectic more as the unity of idealism and materialism" (p. 90). Moreover, Anderson, following Ernst Bloch, attributes doubts in this regard even to Lenin, who, according to this author, was said to have stated that "intelligent idealism is closer to intelligent materialism than stupid materialism" (pp. 91–92).

28 Prusek then adds that "In the social sciences of the 20th century this view was rejected as incompatible with science. This was particularly true of the Marxist view of social development processes, the so-called dialectical and historical materialism" (Prusek, 2014: 10). Przemysław Sadura (2015) notes that the voluntarist position also met with criticism among revolutionary theorists. In this context, he cites the views of Theda Skocpol, who, according to Sadura, considers "any attempt to translate the intentions of revolutionaries into their actions as a 'voluntarist illusion'" (p. 72). Kowalik himself, it seems, very rarely used the term voluntarism, and probably understood it somewhat differently: as the actual attitude of the ruling elites. For example, when asked by Sławomir Sierakowski "how do you assess the economic programmes of the Polish parties, at least as far as they have been revealed?", the author of *From Solidarity to Sellout* answers: "Definitely badly. *Voluntarism* [emphasis mine – G.K.] is taking over again, just like in 1989" (Kowalik & Sierakowski, 2005: 213). And in the text devoted to Włodzimierz Brus, we read that "[Brus] treated [Joseph] Stalin's testament [*Economic Problems of Socialism in the USSR* of 1952 – G.K.] with the utmost seriousness – as a gesture aimed at self-restraint. For Stalin's insistence on the objective character of economic laws in socialism in general, and especially his open acceptance of the law of value, gave Brus the basis for his ever louder, ever more clearly justified insistence on the restriction of the state in the economy in favour of the market, on objective criteria for price-setting, on the incentives for workers. ... Stalin's publication facilitated criticism of the *voluntarism of power* [emphasis mine – G.K.]" (Kowalik, 2013m: 602).

> Whether they [the decision-makers] are capable of publicly declaring a *strong will* [emphasis mine – G.K.] to return to the basic premises of the Constitution in social and economic matters depends on the courage and responsibility of the main political forces in power. This would presuppose the *will* [emphasis mine – G.K.] to take a bold look at the "ugly face" of Polish success and to fight decisively against mass unemployment, pauperisation of the countryside and the housing disaster.
>
> KOWALIK, 2002a: 85

However, in most of his works on systemic change, not just those from the 1980s and 1990s, Kowalik did not present his position in terms of determinism or will as above. Most often he wrote about the possibility of *choice*, which, in his opinion, actually always accompanied the moments in which transformations took place. Thus, in *Spory o ustrój społeczno-gospodarczy Polski 1944–1948* [Disputes over Poland's Socio-Economic System 1944–1948] we read that "We ... can imagine that if Poland had found itself in a situation similar to that of Yugoslavia in 1948, it could have decided to *choose* [emphasis mine – G.K.] a 'competitive' or 'market' model of socialism according to Oskar Lange's classical prescription" (Kowalik, 2006b: 14). Kowalik also presents this view for example in his polemics with Jerzy Kleer's text (Kleer, 1996):

> The divergence or even contradiction of opinions between Kleer and ... left-wing critics is ... enormous. The latter claim (and I am one of them) that ... the shocks [to which society was subjected after 1989 – G.K.] are the result of a more or less conscious *choice* [emphasis mine – G.K.] of one of the possible options towards marketisation and privatisation. It was also a *choice of the path* [emphasis mine – G.K.] towards integration with the European Union. This choice was not at all necessary and did not provide the simplest and shortest route "to Europe". Kleer, on the other hand, believes that it had to be so, that it was the only way. For Kleer, this is a statement of inevitable phenomena, identifying a road devoid of alternatives. And this is what is most surprising. For our generation has experienced first-hand the non-alternative concept of development and its fatal consequences. It would seem, therefore, that it has learnt its lessons. It would also not be out of place to remember that it was the criticism of the previous system from the position of an alternative system, criticism with an alternative (for a long time considered pure quixotism), that laid the intellectual foundations of the pluralistic world of civil society.
>
> KOWALIK, 2013a: 246–247

It seems the author of *From Solidarity to Sellout* held the voluntarist position until the end of his life. Thus, still in the second half of the first decade of the 21st century, he wrote that

> the decomposition of the system and the loss of power by the Communists did not have to mean the introduction of the version of capitalism applied in our case. For years, from the very beginning, I have insisted that "there's many a slip between the cup and the lip". That *in 1989 history gave us an exceptionally large margin of choice, including the choice of socio-economic system* [emphasis mine – G.K.]. And at these moments, the role of the individual, or individuals in leadership, their ability to recognise social forces, to appeal to them, to articulate "directive ideas" is enormous.
>
> KOWALIK, 2006a: 142

And in *From Solidarity to Sellout* we read that "The general shock stabilization-systemic operation was *unnecessary* [emphasis mine – G.K.] and essentially dictated by political considerations. It had no economic substantiation" (Kowalik, 2012a: 226–227) with Kowalik describing the above as one of „the key theses of this book [i.e., *From Solidarity to Sellout*]". It seems that it is due to the voluntarism manifested in this way that Tadeusz Kowalik concentrates on the existence of alternatives to the Balcerowicz Plan while, at the same time, not attempting to answer whether any alternative had a *real* chance of success in the social and political situation of that time.[29] This is well illustrated in the following excerpt from *From Solidarity to Sellout*:

> Defenders of the Balcerowicz Plan cite two kinds of arguments. The first denies the existence of alternative programs; the other admits they exist but denies ... [their] realism. ... There were indeed those who were wiser earlier, and quite a few at that.
>
> KOWALIK, 2012a: 149–150

---

29 A similar assessment of Kowalik's position seems to be made by Ryszard Bugaj, who notes that, in *Polska transformacja* "Tadeusz Kowalik emphasises the existence of numerous alternative concepts during the period of crystallisation of the Polish concept of system reconstruction and suggests that their disregard was almost exclusively rooted in the sympathies (and convictions) of a narrow group of decision-makers at the time. A somewhat similar thesis emerges from a book by American political scientist David Ost [*The Defeat of Solidarity*, see (Ost, 2005) – G.K.]. Both authors *seem to underestimate the dynamics of the political conditions of the time* [emphasis mine – G.K.]" (Bugaj, 2015: 165).

Kowalik cites two types of argument by the "defenders of the Balcerowicz Plan" (the lack of alternative proposals and the lack of realistic alternatives available at the time), but in fact, deals only with the first while quite consistently ignoring the second.[30] He thus seems at least implicitly to identify, in a voluntarist manner, the very existence of alternative visions with a practical possibility of their realisation.

In spite of everything however, Tadeusz Kowalik's position can probably not be regarded as unconditional voluntarism. As I showed in chapter three, Kowalik also repeatedly expressed his belief about the inevitability of real socialism's collapse for largely objective reasons. This further paradox in the views of the author of *From Solidarity to Sellout* is revealed, for example, in an interview from 2005 where he argues that

> Stiglitz speaks the language of Keynes when he reminds us that the primary duty of government is to ensure full employment and adds that we know (since Keynes) how to do it, *we just lack a strong enough will* [emphasis mine – G.K.] ... Of course, it would be good if Stiglitz as a reformer also had the talents and stature [sic!] of Keynes. ... But for today's Poland ..., the thing is not so much the search for an outstanding individual, or the lack of a concept, but *the lack of social movements putting pressure on the authorities* [emphasis mine – G.K.]. To put it in Marx's language, the issue is not so much the strength of the argument, but the argument of power.
> KOWALIK & SIERAKOWSKI, 2005: 203

5

On the eve of formulating the thesis of an "epigonic bourgeois revolution" in Poland, Tadeusz Kowalik agreed with Zygmunt Bauman that, in the context of the changes in Central and Eastern Europe at the turn of the 1980s and 1990s, a "revolution in the theory of revolutions" was needed (Kowalik, 1996a: 289). However, I do not believe that he himself carried out such a revolution. Firstly, because he did not undertake this task at all: Kowalik's reflections on

---

30 Probably the only passage in *From Solidarity to Sellout* in which Kowalik expresses doubts in this regard (but does not develop and very quickly disavows them) reads: "From the purely political point of view, a direct imitation of the Social Democratic Swedish model in 1989 was very difficult, to some politicians bordering on the impossible" (Kowalik, 2012a: 166).

the Polish revolution are, I think, entirely intentionally journalistic,[31] rather perfunctory and above all, in view of the issues he dealt with, simply marginal. Secondly, when writing about the "epigonic bourgeois revolution", the author of *From Solidarity to Sellout* tended to produce more contradictions and misconceptions than complete, innovative proposals (it is, after all, precisely for this reason that this book is a series of reconstructions). Thus I think it is worthwhile, for a moment, to ignore all the limitations to Tadeusz Kowalik's analyses described in the previous sections and to consider, purely hypothetically, what findings his in-depth, theoretical studies of the "epigonic bourgeois revolution" in Poland might have led him to had he ever undertaken them.

Let us first recall that if we adopt a radically consequentialist view of bourgeois revolutions, thus recognising them to be all violent transformations arriving at capitalism (or even just in its direction) without the need to specify as much as their precise historical circumstances, then the adoption of the thesis of an "epigonic bourgeois revolution" in Poland in 1989 – i.e., in a place and time where the "leap" into capitalism undoubtedly occurred – follows immediately and automatically. Although, as I explained in chapter one, Tadeusz Kowalik has never adopted a consequentialist (or probably any other) theory of bourgeois revolutions, it cannot be completely ruled out that he could try to justify his claims precisely in this way, which requires no further discussion.

Perhaps, however, it would be more probable for Kowalik to have created a (still consequentialist) synthesis similar to the one I presented in chapter three or, in a slightly shorter version, along the lines of the argumentation of Barker and Mooers that is summarised above. It is even possible that, similar to me in the reconstruction presented in this book, the author of *From Solidarity to Sellout* would then have consulted the work of Jan Baszkiewicz. Possibly, in such a scenario, Kowalik would even reach for some term other than "epigonic", intended to emphasise the specificity of the events he described: "late bourgeois revolutions" – by analogy with the notion of early bourgeois revolutions, introduced (or, maybe, reintroduced, drawing on Engels) into German

---

31 Jan Toporowski even believes that it is precisely because of the journalistic nature of the texts on the subject of the "epigonic bourgeois revolution" that Kowalik did not develop a precise theoretical argumentation in support of this thesis characteristic of his most outstanding scholarly works. Toporowski also reminds us that Kowalik's excessive entanglement in current discussions and conflicts around the Polish transformation, often with political overtones, may have been significant in this respect. I am very grateful to Professor Jan Toporowski for sharing these insights with me.

historiography a few decades earlier[32] – seems the most obvious candidate. Undoubtedly, Tadeusz Kowalik could not have been indifferent to something that must draw the attention, or even provokes the deep reflection of, every reader of his and Baszkiewicz's works, namely the similarity of a whole series of events in Poland's most recent history to those indicated in the literature as features of bourgeois revolutions from the more distant past.

The author of *From Solidarity to Sellout* would, however, probably have to solve one fundamental theoretical problem himself. For, in the first chapter, I signalled that when discussing the events of 1989 in Poland, Tadeusz Kowalik sometimes hesitated between the terms *revolution* and *counter-revolution* (even referring to "(counter)revolution"[33] in some works).

Leon Trotsky already wrote that real socialism, this "historically unsuccessful systemic experiment" that it was for Kowalik (2005a: 49), could or even must end in a return of capitalism after a *bourgeois counter-revolution*. His position on this issue is summarised by Davidson:

> Trotsky … regarded the Stalinist regime as a historically unique and inherently unstable formation: the socialist property relations he thought were embodied in nationalized property had to be defended, but the regime was doomed to collapse under the impact of the coming world war, either by *bourgeois counterrevolution and capitalist restoration* [emphasis mine – G.K.], or by proletarian political revolution – although, as we shall see, he did allow in his last writings that there might also be a third alternative in which the bureaucracy transformed itself from a parasitic caste into a new ruling class.
>
> DAVIDSON, 2012: 431

It is not out of the question that, had Kowalik decided to deepen his investigations, he would have come to the conclusion that it is the application of the concept of counter-revolution that finds the most justification in the context of the Polish transformation. It is even possible that he would have presented the "epigonism" (or, as he has written elsewhere, the "imitativeness") of this revolution as a term from the outset, at least to some extent, indicating an

---

32 On this subject see especially the now classic text by (Steinmetz, 1979).
33 According to Paweł Kozłowski, it was perhaps under the influence of conversations with him that Tadeusz Kowalik became doubtful that the revolution he was describing was not in fact a counter-revolution. I am extremely grateful to Professor Paweł Kozłowski for sharing this observation with me.

identity with the counter-revolution through the obvious presence in both of an element of opposition to the revolution *proper*.

However, further study could have hypothetically led Kowalik to consider a dichotomy other than revolution/counter-revolution. As I showed in the Introduction, Neil Davidson, in refusing to label the changes of the late 1980s and early 1990s as both bourgeois revolution and counter-revolution, states that "Clearly, the events of … 1989 were revolutions of *some* kind [emphasis N.D.], but which? … Rather than describe them as bourgeois revolutions, they seem to me to be far better understood as examples of the broader category of *political* revolution [emphasis N.D.]" (Davidson, 2012: 380).

And elsewhere, this author explains that,

> As capital increasingly sweeps away even the remnants of previous modes of production and the social formations that include them, the pattern of revolutions has increasingly tended toward *the "political" rather than the "social" type* [emphasis mine – G.K.], starting with the revolutions of 1989 in Eastern Europe that swept away the Stalinist regimes and began … the "sideways" movement from Eastern state capitalism to an approximation of the Western trans-state model.
>
> DAVIDSON, 2012: 464

Importantly, it would probably not have been difficult for Tadeusz Kowalik to link this view of a purely *political* revolution with the interpretation of the Polish transformation in terms of a "revolution from above,"[34] which he presented prior to the formulation of the thesis of the "epigonic bourgeois revolution". However, this would have to mean firstly that Kowalik would have had to withdraw from the thesis because secondly, this time the revolution described would be *from above*, but certainly not *bourgeois*. And such a framing of the issue would not be without precedent in the literature. For example, Sheila

---

34   Or, in an even more nuanced scenario, a revolution that combines features of "from above" and "from below". For example, Davidson (2015), writes about such a possibility in the context of the 20th century history: „[In the] final phase in the history of the bourgeois revolutions … [they] tended to combine elements of earlier bourgeois revolutions from below and above: 'from below' in relation to the existing state, since it required an external military force – usually waging guerrilla warfare in the initial phases – to overcome it; but 'from above' in relation to the popular masses, whose self-activity was either suppressed, minimized or channeled into individual membership in an instrumentally organized party-army apparatus" (p. 132).

Fitzpatrick consistently uses the term "revolution from above" to refer to the beginnings of Stalinism in Russia.[35]

It is worth noting that all the concepts described above – the various variants of consequentialism, bourgeois counter-revolution, revolution from above or the division into political and social revolutions – show strong links with Trotskyist thought in its broadest sense in their contemporary theoretical presentations. Given the already signalled influence that Trotsky's followers have had on Kowalik (evident, for example, in the latter's description of communism as "state capitalism" or in his references to the role of the bureaucracy in the evolution of real socialism), it does not seem entirely implausible that, hypothetically, he could have made use of this set of instruments. Moreover, it seems that if Kowalik had combined an in-depth study of the literature on the theory of revolution with a return to his Trotskyist inspirations of the 1960s, he could also have *rejected* his thesis of an epigonic bourgeois revolution, recognising the distinction between bourgeois and bourgeois-democratic revolutions, that the "cycle of bourgeois revolutions" ended around 1918, and that what remained were merely the *unfulfilled tasks* of the bourgeois-democratic revolution, which only a future proletarian revolution could complete.

However, it cannot be ruled out that Kowalik, as a result of hypothetical literature studies, would end up agreeing with the *Capital*-centric Marxists who deny the events of the late 1980s and early 1990s in Eastern Europe to be either revolutionary or counter-revolutionary. This is the position of, for example, Zbigniew M. Kowalewski, who explains that,

> The Soviet Union, [as Donald] Filtzer wrote, constituted "a historically unstable social formation that is neither capitalist nor socialist, and as such has no effective regulator either of the economy or of the reproduction of its social structure". "It operated at such a high level of internal contradiction and instability that it could never be more than a historically transient social formation". For some time after the 1917 revolution, Soviet *society was in transition between capitalism and socialism. In between, that is, not necessarily moving from capitalism to socialism and "building socialism"* (or, even less, one that had already "built socialism" [emphasis mine – G.K.], contrary to what Stalin had proclaimed even before [Second World War]). It could have evolved either one way or the other – towards socialism or back to capitalism, and it could have

---

35   For example when she writes that "at the end of the 1920s, Russia plunged into another upheaval – *Stalin's 'revolution from above'* [emphasis mine – G.K.]" (Fitzpatrick, 2017: 3).

gotten stuck and degenerated somewhere along this two-way road. Not only because of underdevelopment but above all because socialism in one country or even in a group of countries is impossible, the fate of Soviet society depended on revolutions in other, mainly highly developed regions of the world. The bureaucratic degeneration of the October Revolution, crowned by the *Stalinist counter-revolution* [emphasis mine – G.K.],[36] ultimately blocked the possibility of evolution towards socialism. A return to a transitional society between capitalism and socialism was not possible without a new workers' revolution that would overthrow the bureaucratic regime and establish its authority. Without it, Soviet society could only be *transitional* [emphasis mine – G.K.] in the sense: *temporarily "disconnected" from the world capitalist system* [emphasis mine – G.K.].

KOWALEWSKI, 2020: 410–411[37]

Next Kowalewski argues that,

The mode of exploitation introduced first in the Soviet Union by the Stalinist regime and then in the peripheral states of the Soviet bloc was not a mode of production [emphasis mine – G.K.]. It did not formally and realistically subordinate the productive forces. In these countries, the industrial revolution, historically delayed and, as its delay deepened, increasingly difficult to carry out under capitalism, took place on a large scale only after its overthrow – already under the rule of the bureaucracy. The productive forces that developed in the course, and as a result of, this revolution and the subsequent processes of modernisation and socio-economic development were entirely shaped by the capitalist mode of production. They were partly inherited and now multiplied, and partly obtained by importing from capitalist countries and by imitation or borrowing. The contribution of the post-war transfer to the USSR of the most modern industrial equipment, devices and technologies, together with thousands of scientists and specialists, from the highly industrialised Soviet occupation

---

36 Significantly, such a view is not exclusively characteristic of *Capital*-centric Marxists, but is shared by a much more diverse group of Marxist authors whose common denominator appears to be drawing inspiration from the work of Leon Trotsky. Thus, for example, Neil Faulkner (2017) writes that "The party-state bureaucracy that had emerged in Russia under Stalin's leadership was, by 1928, strong enough to complete what was, in effect, *a counter-revolution* [emphasis mine – G.K.]" (p. 245). Let us just note that this view contradicts Fitzpatrick's position quoted earlier.

37 The excerpts from Filtzer's works quoted by Kowalewski are, respectively, (Filtzer, 2002: 122) and (Filtzer, 1996: 24).

> zone of Germany was simply enormous. In all these productive forces, capital materialised – they embodied it, but at the same time they were now stripped of their capitalist social form. The ruling bureaucracy did not materially transform them, so they permanently remained what they had been when they were taken over from the capitalists – a materialisation of capital and thus did not subsume them to itself in real terms. Nor did it give them a new social form and thus did not formally subsume them to itself. ... In short, "socialism was proclaimed without radically overcoming the material embodiment of capital".
>
> KOWALEWSKI, 2020: 418–420[38]

It is therefore not surprising that, from this point of view, in the context of the events of 1989 in Poland, there can be no question of either a bourgeois revolution, even "from above", or a counter-revolution. In his work, Kowalewski sees *workers'* revolutions in Russia (in 1917), Bolivia (in 1952), Cuba (in the 1950s) or Poland (in 1980–1981),[39] among others, while he refers to Stalinism in the Soviet Union in the 1920s and 1930s as a counter-revolution. Everything that happened in Eastern Europe in 1989 and the following years is, in this view, at best – not deserving of the name (counter)revolution – the inevitable return of a "temporarily disconnected" society back to the world capitalist system.

Even this, however, does not yet exhaust the list of positions that Kowalik could hypothetically have taken if he had devoted himself to in-depth studies of theories of bourgeois revolutions. Remaining in the circle of *Capital*-centric Marxism, let us also note that its representatives, criticising the use of the term bourgeois revolution, even abandon the term itself replacing it, in cases they consider deserving of the name, with *capitalist revolution*. As Charles Post explains:

> We abandon the conventional term "bourgeois revolutions" for two reasons. First, we seek to avoid the confusions concerning the social character [of] the "bourgeoisie" – *urban, non-capitalist* [emphasis C.P.] groups of lawyers, merchants, office-holders and the like. Second, we want to emphasise that these revolutions are characterised not by "class agency",

---

38 The last sentence quoted by Kowalewski is from (Arthur, 2004: 208).
39 As I mentioned in chapter one, Michał Siermiński's entire book, to which Kowalewski's text is an afterword, provides a detailed and convincing argumentation for this claim. See (Siermiński, 2020) as well as an earlier study by this author (Siermiński, 2016).

but by their *consequences* [emphasis C.P.] – the establishment of capitalist states and the promotion of capitalist accumulation.

POST, 2019: 175[40]

Given that, as I showed in chapter one, Kowalik also referred to the "epigonic bourgeois revolution" in Poland as a "capitalist revolution", he might have attempted to reconcile this terminological convergence with the theoretical incompatibility of his proposal and the views of the *Capital*-centric Marxists. Thus, the author of *From Solidarity to Sellout* could, for example, agree with Post on the necessity of using the term "capitalist revolution" (rather than "bourgeois") and on how few historical events can be included in this group, but reject the *Capital*-centric view of the inadequacy of such a category for the Polish late twentieth-century transformations, thus potentially making some serious redefinition, which amounts to proposing that the concept (changed to, for example, *new capitalist revolutions*) be applied *exclusively* to the transformation from real socialism to capitalism.

Finally, at the very end of this list of hypothetical situations in which I place Tadeusz Kowalik, it is worthwhile, I think, to carry out a slightly different mental exercise. Neil Davidson states categorically that

> bourgeois commentators have recently begun to use their own interpretation of the term [i.e. bourgeois revolution – G.K.]. In effect, the *only* [emphasis N.D.] type of social revolutions that bourgeois ideology recognized before 1989 were the so-called communist revolutions, since these supposedly involved a break with the evolutionary development of capitalism and the imposition of a different type of economy. Following the Eastern European revolutions of that year [i.e. 1989] *an additional type was identified: those which undid the original revolutions and allowed the economies to revert to capitalism. It was in the context of these events that the bourgeoisie reappropriated both the concept of bourgeois revolution and its link with capitalism but in a way opposed to any Marxist conception* [emphasis mine – G.K.].
>
> DAVIDSON, 2012: XV

---

40 Similarly Teschke (2005), who argues that "we need to radically dissociate the two sides of the conceptual pair bourgeoisie-capitalism. If capitalism is not simply urban commerce on a greater scale, then we cannot assume that a town-based class of burghers (or even a class of merchants and financiers) is the necessary carrier of the capitalist project. You can have a non-capitalist bourgeoisie, as you can have a capitalist aristocracy" (p. 11).

This poses a fundamental question: in the face of such an accusation, which can undoubtedly also be applied to the thesis of an "epigonic bourgeois revolution" in Poland, would Kowalik defend his proposal and its progressive character? Or, on the contrary, would he consider it a mistake, putting the use of such a formulation down to the nonchalance, so characteristic of many economists, in the use of concepts from the area of social sciences? Or would he have maintained the thesis openly (which was, after all, the principle of his *value disclosure*) thus accepting to be counted among the bourgeois thinkers?

Although we will never know the answers to these questions, approaching them is probably not entirely impossible. This is, however, a task that lies ahead of the future authors of Tadeusz Kowalik's intellectual biography.

References

Anderson, K. (1992). Lenin, Hegel and Western Marxism: From the 1920s to 1953. *Studies in Soviet Thought, 44*(2), 79–129.

Anderson, P. (1992). *A Zone of Engagement*. London: Verso.

Anievas, A. & Nişancıoğlu, K. (2015). *How the West Came to Rule. The Geopolitical Origins of Capitalism*. London: Pluto Press.

Arato, A. (1993). Interpreting 1989. *Social Research, 60*(3), 609–646.

Arthur, C.J. (2004). *The New Dialectic and Marx's Capital*. Leiden-Boston: Brill.

Baka, W. (2007). *Zmagania o reformę. Z dziennika politycznego 1980–1990*. Warszawa: Iskry.

Banaszkiewicz, M. (2011). Profesor Jan Baszkiewicz (3 stycznia 1930 – 27 stycznia 2011). *Politeja, 15*(1), 21–48.

Barker, C. & Mooers, C. (1994). Marxism and the 1989 Revolution. In P. Dunleavy & J. Stanyer (Eds.), *Contemporary Political Studies: Proceedings of the Annual Conference Held at the University of Wales Swansea March 29th-31st 1994* (Vol. 2, pp. 987–1001). Newcastle upon Tyne: Political Studies Association of the United Kingdom.

Barker, C. & Mooers, C. (1997). Theories of Revolution in the Light of 1989 in Eastern Europe. *Cultural Dynamics, 9*(1), 17–43.

Baszkiewicz, J. (1981). *Wolność. Równość. Własność. Rewolucje burżuazyjne*. Warszawa: Czytelnik.

Baszkiewicz, J. (1983). W sprawie teorii rewolucji. *Colloquia Communia*(6), 135–148.

Baszkiewicz, J. (1999). *Władza*. Wrocław: Zakład Narodowy im. Ossolińskich.

Baszkiewicz, J. (2009a). Rewolucja: kilka uwag o zmienności pojęcia. In J. Baszkiewicz, *Państwo. Rewolucja. Kultura polityczna* (pp. 799–813). Poznań: Wydawnictwo Poznańskie.

Baszkiewicz, J. (2009b). Władza państwowa i klasa panująca w teorii Karola Marksa. In J. Baszkiewicz, *Państwo. Rewolucja. Kultura polityczna* (pp. 371–388). Poznań: Wydawnictwo Poznańskie.

Baszkiewicz, J., Rykowski, Z. & Władyka, W. (1982, December 8). Sztuka stosowana. O rewolucji i reformie z profesorem Janem Baszkiewiczem rozmawiają Zbysław Rykowski i Wiesław Władyka. *Tu i Teraz*(28), 1, 4.

Bates, T. (1975). Gramsci and the Theory of Hegemony. *Journal of the History of Ideas, 36*(2), 351–366.

Bauman, Z. (1993). Dismantling a Patronage State. In J. Frentzel-Zagórska (Ed.), *From a One-Party State to Democracy: Transition in Eastern Europe* (*Poznań Studies in the Philosophy of the Sciences and the Humanities*, Vol. 32, pp. 139–154). Amsterdam-Atlanta: Rodopi.

Bauman, Z. (1994). A Revolution in the Theory of Revolutions?. *International Political Science Review, 15*(1), 15–24.

Bellofiore, R., Karwowski, E. & Toporowski, J. (Eds.). (2014a). *Economic Crisis and Political Economy. Essays in Honour of Tadeusz Kowalik* (Vol. 2). London: Palgrave Macmillan.

Bellofiore, R., Karwowski, E. & Toporowski, J. (2014b). Introduction: Tadeusz Kowalik and the Political Economy of the 20th Century. In R. Bellofiore, E. Karwowski & J. Toporowski (Eds.), *The Legacy of Rosa Luxemburg, Oskar Lange and Michał Kalecki. Essays in Honour of Tadeusz Kowalik* (Vol. 1, pp. 1–8). London: Palgrave Macmillan.

Bellofiore, R., Karwowski, E. & Toporowski, J. (Eds.). (2014c). *The Legacy of Rosa Luxemburg, Oskar Lange and Michał Kalecki. Essays in Honour of Tadeusz Kowalik* (Vol. 1). London: Palgrave Macmillan.

Bińczyk, E. (2015). Beyond Neoliberal Economics: The Postulates of Social Justice in Polish Social Economics. *International Journal of Social Economics, 42*(9), 791–803.

Bochenek, M. (2020). O nieporozumieniach wokół nazwy i istoty niemieckiego modelu gospodarczego. *Nierówności Społeczne a Wzrost Gospodarczy*(61), 73–91.

Bohle, D. (2006). Neoliberal Hegemony, Transnational Capital and the Terms of the EU's Eastward Expansion. *Capital & Class, 30*(1), 57–86.

Bolesta-Kukułka, K. (1992). *Gra o władzę a gospodarka. Polska 1944–1991*. Warszawa: Państwowe Wydawnictwo Ekonomiczne.

Borodziej, W. & Garlicki, A. (Eds.). (2004). *Okrągły Stół. Dokumenty i materiały* (Vol. 1: *wrzesień 1986 – luty 1989*). Warszawa: Kancelaria Prezydenta Rzeczypospolitej Polskiej.

Borowiec, P. (2013). *Czas polityczny po rewolucji. Czas w polskim dyskursie politycznym po 1989 roku*. Kraków: Wydawnictwo Uniwersytetu Jagiellońskiego.

Brenner, R. (1989). Bourgeois Revolution and Transition to Capitalism. In A.L. Beier, D. Cannadine & J. Rosenheim (Eds.), *The First Modern Society: Essays in English History in Honour of Lawrence Stone* (pp. 271–304). Cambridge: Cambridge University Press.

Brinton, C. (1938). *The Anatomy of Revolution*. New York: W.W. Norton and Company.

Brus, W. (1992). Refleksje o postępującej nieoznaczoności socjalizmu. In A. Jasińska-Kania, W. Wesołowski & J. Wiatr (Eds.), *Demokracja i socjalizm. Księga poświęcona pamięci Juliana Hochfelda* (pp. 41–54). Wrocław-Warszawa: Zakład Narodowy im. Ossolińskich.

Brus, W. & Kowalik, T. (1983). Socialism and Development. *Cambridge Journal of Economics, 7*(3/4), 243–255.

Brus, W. & Łaski, K. (1989). *From Marx to the Market: Socialism in Search of an Economic System*. Oxford: Clarendon Press.

Bugaj, R. (2015). *Plusy dodatnie i ujemne czyli polski kapitalizm bez solidarności*. Warszawa: Poltext.

Bugaj, R. & Kowalik, T. (1990). W kierunku gospodarki mieszanej. *Życie Gospodarcze*(39), 1, 3.

Bukvić, R.M. (2013). Tadeusz Kowalik – veliki politekonomist. *Zbornik Matice srpske za društvene nauke*, 64(142), 193–201.

Bywalec, C. (1995). Poziom życia społeczeństwa polskiego na tle procesów transformacji gospodarczej (1989–1993). *Procesy transformacji w Polsce*(10), 1–44.

Callinicos, A. (2010). The Limits of Passive Revolution. *Capital & Class*, 34(3), 491–507.

Carr, E.H. (1990). *What is History?*. London: Penguin.

Celiński, A. (1989, October 9). Trudno postawić konia przed wozem. *Życie Warszawy*(235), 3.

Chodak, J. (2012). *Teorie rewolucji w naukach społecznych*. Lublin: Wydawnictwo Uniwersytetu Marii Curie-Skłodowskiej.

Clarke, S. (1994). *Marx's Theory of Crisis*. New York: St. Martin's Press.

Comninel, G. (1987). *Rethinking the French Revolution: Marxism and the Revisionist Challenge*. New York: Verso.

Connelly, J. (1996). Internal Bolshevisation? Elite Social Science Training in Stalinist Poland. *Minerva*, 34(4), 323–346.

Czarnota, A. & Zybertowicz, A. (1983). Teoria rewolucji w powijakach. Rozważania teoretyczno-metodologiczne nad książką Jana Baszkiewicza «Wolność, Równość, Własność». *Colloquia Communia*(3), 123–152.

Davidson, N. (2012). *How Revolutionary Were the Bourgeois Revolutions?*. Chicago: Haymarket Books.

Davidson, N. (2015). Is Social Revolution Still Possible in the Twenty-First Century?. *Journal of Contemporary Central and Eastern Europe*, 23(2–3), 105–150.

Davidson, N. (2017). *How Revolutionary Were the Bourgeois Revolutions?* (Abridged ed.). Chicago: Haymarket Books.

Davidson, N. (2019). Capitalist Outcomes, Ideal Types, Historical Realities. *Historical Materialism*, 27(3), 210–276.

Djilas, M. (1957). *The New Class: An Analysis of the Communist System*. New York: Frederick A. Praeger.

Doktorat honoris causa dla Profesora Jana Baszkiewicza. (2008). *Annales Universitatis Mariae Curie Skłodowska. Sectio K*, 15(2), 225–230.

Dow, S. (2002). *Economic Methodology: An Inquiry*. Oxford: Oxford University Press.

Dunn, J. (1972). *Modern Revolutions: An Introduction to the Analysis of a Political Phenomenon*. Cambridge: Cambridge University Press.

Dymski, G. (2014). «Crucial Reform» in Post-War Socialism and Capitalism: Kowalik's Analysis and the Polish Transition. In R. Bellofiore, E. Karwowski & J. Toporowski (Eds.), *Economic Crisis and Political Economy. Essays in Honour of Tadeusz Kowalik* (Vol. 2, pp. 42–61). London: Palgrave Macmillan.

Engels, F. (1987). Anti-Dühring. Herr Eugen Dühring's Revolution in Science. In K. Marx, F. Engels, *Collected Works* (Vol. 25, pp. 1–309). London: Lawrence & Wishart.

Engels, F. (1988). The «Crisis» in Prussia. In K. Marx, F. Engels, *Collected Works* (Vol. 23, pp. 400–405). London: Lawrence & Wishart.

Engels, F. (1989). On Social Relations in Russia. In K. Marx, F. Engels, *Collected Works* (Vol. 24, pp. 39–50). London: Lawrence & Wishart.

Engels, F. (1990a). Preface [to the Pamphlet *Karl Marx Before The Cologne Jury*]. In K. Marx, F. Engels, *Collected Works* (Vol. 26, pp. 304–310). London: Lawrence & Wishart.

Engels, F. (1990b). Preface [to the 1892 English Edition of *The Condition Of The Working-Class In England in 1844*]. In K. Marx, F. Engels, *Collected Works* (Vol. 27, pp. 257–269). London: Lawrence & Wishart.

Eyal, G., Szelényi, I. & Townsley, E. (1997). The Theory of Post-Communist Managerialism. *New Left Review*(222), 60–92.

Eyal, G., Szelényi, I. & Townsley, E. (1998). *Making Capitalism Without Capitalists: Class Formation and Elite Struggles in Post-Communist Central Europe.* London: Verso.

Falkowski, M. & Kowalik, T. (1957). Posłowie. In M. Falkowski & T. Kowalik (Eds.), *Początki marksistowskiej myśli ekonomicznej w Polsce. Wybór publicystyki z lat 1880–1885* (pp. 641–693). Warszawa: Państwowe Wydawnictwo Naukowe.

Faulkner, N. (2017). *A People's History of the Russian Revolution.* London: Pluto Press.

Fetscher, I. (1991). Class Consciousness. In T. Bottomore, L. Harris, V. Kiernan & R. Miliband (Eds.), *A Dictionary of Marxist Thought* (2nd ed., pp. 89–91). Oxford: Blackwell.

Filtzer, D. (1992). *Soviet Workers and De-Stalinization. The Consolidation of the Modern System of Soviet Production Relations, 1953–1964.* Cambridge: Cambridge University Press.

Filtzer, D. (1996). Labor Discipline, the Use of Work Time, and the Decline of the Soviet System, 1928–1991. *International Labor and Working-Class History*(50), 9–28.

Fitzpatrick, S. (2017). *The Russian Revolution* (4th ed.). Oxford: Oxford University Press.

Foster, J. (2014). Polish Marxian Political Economy and US Monopoly Capital Theory: The Influence of Luxemburg, Kalecki and Lange on Baran and Sweezy and Monthly Review. In R. Bellofiore, E. Karwowski & J. Toporowski (Eds.), *The Legacy of Rosa Luxemburg, Oskar Lange and Michał Kalecki. Essays in Honour of Tadeusz Kowalik* (Vol. 1, pp. 104–121). London: Palgrave Macmillan.

Foster, J.B. & McChesney, R.W. (2012). *The Endless Crisis: How Monopoly-Finance Capital Produces Stagnation and Upheaval from the U.S.A. to China.* New York: Monthly Review Press.

Galbraith, J.K. (1996). *The Good Society: The Humane Agenda.* Boston: Houghton Mifflin.

Gardawski, J. (2009). *Polacy pracujący a kryzys fordyzmu.* Warszawa: Wydawnictwo Naukowe Scholar.

Geremek, B. & Żakowski, J. (1990). *Rok 1989: Bronisław Geremek odpowiada, Jacek Żakowski pyta.* Warszawa: Plejada.

Gerschenkron, A. (1962). *Economic Backwardness in Historical Perspective.* Cambridge: Harvard University Press.

Gerstenberger, H. (2019). «How Bourgeois Were the Bourgeois Revolutions?»: Remarks on Neil Davidson's Book. *Historical Materialism,* 27(3), 191–209.

Glasman, M. (1994). The Great Deformation: Polanyi, Poland and the Terrors of Planned Spontaneity. *New Left Review*(205), 59–86.

Goldstone, J. (2003). Comparative Historical Analysis and Knowledge Accumulation in the Study of Revolutions. In J. Mahoney & D. Rueschemeyer (Eds.), *Comparative Historical Analysis in the Social Sciences* (pp. 41–90). Cambridge: Cambridge University Press.

Gomułka, S. (1989, August 19). Shock Needed for Polish Economy. *The Guardian,* 5.

Gomułka, S. (1994). Polityka stabilizacyjna w Polsce 1990–93: odpowiedzi na pytania. In E. Rychlewski (Ed.), *Gospodarka polska 1990–1993. Kontrowersje wokół oceny doświadczeń i polityki gospodarczej* (*Studia i Materiały INE PAN,* Vol. 44, pp. 75–81). Warszawa: Instytut Nauk Ekonomicznych PAN.

Gomułka, S. & Kowalik, T. (Eds.). (2011). *Transformacja polska. Dokumenty i analizy 1990.* Warszawa: Wydawnictwo Naukowe Scholar.

Górski, J., Kowalik, T. & Sierpiński, W. (1967). *Historia powszechnej myśli ekonomicznej 1870–1950.* Warszawa: Państwowe Wydawnictwo Naukowe.

Górski, J. & Sierpiński, W. (1972). *Historia powszechnej myśli ekonomicznej 1870–1950.* Warszawa: Państwowe Wydawnictwo Naukowe.

Gregory, P.R. (1992). The Role of the State in Promoting Economic Development: the Russian Case and its General Implications. In R. Sylla & G. Toniolo (Eds.), *Patterns of European Industrialisation. The Nineteenth Century* (pp. 64–79). London: Routledge.

Grinberg, D., Kochanowicz, J. & Meller, S. (1983). Rewolucje burżuazyjne. *Przegląd Historyczny,* 74(4), 739–748.

Habermas, J. (1990). What Does Socialism Mean Today? The Rectifying Revolution and the Need for New. *New Left Review*(183), 3–22.

Hankiss, E. (1994). Our Recent Pasts: Recent Developments in East Central Europe in the Light of Various Social Philosophies. *East European Politics and Societies: and Cultures,* 8(3), 531–542.

Hardy, J. (2009). *Poland's New Capitalism.* London: Pluto Press.

Harman, C. (1990). The Storm Breaks. *International Socialism,* 2(46), 3–93.

Herer, W., Kowalik, T. & Sadowski, W. (1989). *Uwagi do programu dostosowawczego* [Unpublished typescript].

Himmelweit, S. (1991). Mode of Production. In T. Bottomore, L. Harris, V. Kiernan & R. Miliband (Eds.), *A Dictionary of Marxis^t Thought* (2nd ed., pp. 379–381). Oxford: Blackwell.

Hobsbawm, E.J. (2004). The Making of a «Bourgeois Revolution». *Social Research, 71*(3), 455–480.

Hutchful, E. (1991). Eastern Europe: Consequences for Africa. *Review of African Political Economy, 18*(50), 51–59.

Janczak [Kurowski], H. [S.] (1986). *Reforma gospodarcza w PRL. Trzecie podejście*. Warszawa: Wydawnictwo CDN.

Kabaj, M. & Kowalik, T. (1995). Letter to the Editor: Who Is Responsible for Postcommunist Successes in Eastern Europe?. *Transition: The Newsletter about Reforming Economies, 6*(7–8), 7–8.

Kalecki, M. (1971). Class Struggle and the Distribution of National Income. *Kyklos, 24*(1), 1–9.

Kalecki, M. & Kowalik, T. (1991). Observations on the «Crucial Reform». In J. Osiatyński (Ed.), *Collected Works of Michał Kalecki* (Vol. 2, pp. 467–476). Oxford: Clarendon Press.

Karwowski, E., Szymborska, H. & Toporowski, J. (2014). Bibliography of Published Works by Tadeusz Kowalik. In R. Bellofiore, E. Karwowski & J. Toporowski (Eds.), *The Legacy of Rosa Luxemburg, Oskar Lange and Michał Kalecki. Essays in Honour of Tadeusz Kowalik* (Vol. 1, pp. 230–248). London: Palgrave Macmillan.

Katznelson, I. (1996). *Liberalism's Crooked Circle. Letters to Adam Michnik*. Princeton: Princeton University Press.

Katznelson, I. (2006). *Krzywe koło liberalizmu. Listy do Adama Michnika*. Wrocław: Wydawnictwo Naukowe Dolnośląskiej Szkoły Wyższej Edukacji TWP.

King, J.E. (2014). Whatever Happened to the «Crucial Reform»?. In R. Bellofiore, E. Karwowski & J. Toporowski (Eds.), *Economic Crisis and Political Economy. Essays in Honour of Tadeusz Kowalik* (Vol. 2, pp. 29–41). London: Palgrave Macmillan.

Kisielewski, S. & Gabryel, P. (1991, January 20). Uwieść i zdradzić. *Wprost*(3), 6.

Klaes, M. (2003). Historiography. In W. Samuels, J. Biddle & J. Davis (Eds.), *A Companion to the History of Economic Thought* (pp. 491–506). Malden: Blackwell.

Kleer, J. (1996). Marginalizacja sektora spółdzielczego w Polsce. *Ekonomista*(4), 473–489.

Klein, N. (2007). *The Shock Doctrine: The Rise of Disaster Capitalism*. New York: Metropolitan Books.

Kołodziejczyk, R. (1979). *Miasta, mieszczaństwo, burżuazja w Polsce w XIX w. Szkice i rozprawy historyczne*. Warszawa: Państwowe Wydawnictwo Naukowe.

Komitet Obywatelski "Solidarności" (1989, May 10). Program wyborczy. *Gazeta Wyborcza*(3), 5–6.

Konat, G. (2014, December 2). Krzywicki, Kalecki, Kowalik – kapitał monopolistyczny w polskiej myśli ekonomicznej [Conference paper]. *Idee na kryzys: Michał Kalecki*, Warszawa.

Konat, G. (2015, November 30). Tadeusz Kowalik – twórca polskiej szkoły w ekonomii? [Conference paper]. *Idee na kryzys: polscy ekonomiści odkrywani na nowo*, Warszawa.

Konat, G. (2019). Wkład Tadeusza Kowalika do ekonomii w świetle opinii polskich ekonomistów. *Ekonomista*(3), 369–373.

Konat, G. (2021a). Linking Economics with Economic Policy-making: Interview with Jerzy Osiatyński. *European Journal of Economics and Economic Policies: Intervention, 18*(1), 1–10.

Konat, G. (2021b). *Polska rewolucja. Tadeusz Kowalik o epigońsko-mieszczańskiej transformacji roku 1989*. Warszawa: Instytut Wydawniczy Książka i Prasa.

Konat, G. (2022). Oskar Lange and Tadeusz Kowalik on the Bourgeois Revolutions in Twentieth-Century Poland: A Note on Two Papers. In J. Toporowski (Ed.), *Polish Marxism after Luxemburg (Research in Political Economy*, Vol. 37, pp. 187–201). Bingley: Emerald.

Konat, G. & Foster, J. (2018). «The Present as History» and the Theory of Monopoly Capital. *Monthly Review, 69*(9), 1–13.

Konat, G., Karpińska-Mizielińska, W., Kloc, K., Smuga, T. & Witkowski, B. (2019). Self-Identification of Polish Academic Economists with Schools of Economic Thought. *Acta Oeconomica, 69*(2), 241–272.

Konat, G. & Smuga, T. (Eds.). (2016). *Paradoksy ekonomii. Rozmowy z polskimi ekonomistami*. Warszawa: Wydawnictwo Naukowe PWN.

Konat, G. & Szlajfer, H. (2019). Liberated Capitalism. *Monthly Review, 71*(7), 37–53.

Konat, G. & Wielgosz, P. (Eds.). (2018). *Realny kapitalizm. Wokół teorii kapitału monopolistycznego* (2nd ed.). Warszawa: Instytut Wydawniczy Książka i Prasa.

Koredczuk, J. (2015). Wrocławski okres w życiu Jana Baszkiewicza. *Miscellanea Historico-Iuridica, XIV*(1), 269–285.

Kovács J.M. (1992). Engineers of the Transition (Interventionist Temptations in Eastern European Economic Thought). *Acta Oeconomica, 44*(1/2), 37–52.

Kowalewski, Z.M. (2005). Sierpień – zdradzona rewolucja. *Nowy Robotnik*(7), 9.

Kowalewski, Z.M. (2020). Robotnicy i biurokraci. Jak w bloku radzieckim ukształtowały się i funkcjonowały stosunki wyzysku. In M. Siermiński, *Pęknięta Solidarność. Inteligencja opozycyjna a robotnicy 1964–1981* (pp. 355–436). Warszawa: Instytut Wydawniczy Książka i Prasa.

Kowalik, T. (1955). Z historii marksistowskiej myśli ekonomicznej w Polsce (O pierwszych publikacjach Ludwika Krzywickiego). *Ekonomista*(5–6), 155–179.

Kowalik, T. (1958). Stanisław Krusiński i «krusińszczycy». In S. Krusiński, *Pisma zebrane* (pp. VII–LXIII). Warszawa: Książka i Wiedza.

Kowalik, T. (1959). *O Ludwiku Krzywickim. Studium społeczno-ekonomiczne*. Warszawa: Państwowe Wydawnictwo Naukowe.

Kowalik, T. (1965). *Krzywicki*. Warszawa: Wiedza Powszechna.

Kowalik, T. (1975). Filozofia społeczna Ludwika Krzywickiego. In B. Skarga (Ed.), *Polska myśl filozoficzna i społeczna* (pp. 400–455). Warszawa: Państwowe Wydawnictwo Naukowe.

Kowalik, T. (1977a). Capitale. In *Enciclopedia Einaudi* (Vol. 2, pp. 589-667). Torino: Einaudi.

Kowalik, T. (1977b). *Rosa Luxemburg. Il pensiero economico*. Roma: Editori Riuniti.

Kowalik, T. (1978). Crisi. In *Enciclopedia Einaudi* (Vol. 4, pp. 128-179). Torino: Einaudi.

Kowalik, T. (1979). *Teoria de la acumulacion y del imperialismo en Rosa Luxemburg*. Mexico: Ediciones Era.

Kowalik, T. (1980). *Spory o ustrój społeczno-gospodarczy Polski 1944-1948*. Warszawa: Niezależna Oficyna Wydawnicza NOWA.

Kowalik, T. (1982). Planning and Freedom: A Polish Dilemma 1944-1981 [Colloquium paper]. Washington: Woodrow Wilson International Center for Scholars.

Kowalik, T. (1989). On Crucial Reform of Real Socialism. In H. Gabrisch (Ed.), *Economic Reforms in Eastern Europe and the Soviet Union* (pp. 23-86). Boulder-London: Westview Press.

Kowalik, T. (1991a, March 23). Rewolucja ponad społeczeństwem. *Polityka*, 12(1768), 7.

Kowalik, T. (1991b). Wobec socjalizmu realnego i postulowanego. In A. Siciński (Ed.), *Sens uczestnictwa. Wokół idei Jana Strzeleckiego* (pp. 81-93). Warszawa: Instytut Filozofii i Socjologii PAN.

Kowalik, T. (1991c). Zmiana ustroju – wielka operacja czy proces społeczny?. In R. Gortat (Ed.), *Społeczeństwo uczestniczące, gospodarka rynkowa, sprawiedliwość społeczna* (pp. 29-50). Warszawa: Instytut Nauk Politycznych PAN.

Kowalik, T. (1992a). *Historia ekonomii w Polsce 1864-1950*. Wrocław-Warszawa: Zakład Narodowy im. Ossolińskich.

Kowalik, T. (1992b). Reform Economics and Bureaucracy. In J. Kovacs & M. Tardos (Eds.), *Reform and Transformation in Eastern Europe* (pp. 164-176). London: Routledge.

Kowalik, T. (1994). A Reply to Maurice Glasman. *New Left Review*(206), 133-144.

Kowalik, T. (1995). From «Self-Governing Republic» to Capitalism: Polish Workers and Intellectuals. In M. Mendell & K. Nielsen (Eds.), *Europe: Central and East* (pp. 92-110). Montreal-New York-London: Black Rose Books.

Kowalik, T. (1996a). On the Transformation of Post-communist Societies: The Inefficiency of Primitive Capital Accumulation. *International Political Science Review*, 17(3), 289-296.

Kowalik, T. (1996b). Sierpień – epigońska rewolucja mieszczańska. *Nowe Życie Gospodarcze*(37), 22-24.

Kowalik, T. (1997a). August – A Bourgeois Epigone Revolution. *Labour Focus on Eastern Europe*(57), 49-57.

Kowalik, T. (1997b). Spór o Marksa i ZSRR ciągle otwarty (Dwóch Marksów, wiele marksizmów). *Zdanie*(1-2), 62-65.

Kowalik, T. (1997c). The Polish Revolution. *Dissent*(2), 26-30.

Kowalik, T. (1997d). «Wybór» systemu ekonomicznego jako proces społeczny. *Roczniki Kolegium Analiz Ekonomicznych*(4), 84-110.

Kowalik, T. (2000). *Współczesne systemy ekonomiczne. Powstawanie. Ewolucja. Kryzys.* Warszawa: Wydawnictwo Wyższej Szkoły Przedsiębiorczości i Zarządzania im. Leona Koźmińskiego.

Kowalik, T. (2001a). The Ugly Face of Polish Success: Social Aspects of Transformation. In R. Rapacki & G. Blazyca (Eds.), *Poland into the New Millennium* (pp. 33–53). Cheltenham: Edward Elgar.

Kowalik, T. (2001b). Why the Social Democratic Option Failed: Poland's Experience of Systemic Change. In A. Glyn (Ed.), *Social Democracy in Neoliberal Time: The Left and Economic Policy since 1980* (pp. 223–252). Oxford: Oxford University Press.

Kowalik, T. (2002a). Dystrybucyjna sprawiedliwość w transformacji polskiej. In T. Kowalik (Ed.), *Nierówni i równiejsi. Sprawiedliwość dystrybucyjna czasu transformacji w Polsce* (pp. 52–89). Warszawa: Fundacja Innowacja.

Kowalik, T. (2002b, March 23). Mój rok osiemdziesiąty dziewiąty. *Gazeta Wyborcza* (70), 20.

Kowalik, T. (Ed.). (2002c). *Nierówni i równiejsi. Sprawiedliwość dystrybucyjna czasu transformacji w Polsce.* Warszawa: Fundacja Innowacja.

Kowalik, T. (2002d). Nowe tendencje w świecie. In T. Kowalik (Ed.), *Nierówni i równiejsi. Sprawiedliwość dystrybucyjna czasu transformacji w Polsce* (pp. 12–51). Warszawa: Fundacja Innowacja.

Kowalik, T. (2002e). Zmiany systemowe ostatniej dekady: spojrzenie ogólne. In E. Bowden & J. Bowden (Eds.), *Ekonomia. Nauka zdrowego rozsądku* (pp. 615–642). Warszawa: Fundacja Innowacja.

Kowalik, T. (2003). Polska rewolucja epigońsko-mieszczańska na drodze do Europy. In J. Gardawski & J. Polakowska-Kujawa (Eds.), *Globalizacja. Gospodarka. Praca. Kultura. W 70 rocznicę urodzin prof. zw. dr. hab. Leszka Gilejko* (pp. 219–235). Warszawa: Szkoła Główna Handlowa.

Kowalik, T. (2004a). Kaleckian Crucial Reform of Capitalism and After. In Z. Sadowski & A. Szeworski (Eds.), *Kalecki's Economics Today* (pp. 42–50). London: Routledge.

Kowalik, T. (2004b). Państwo dobrobytu – druga fala. *Problemy Polityki Społecznej* (6), 69–77.

Kowalik, T. (2005a). *Systemy gospodarcze. Efekty i defekty reform i zmian ustrojowych.* Warszawa: Fundacja Innowacja.

Kowalik, T. (2005b, March 6). Transformacja według noblisty. Laureat Nobla ocenia polską drogę do gospodarki rynkowej. *Przegląd*(9), 52–54.

Kowalik, T. (2006a). Robotnicy i rewolucja. *Dziś. Przegląd społeczny*(5), 135–147.

Kowalik, T. (2006b). *Spory o ustrój społeczno-gospodarczy w Polsce. Lata 1944–1948.* Warszawa: Instytut Nauk Ekonomicznych PAN.

Kowalik, T. (2007). Blaski i cienie transformacji polskiej. In M. Kaltwasser, E. Majewska & K. Szreder (Eds.), *Futuryzm miast przemysłowych: 100 lat Wolfsburga i Nowej Huty* (pp. 267–279). Kraków: Korporacja Ha!art.

Kowalik, T. (2008). Czy kapitalizm może być etyczny?. *Annales. Etyka w życiu gospodarczym*, 11(1), 23–30.

Kowalik, T. (2009a). Koszty transformacji wpisane w cechy systemu. Rozmowa z prof. dr. hab. Tadeuszem Kowalikiem. *Przegląd Socjalistyczny*, 23(2), 11–15.

Kowalik, T. (2009b). *Polska transformacja*. Warszawa: MUZA.

Kowalik, T. (2010a). Przedmowa. In T. Kowalik (Ed.), *Stanisław Gomułka i transformacja polska. Dokumenty i analizy 1968–1989* (pp. 13–19). Warszawa: Wydawnictwo Naukowe Scholar.

Kowalik, T. (Ed.). (2010b). *Stanisław Gomułka i transformacja polska. Dokumenty i analizy 1968–1989*. Warszawa: Wydawnictwo Naukowe Scholar.

Kowalik, T. (2011a). Animal spirits w transformacji polskiej. In P. Kozłowski (Ed.), *Węzeł polski. Bariery rozwoju z perspektywy ekonomicznej i psychologicznej* (pp. 11–26). Warszawa: Instytut Nauk Ekonomicznych PAN & Instytut Psychologii PAN.

Kowalik, T. (2011b). Poglądy ekonomiczne Josepha Stiglitza. *Ekonomista*(5), 747–763.

Kowalik, T. (2011c). Urynkowienie bez modernizacji. In P. Kozłowski (Ed.), *Dwudziestolecie polskich przemian. Konserwatywna modernizacja* (pp. 23–68). Warszawa: Instytut Nauk Ekonomicznych PAN.

Kowalik, T. (2012a). *From Solidarity to Sellout. The Restoration of Capitalism in Poland*. New York: Monthly Review Press.

Kowalik, T. (2012b). *Róża Luksemburg. Teoria akumulacji i imperializmu*. Warszawa: Instytut Wydawniczy Książka i Prasa.

Kowalik, T. (2012c). Status i pożytki ekonomii porównawczej (tezy referatu). *Studia Ekonomiczne*, LXXV(4), 569–572.

Kowalik, T. (2012d). W czynów uderzaj stal!. In Ph. Askenazy, Th. Coutrot, A. Orléan, H. Sterdyniak, *Manifest oburzonych ekonomistów. Kryzys i dług w Europie: 10 fałszywych oczywistości, 22 sposoby na wyprowadzenie debaty z impasu* (pp. 68–76). Warszawa: Wydawnictwo Krytyki Politycznej.

Kowalik, T. (2012e). What Went Wrong with the Transformation? Social Failures of the New System [Tribute of the Editorial Board to the memory of Tadeusz Kowalik, edited by K. Kozłowski, J. Czarzasty & H. Dębowski]. *Warsaw Forum of Economic Sociology*, 3(6), 9–26.

Kowalik, T. (2013a). Czy sprawiedliwość społeczna kosztuje?. In T. Kowalik, *O lepszy ład społeczno-ekonomiczny* (pp. 238–266). Warszawa: Polskie Towarzystwo Ekonomiczne & Instytut Nauk Ekonomicznych PAN.

Kowalik, T. (2013b). Ekonomia polityczna klęski socjaldemokratycznej opcji. In T. Kowalik, *O lepszy ład społeczno-ekonomiczny* (pp. 209–237). Warszawa: Polskie Towarzystwo Ekonomiczne & Instytut Nauk Ekonomicznych PAN.

Kowalik, T. (2013c). Michał Kalecki, kim był, jakim go znałem i podziwiałem. In T. Kowalik, *O lepszy ład społeczno-ekonomiczny* (pp. 573–595). Warszawa: Polskie Towarzystwo Ekonomiczne & Instytut Nauk Ekonomicznych PAN.

Kowalik, T. (2013d). *O lepszy ład społeczno-ekonomiczny*. Warszawa: Polskie Towarzystwo Ekonomiczne & Instytut Nauk Ekonomicznych PAN.

Kowalik, T. (2013e). O możliwości wyboru systemu ekonomicznego. Dahrendorf po 10 latach. In T. Kowalik, *O lepszy ład społeczno-ekonomiczny* (pp. 142–156). Warszawa: Polskie Towarzystwo Ekonomiczne & Instytut Nauk Ekonomicznych PAN.

Kowalik, T. (2013f). O socjalizmie bez mistyki. Uwagi jak najbardziej osobiste. In T. Kowalik, *O lepszy ład społeczno-ekonomiczny* (pp. 429–437). Warszawa: Polskie Towarzystwo Ekonomiczne & Instytut Nauk Ekonomicznych PAN.

Kowalik, T. (2013g). Oskar Lange odczytywany na nowo. In T. Kowalik, *O lepszy ład społeczno-ekonomiczny* (pp. 557–572). Warszawa: Polskie Towarzystwo Ekonomiczne & Instytut Nauk Ekonomicznych PAN.

Kowalik, T. (2013h). Polska transformacja a nurty liberalne. In T. Kowalik, *O lepszy ład społeczno-ekonomiczny* (pp. 186–202). Warszawa: Polskie Towarzystwo Ekonomiczne & Instytut Nauk Ekonomicznych PAN.

Kowalik, T. (2013i). Sierpień – epigońska rewolucja mieszczańska. In T. Kowalik, *O lepszy ład społeczno-ekonomiczny* (pp. 520–526). Warszawa: Polskie Towarzystwo Ekonomiczne & Instytut Nauk Ekonomicznych PAN.

Kowalik, T. (2013j). Słuchany doradca. In T. Kowalik, *O lepszy ład społeczno-ekonomiczny* (pp. 348–354). Warszawa: Polskie Towarzystwo Ekonomiczne & Instytut Nauk Ekonomicznych PAN.

Kowalik, T. (2013k). Społeczna gospodarka rynkowa – demokracja czy program działania?. In T. Kowalik, *O lepszy ład społeczno-ekonomiczny* (pp. 118–141). Warszawa: Polskie Towarzystwo Ekonomiczne & Instytut Nauk Ekonomicznych PAN.

Kowalik, T. (2013l). Spory wokół Nowej Trzeciej Drogi. In T. Kowalik, *O lepszy ład społeczno-ekonomiczny* (pp. 86–117). Warszawa: Polskie Towarzystwo Ekonomiczne & Instytut Nauk Ekonomicznych PAN.

Kowalik, T. (2013m). Włodzimierz Brus. W czyśćcu historii. In T. Kowalik, *O lepszy ład społeczno-ekonomiczny* (pp. 596–612). Warszawa: Polskie Towarzystwo Ekonomiczne & Instytut Nauk Ekonomicznych PAN.

Kowalik, T. (2014). *Rosa Luxemburg. Theory of Accumulation and Imperialism*. London: Palgrave Macmillan.

Kowalik, T., Chudziński, E., Kozłowski, P. & Ratkowski, F. (2013). Trzech na jednego. Musztarda przed obiadem. In T. Kowalik, *O lepszy ład społeczno-ekonomiczny* (pp. 618–652). Warszawa: Polskie Towarzystwo Ekonomiczne & Instytut Nauk Ekonomicznych PAN.

Kowalik, T. & Dryszel, A. (2010, January 17). Plan Balcerowicza: operacja niepotrzebna i chybiona. *Przegląd*(2), 38–41.

Kowalik, T. & Hołda-Róziewicz, H. (1976). *Ludwik Krzywicki*. Warszawa: Wydawnictwo Interpress.

Kowalik, T. & Leszkowska, A. (2010, April 14). Niespodzianki są możliwe. *Sprawy Nauki,* 4(149). https://www.sprawynauki.edu.pl/archiwum/dzialy-wyd-elektron/312-ekono mia-el3/1549-niespodzianki-sa-mozliwe.

Kowalik, T. & Lubczyński, K. (2013). Bez buntu się nie obejdzie. In T. Kowalik, *O lepszy ład społeczno-ekonomiczny* (pp. 342–347). Warszawa: Polskie Towarzystwo Ekonomiczne & Instytut Nauk Ekonomicznych PAN.

Kowalik, T. & Sierakowski, S. (2005). Od Stiglitza do Keynesa. *Krytyka Polityczna*(9/10), 198–213.

Kowalik, T. & Wielgosz, P. (2004, February 14–15). Porozmawiajmy o kapitalizmie. *Trybuna,* 38(4241), A, C.

Kowalik, T. & Zybała, A. (2005). Bezdroża Solidarności. *Obywatel,* 5(25), 38–41.

Kozłowski, P. (1997). *Szukanie sposobu. Społeczne uwarunkowania procesu transformacji gospodarczej w Polsce.* Warszawa: Wydawnictwo Instytutu Filozofii i Socjologii PAN.

Kozłowski, P. (2012). Wspomnienie o profesorze Tadeuszu Kowaliku. *Studia Ekonomiczne,* LXXV(4), 567–568.

Kozłowski, P. (2013a). Tadeusz Kowalik (1926–2012) – krytyczne spojrzenie na transformację. *Kwartalnik Historii Nauki i Techniki,* 58(2), 255–261.

Kozłowski, P. (2013b). Wprowadzenie. In T. Kowalik, *O lepszy ład społecznoekonomiczny* (pp. 11–12). Warszawa: Polskie Towarzystwo Ekonomiczne & Instytut Nauk Ekonomicznych PAN.

Kozłowski, P. (2014). Ekonomia i historia idei. *Przegląd Humanistyczny,* LVIII(3), 47–54.

Kryshtanovskaya, O. & White, S. (1996). From Soviet Nomenklatura to Russian Élite. *Europe-Asia Studies,* 48(5), 711–733.

Krzywicki, L. (1959). *Dzieła* (Vol. 3: *Artykuły i rozprawy 1886–1888*). Warszawa: Państwowe Wydawnictwo Naukowe.

Kuczyński, W. (1992). *Zwierzenia zausznika.* Warszawa: Wydawnictwo BGW.

Kuczyński, W. (1996). *Agonia systemu. Szkice z niedawnej przeszłości.* Warszawa: Presspublica.

Kula, M. (1984). Rewolucja burżuazyjna. Przyczynek do dyskusji nad użytecznością pojęcia. *Dzieje Najnowsze,* XVI(3–4), 135–146.

Kulas, P. (2015). Młodzi intelektualiści wobec inteligencji. Analiza wyobrażeń na temat inteligencji i intelektualistów. *Kultura Współczesna. Teoria. Interpretacje. Praktyka*(4), 65–79.

Kumar, K. (1992). The Revolutions of 1989: Socialism, Capitalism, and Democracy. *Theory and Society,* 21(3), 309–356.

Kurczewski, J. (1995, January 27–28). Taka młoda a taka brzydka. *Gazeta Wyborcza*(24), 12–13.

Kuroń, J. (1991). *Moja zupa.* Warszawa: Wydawnictwo BGW.

Kuroń, J. & Żakowski, J. (1997). *Siedmiolatka, czyli kto ukradł Polskę?.* Wrocław: Wydawnictwo Dolnośląskie.

Lakatos, I. (1976). *Proofs and Refutations: The Logic of Mathematical Discovery.* Cambridge: Cambridge University Press.
Lange, O. (1994). *Economic Theory and Market Socialism. Selected Essays of Oskar Lange.* Aldershot: Edward Elgar.
Lange, O. (1990). Kryzys socjalizmu. In O. Lange, *Wybór pism* (Vol. 1: *Drogi do socjalizmu*, pp. 89–103). Warszawa: Państwowe Wydawnictwo Naukowe.
Leder, A. (2014). *Prześniona rewolucja. Ćwiczenie z logiki historycznej.* Warszawa: Wydawnictwo Krytyki Politycznej.
Lenin, V.I. (1962). Two Tactics of Social-Democracy in the Democratic Revolution. In V.I. Lenin, *Collected Works* (Vol. 9, pp. 15–140). London: Lawrence & Wishart.
Lenin, V.I. (1963). May Day Action by the Revolutionary Proletariat. In V.I. Lenin, *Collected Works* (Vol. 19, pp. 218–227). London: Lawrence & Wishart.
Lenin, V.I. (1964a). Letters on Tactics. In V.I. Lenin, *Collected Works* (Vol. 24, pp. 42–54). London: Lawrence & Wishart.
Lenin, V.I. (1964b). From A Publicist's Diary. The Mistakes Of Our Party. In V.I. Lenin, *Collected Works* (Vol. 26, pp. 52–58). London: Lawrence & Wishart.
Lenin, V.I. (1964c). The Collapse of the Second International. In V.I. Lenin, *Collected Works* (Vol. 21, pp. 205–259). London: Lawrence & Wishart.
Lenin, V.I. (1965). Deception of the People with Slogans of Freedom and Equality. May 19. (First All-Russia Congress on Adult Education. May 6–19, 1919). In V.I. Lenin, *Collected Works* (Vol. 29, pp. 339–376). London: Lawrence & Wishart.
Lipiński, E. (1981). *Problemy, pytania, wątpliwości. Z warsztatu ekonomisty.* Warszawa: Państwowe Wydawnictwo Ekonomiczne.
Lowenthal, R. (1970). Development vs. Utopia in Communist Policy. In C. Johnson (Ed.), *Change in Communist Systems* (pp. 33–116). Stanford: Stanford University Press.
Łagowski, B. (2010, April 13). Historia alternatywna. *Przegląd*(13), 11.
Łaski, K. & Kowalik, T. (2007). *Kazimierz Łaski o sobie, ekonomii, Polsce i Unii Europejskiej w rozmowie z Tadeuszem Kowalikiem* [Unpublished typescript].
Łepkowski, T. (1983). Jan Baszkiewicz, Wolność, Równość, Własność. Rewolucje burżuazyjne [Liberté, Egalité, Propriété. Révolutions bourgeoises]. *Acta Poloniae Historica, 48*, 232–236.
Łukawer, E. (2008). *O tych z najwyższej półki, czyli rzecz w sprawie naszego środowiska ekonomicznego.* Kraków: Polskie Towarzystwo Ekonomiczne.
Maas, H. (2013). A 2x2=4 Hobbyhorse: Mark Blaug on Rational and Historical Reconstructions. *Erasmus Journal for Philosophy and Economics, 6*(3), 64–86.
Magala, S. (1983). Rewolucja jako próba sił i środków. *Colloquia Communia*(6), 149–156.
Marcuzzo, M.C. (2008). Is History of Economic Thought a «Serious» Subject?. *Erasmus Journal for Philosophy and Economics, 1*(1), 107–123.
Marx, K. (1987). A Contribution to the Critique of Political Economy. In K. Marx, F. Engels, *Collected Works* (Vol. 29, pp. 257–417). London: Lawrence & Wishart.

Marx, K. (1998). *Capital: A Critique of Political Economy*. Volume III. In K. Marx, F. Engels, *Collected Works* (Vol. 37). London: Lawrence & Wishart.

Marx, K. & Engels, F. (1990). *Collected Works* (Vol. 27). New York: International Publishers.

Meiksins Wood, E. (1994). From Opportunity to Imperative: The History of the Market. *Monthly Review*, 46(3), 14–40.

Meiksins Wood, E. (1996). Capitalism, Merchants and Bourgeois Revolution: Reflections on the Brenner Debate and its Sequel. *International Review of Social History*, 41(2), 209–232.

Mikołajczyk, M. (2015). «Znikająca lewica». O dyskursie zawierającym diagnozę zmian polskiej sceny politycznej. *Annales Universitatis Paedagogicae Cracoviensi. Studia Politologica*, 15(194), 89–114.

Modzelewski, K. (2013). *Zajeździmy kobyłę historii. Wyznania poobijanego jeźdźca*. Warszawa: Wydawnictwo Iskry.

Morawski, W. (1998). Change as Institutional Change: Universal Challenges and Polish Adaptations. *Polish Sociological Review*(121), 57–67.

Myrdal, G. (1969). *Objectivity in Social Research*. New York: Pantheon Books.

Nolte, E. (1991). Die unvollstandige Revolution. Die Rehabilitierung des Burgertums und der defensive Nationalismus. *Frankfurter Allgemeine Zeitung*(24), 27.

Nygaard, B. (2007). The Meanings of «Bourgeois Revolutions»: Conceptualizing the French Revolution. *Science & Society*, 71(2), 146–172.

Olszewski, H. (2009). Jana Baszkiewicza badania nad władzą, społeczeństwem i kulturą polityczną. In J. Baszkiewicz, *Państwo. Rewolucja. Kultura polityczna* (pp. 5–17). Poznań: Wydawnictwo Poznańskie.

Olszewski, H. (2011). Jan Baszkiewicz (1930–2011). *Nauka*(1), 177–182.

Orsi, P.L. (2009). *Teoria generale della rivoluzione borghese*. Pisa: Edizioni II Campano.

Osiatyński, J. (2012, September 7). Tadeusz Kowalik: 1926–2012. *Gazeta Wyborcza*(183), 9.

Ost, D. (2005). *The Defeat of Solidarity: Anger and Politics in Postcommunist Europe*. Ithaca: Cornell University Press.

Paine, T. (1986). *Common Sense*. London: Penguin Books.

Podziały w Solidarności. Dlaczego?. (1991). *Życie Gospodarcze*(23), 1, 3–9 [Editorial discussion].

Pospiszyl, M. (2013). Prześniona walka klas. Leder, Marks i mieszczańska rewolucja. *Praktyka Teoretyczna*, 4(10), 205–215.

Post, C. (2011). *The American Road to Capitalism. Studies in Class Structure, Economic Development and Political Conflict, 1620–1877*. Leiden-Boston: Brill.

Post, C. (2018). The Use and Misuse of Uneven and Combined Development: A Critique of Anievas and Nişancıoğlu. *Historical Materialism*, 26(3), 79–98.

Post, C. (2019). How Capitalist Were the «Bourgeois Revolutions»?. *Historical Materialism*, 27(3), 157–190.

Prusek, A. (2014). Woluntaryzm ekonomiczny w Unii Europejskiej a nowy model jej funkcjonowania w warunkach kryzysu. *Studia Ekonomiczne / Uniwersytet Ekonomiczny w Katowicach*(166), 9–19.

Rae, G. (2012). Tadeusz Kowalik 1926–2012. Debatte: *Journal of Contemporary Central and Eastern Europe*, 20(1), 99–102.

Rae, G. (2020). In the Polish Mirror. *New Left Review*(124), 89–104.

Rae, G. (2022). False Dawns: The Failed Crucial Reforms of Capitalism and Socialism. In J. Toporowski (Ed.), *Polish Marxism after Luxemburg (Research in Political Economy*, Vol. 37, pp. 217–233). Bingley: Emerald.

Rae, G. (2024). *Full Circle. The Intellectual and Political Life of Tadeusz Kowalik*. Manchester: Manchester University Press (forthcoming).

Rorty, R. (1984). The Historiography of Philosophy: Four Genres. In R. Rorty, J. Schneewind & Q. Skinner (Eds.), *Philosophy in History. Essays on the Historiography of Philosophy* (pp. 49–75). Cambridge: Cambridge University Press.

Rothschild, K.W. (1989). Political Economy or Economics? Some Terminological and Normative Considerations. *European Journal of Political Economy*(5), 1–12.

Rupnik, J. (2018). The Crisis of Liberalism. *Journal of Democracy*, 29(3), 24–38.

Sadowski, Z. (2012). Tadeusz Kowalik (1926–2012). *Ekonomista*(5), 547.

Sadura, P. (2015). *Upadek komunizmu w Europie Środkowo-Wschodniej w perspektywie współczesnych teorii rewolucji*. Warszawa: Oficyna Naukowa.

Sady, W. (1990). *Racjonalna rekonstrukcja odkryć naukowych*. Lublin: Wydawnictwo UMCS.

Sakwa, R. (2001). The Age of Paradox: the Anti-revolutionary Revolutions of 1989–91. In M. Donald & T. Rees (Eds.), *Reinterpreting Revolution in Twentieth-Century Europe* (pp. 159–176). Basingstoke: Palgrave Macmillan.

Salmonowicz, S. (1983). Rewolty ludowe, rewolucje burżuazyjne, reformy odgórne. Uwagi o trudnościach klasyfikacji. *Czasopismo Prawno-Historyczne*, 35(1), 249–259.

Samary, C. (2020, May). In the Name of the Communist Ideal. *Le Monde diplomatique*. https://mondediplo.com/2020/05/13ussr.

Sandelin, B., Trautwein, H.-M. & Wundrak, R. (2014). *A Short History of Economic Thought* (3rd ed.). Abingdon: Routledge.

Savelsberg, J.J. (1995). Crime, Inequality, and Justice in Eastern Europe: Anomie, Domination, and Revolutionary Change. In J. Hagan & R. Peterson (Eds.), *Crime and Inequality* (pp. 206–225). Stanford: Stanford University Press.

Siemek, M.J. (1988). Marksizm jako filozofia. In G. Lukács, *Historia i świadomość klasowa. Studia o marksistowskiej dialektyce* (pp. VII–XLII). Warszawa: Państwowe Wydawnictwo Naukowe.

Siermiński, M. (2016). *Dekada przełomu. Polska lewica opozycyjna 1968–1980*. Warszawa: Instytut Wydawniczy Książka i Prasa.

Siermiński, M. (2020). *Pęknięta Solidarność Inteligencja opozycyjna a robotnicy 1964–1981*. Warszawa: Instytut Wydawniczy Książka i Prasa.

Signorino, R. (2003). Rational vs Historical Reconstructions. A Note on Blaug. *European Journal of the History of Economic Thought, 10*(2), 329–338.
Singer, D. (1989). On Revolution. *Monthly Review, 41*(2), 33–36.
Singer, D. (1990). Prometheus Rebound?. *Monthly Review, 42*(3), 73–92.
Skinner, Q. (1969). Meaning and Understanding in the History of Ideas. *History and Theory, 8*(1), 3–53.
Słabek, H. (2004). *Obraz robotników polskich w świetle ich świadectw własnych i statystyki 1945–1989*. Warszawa-Kutno: Instytut Historii PAN & Wyższa Szkoła Gospodarki Krajowej w Kutnie.
Staniszkis, J. (1989). Gesty jako argumenty. *Tygodnik Solidarność*(26), 4.
Stankiewicz, W. (2007). *Historia myśli ekonomicznej* (3rd ed.). Warszawa: Polskie Wydawnictwo Ekonomiczne.
Statut. Uchwała programowa z Aneksem. Dokumenty Zjazdu (1981). Gdańsk: Biuro Informacji Prasowej Komisji Krajowej NSZZ «Solidarność».
Ste. Croix, G.E.M. de (1981). *The Class Struggle in the Ancient Greek World. From the Archaic Age to the Arab Conquests*. Ithaca: Cornell University Press.
Steinmetz, M. (1979). Theses on the Early Bourgeois Revolution in Germany, 1476–1535. In B. Scribner, G. Benecke (Eds.), *The German Peasant War of 1525: New Viewpoints* (pp. 9–18), London-Boston: Allen & Unwin.
Stiglitz, J. (2001). Development Thinking at the Millennium. In B. Pleskovic & N. Stern (Eds.), *Annual World Bank Conference on Development Economics 2000* (pp. 13–38). Washington: The World Bank.
Stone, B. (2020). *Rethinking Revolutionary Change in Europe: A Neostructuralist Approach*. London: Rowman & Littlefield.
Surdykowski, J. (1990, August 4). Między demokracją a polskim piekłem. *Gazeta Wyborcza*(180), 6–7.
Szelényi, I. (1991). Foreword. In J. Staniszkis, *The Dynamics of the Breakthrough in Eastern Europe: The Polish Experience* (pp. vii–xiii). Berkeley-Los Angeles-Oxford: University of California Press.
Szelényi, S., Szelényi, I. & Kovách, I. (1995). The Making of the Hungarian Postcommunist Elite: Circulation in Politics, Reproduction in the Economy. *Theory and Society, 24*(5), 697–722.
Szwarc, K. (2012). Z lewicowym życiorysem (Profesor Tadeusz Kowalik 1926–2012). *Nowe Życie Gospodarcze*(7/8), 13.
Szymborska, H., Toporowski, J. (2022). Industrial Feudalism and the Distribution of Wealth. In J. Toporowski (Ed.), *Polish Marxism after Luxemburg (Research in Political Economy*, Vol. 37, pp. 61–75). Bingley: Emerald.
Tabin, M. (2014). Tadeusz Kowalik – ekonomista obywatelski. *Zdanie*(3–4), 62–65.
Tanewski, P. (2014). *Polska myśl ekonomiczna w latach 1956–1989 wobec zagadnienia przemian systemowych w gospodarce PRL*. Warszawa: Oficyna Wydawnicza SGH.

Tatur, M. (1992). Why is There No Women's Movement in Eastern Europe?. In P.G. Lewis (Ed.), *Democracy and Civil Society in Eastern Europe. Selected Papers from the Fourth World Congress for Soviet and East European Studies, Harrogate, 1990* (pp. 61–75). Basingstoke: Palgrave Macmillan.

Teschke, B. (2005). Bourgeois Revolution, State Formation and the Absence of the International. *Historical Materialism, 13*(2), 3–26.

Tittenbrun, J. (2007). *Z deszczu pod rynnę. Meandry polskiej prywatyzacji* (Vols. 1–4). Poznań: Wydawnictwo Zysk i S-ka.

Toporowski, J. (1995). The Contradictions of Market Socialism. *Monthly Review, 46*(11), 1–7.

Toporowski, J. (2012). Tadeusz Kowalik a współczesna ekonomia polityczna. In T. Kowalik, *Róża Luksemburg. Teoria akumulacji i imperializmu* (pp. 7–14). Warszawa: Instytut Wydawniczy Książka i Prasa.

Toporowski, J. (2013a). Tadeusz Kowalik and the Accumulation of Capital. *Monthly Review, 64*(8), 33–44.

Toporowski, J. (2013b). Tadeusz Kowalik: Radical Political Economist, Solidarity Advisor and Critic of Globalised Capitalism. *PSL Quarterly Review, 66*(264), 49–57.

Toporowski, J. (2022). Industrial Feudalism and American Capitalism. In J. Toporowski (Ed.), *Polish Marxism after Luxemburg* (Research in Political Economy, Vol. 37, pp. 43–59). Bingley: Emerald.

Tymowski, A. (1993). Poland's Unwanted Social Revolution. *East European Politics and Societies, 7*(2), 169–202.

Walicki, A. (1996). *Marksizm i skok do królestwa wolności. Dzieje komunistycznej utopii.* Warszawa: Wydawnictwo Naukowe PWN.

Walicki, A. (1997). Sporu ciąg dalszy. Odpowiedź prof. Tadeuszowi Kowalikowi. *Zdanie* (3–4), 33–39.

Walicki, A. (2000). Liberalizm w Polsce. In A. Walicki, *Polskie zmagania z wolnością: widziane z boku* (pp. 35–64). Kraków: Universitas.

Wałęsa, L. & Merkel, J. (1989, July 6). *International Assistance Program for Poland* [Unpublished typescript].

Wierzbicki, P. (1989, August 6). Przeklęte piętno. *Tygodnik Powszechny*(32), 8.

Założenia i kierunki polityki gospodarczej. (1989, October 12). *Rzeczpospolita* [Supplement].

Założenia programu gospodarczego na lata 1989–1992. (1989, July 13). *Rzeczpospolita* [Supplement «Reforma gospodarcza»].

Index

Abramowski, Edward 171
administrative-command economy. *See* central planning
Anderson, Kevin 177*n*27
Anderson, Perry 28*n*56, 65*n*11
Anglo-Saxon (economic) system. *See* Anglo-Saxon model
Anglo-Saxon model 42, 92*n*3, 148
Anglo-Saxon version of capitalism. *See* Anglo-Saxon model
Anievas, Alexander 17*n*37
anti-revisionism 6*n*19
anti-zionism 6*n*19
Arato, Andrew 13
Arthur, Christopher J 186*n*38
Asian tigers 49
August '80 15, 38, 39, 40, 41, 45, 45*n*9, 53, 160
August Agreements 41
Austria 1*n*5, 37, 46*n*12, 49, 102*n*18, 117*n*32, 172*n*24
authoritarianism 143, 157

Babeuf, François Noël 87
Baka, Władysław 107, 121*n*35, 126
Balcerowicz, Leszek 52, 118, 118*n*33, 121*n*35, 124, 136*n*51, 145, 150
Balcerowicz Plan 42*n*6, 52*n*19, 53, 110, 118, 119, 121, 121*n*35, 122, 123*n*37, 124, 124*n*39, 125, 128, 128*n*42, 128*n*43, 129, 131, 131*n*46, 142, 146, 146*n*68, 150, 154, 160*n*6, 179, 180
Banaszkiewicz, Mikołaj 27*n*54, 31
Barker, Colin 14, 14*n*29, 16, 20*n*39, 24, 158, 158*n*3, 158*n*4, 159, 159*n*5, 160, 161, 181
Baszkiewicz, Jan 16*n*35, 20*n*41, 24, 24*n*48, 25, 26*n*53, 27, 27*n*53, 27*n*54, 27*n*55, 28, 28*n*56, 29, 30, 30*n*59, 31, 31*n*60, 31*n*61, 32, 33, 35, 43*n*8, 44*n*8, 48, 48*n*13, 57, 57*n*1, 57*n*2, 58, 58*n*3, 59, 59*n*4, 60, 61, 62, 63, 63*n*9, 64, 65, 66, 66*n*12, 67, 68, 68*n*17, 68*n*18, 69, 69*n*19, 70, 70*n*20, 70*n*21, 71, 71*n*22, 72, 72*n*24, 73, 74, 74*n*26, 75, 75*n*28, 75*n*29, 76, 77, 78, 79, 79*n*30, 80, 81, 81*n*32, 82, 83, 84, 85, 86, 87, 87*n*33, 88, 89, 89*n*34, 90, 91, 100, 106, 129, 133, 142, 144, 146*n*68, 147*n*68, 152, 154, 155, 156, 157, 158, 160, 161, 181, 182

Bates, Thomas R 80*n*31
Bauer, Otto 48
Bauman, Zygmunt 11*n*26, 92*n*2, 170*n*20, 180
Beksiak, Janusz 115, 116, 120, 121
Belgium 105
Bellofiore, Riccardo 1*n*6, 2, 5*n*15, 6*n*17, 95*n*10
Big Bang. *See* shock therapy
Bińczyk, Ewa 2
Bismarck, Otto 27, 29, 162
Blanc, Louis 16, 90
Blaug, Mark 35*n*65
Bloch, Ernst 177*n*27
Bochenek, Mirosław 2
Bohle, Dorothee 14
Bolesta-Kukułka, Krystyna 118, 118*n*33
Bolivia 186
Bonaparte, Louis-Napoléon [Napoleon III] 29*n*57
Bonaparte, Napoleon [Napoleon I] 77, 91
Borodziej, Włodzimierz 107
Borowiec, Piotr 15, 15*n*31, 16, 16*n*32
bourgeoisie 11, 11*n*26, 12, 13, 13*n*27, 14*n*30, 16, 17, 18, 19, 20, 27, 28, 33, 39, 44*n*8, 47, 48, 49, 51, 52, 54, 63*n*9, 66*n*12, 70, 73, 75, 75*n*29, 76, 79, 80, 81, 81*n*32, 82, 83, 84, 85, 89, 90, 93, 93*n*7, 104, 133, 134, 136, 136*n*52, 137, 143, 143*n*65, 153, 162, 169*n*16, 172*n*24, 186, 187, 187*n*40
  non-capitalist 187*n*40
  petty 76, 80
  surrogate 143*n*65
Brenner, Robert 19
Brinton, Crane 30*n*59, 84
Bruno, Michael 147*n*68
Brus, Włodzimierz 51, 52, 100*n*15, 101, 101*n*17, 173, 174, 177*n*28
Bugaj, Ryszard 55, 149, 179*n*29
Bukvić, Rajko 1, 2
Bulgaria 13
bureaucracy 93, 93*n*6, 94, 94*n*10, 103, 134, 182, 184, 185, 186
  bureaucratic capitalism 5*n*14
  bureaucratic collectivism 67
  bureaucratic socialism 5*n*14
  party-state 94*n*10, 104*n*21, 156, 185*n*36

INDEX 207

burghers 16, 47, 48, 48n14, 49, 54, 187n40
Bywalec, Czesław 127

Callinicos, Alex 28n56, 29n57
Calvinism 90
Canada 1n5
capital 21n43, 50n17, 97, 112, 136n50, 141, 143n65, 162, 163, 183, 186
   accumulation of 49
      primitive 41, 46, 46n12, 49, 50, 50n17, 54, 110, 128n42
   cultural 143n65
   foreign 30, 82, 83, 144, 145, 147
   formation 96
      domestic 143n65
      state 143n65
   human 46n12, 136n50
   market 117n32, 119, 133
   owners of. *See* bourgeoisie
capitalism 2, 4, 6, 7, 8, 8n22, 10, 13, 14n28, 15n31, 16, 16n35, 18, 19, 20n39, 21, 21n42, 22n44, 23, 26, 27, 29n57, 33, 38, 38n3, 41, 42, 47, 50n17, 51, 53, 54, 55, 57n2, 63, 64, 64n10, 65, 68, 79, 82, 92n3, 94n10, 96n12, 100n15, 101, 101n18, 105, 107, 108, 110, 112, 113, 115, 116, 117n32, 118, 119, 120, 121n35, 126, 128n44, 129, 132, 133, 134, 136n51, 140, 141n61, 145n66, 148, 152, 153n2, 158n3, 161, 161n8, 162, 162n9, 163, 164, 166n12, 166n13, 167, 168n16, 169n19, 170n20, 171n22, 172, 172n24, 173, 175, 179, 181, 182, 184, 185, 186, 187, 187n40
   Anglo-Saxon version of. *See* Anglo-Saxon model
   contemporary 172n24
   crucial reform of. *See* reform
   democratic 150
   (free) market 8n22, 14n28, 94n9, 104n22, 108, 175
   neoliberal 4n10
   restoration of 39, 42, 94n8, 129, 130
   state 5n14, 13n27, 14, 21n43, 67, 94, 94n9, 104n22, 158n3, 183, 184
Carr, Edward H 7n21, 36n66
Carranza, Venustiano 90
Cavaignac, Louis-Eugène 90
Cavour, Camillo 90
Celiński, Andrzej 138, 138n53
Central and Eastern Europe (CEE) 10, 11, 12, 13n27, 14, 14n30, 21n43, 29n58, 44, 45, 49, 83, 102, 129, 133, 134, 140, 156, 158, 158n3, 159, 169n19, 175, 180, 183, 184, 186
central planning 5n14, 107, 108, 113, 117n32, 126, 166n12
centrally controlled economy. *See* central planning
Chateaubriand, François-Rene de 91
Chodak, Jarosław 17n37, 26n51, 27n53, 29n58
Church 85, 90, 157
   Anglican 90
   Catholic 10, 37n2, 38, 39, 55, 90, 106n24
   Orthodox 90
civil society 11n26, 140, 159, 178
civil war 44n8
   American 27
Clarke, Simon 67n14
class 19, 20n41, 33, 47, 65, 66, 68n18, 71, 74, 74n27, 75, 75n27, 75n28, 79, 80, 81, 84, 93, 93n6, 94n8, 95, 97, 97n14, 98, 100, 131, 132, 132n47, 133, 134, 135, 136, 153, 159n5, 163, 164, 166n12, 168n16, 187n40
   agency 186
   analysis 14n30
   -based tensions 100, 153
   basis of the system
      significant transformations in 43n8, 60, 61, 62, 74, 100, 152, 154
   bourgeois. *See* bourgeoisie
   capitalist. *See* bourgeoisie
   conflict (antagonism) 19, 59, 66n12, 93, 96n13, 97n14, 98, 111
   consciousness 43n8, 71n23, 170n21, 171n21
   division 161
   dominant 134, 135, 137, 154
   interest 79, 81
   middle 11n26, 13n27, 52, 93n7, 128, 135, 136, 139n55, 141n61, 143n65, 172n24
      middle-class-to-be 39, 47, 93, 99, 100, 153
   new 93, 93n6
   oppressed 70
   popular (masses) 13, 16n35, 43n8, 44n8, 46n12, 51, 69, 70, 70n20, 73, 75, 75n29, 76, 77, 79, 82, 130, 152, 153, 158, 168n16, 169n16, 183n34
      activity of 16n35, 48n13, 58n3, 61, 62, 63, 68, 69, 69n19, 75, 76, 106, 130, 144, 152, 155, 157
      passivity of 130, 131, 131n46, 132, 133, 158

class (*cont.*)
  possessing (propertied)   18, 56, 69, 82, 135, 135*n*49
  proletarian (working). *See* workers
  relations   70, 80
  revolutionary   20, 70, 80, 81, 133
  rule   20, 22*n*43, 48, 69, 75*n*28, 82, 152, 158, 182
    changes in   43*n*8, 60, 61, 62, 74, 75, 100, 154
  society (social structure)   67, 95, 127, 133, 143*n*65
  struggle   26*n*50, 65, 67, 67*n*14, 68, 90, 96, 97, 97*n*14, 98, 100, 152, 161, 161*n*8, 163, 164, 165, 167*n*13, 168*n*16, 169*n*16
  substrate of power
    change in   61, 62, 74, 75
  unheroic   75*n*29
  working. *See* workers
Cold War   102*n*19
Colloquia Communia (academic journal)   58
colonial rule   82, 144, 153
command economy. *See* central planning
command-distributive system. *See* central planning
communism   5*n*14, 11*n*26, 43, 55, 93, 94*n*9, 94*n*10, 101*n*17, 102, 102*n*18, 102*n*19, 104*n*22, 105, 106*n*23, 106*n*24, 109, 111, 119, 129, 132*n*47, 134, 136, 136*n*51, 141*n*61, 154, 156, 161, 161*n*8, 165, 171*n*22, 172*n*24, 174, 179, 184
  anti-   86, 138, 151
  communist party. *See* Polish United Workers' Party (PUWP)
  post-   46*n*12, 128*n*40, 134, 139*n*55, 141*n*61, 165, 168
  Soviet bloc (Eastern bloc)   5*n*14, 67, 100*n*15, 101*n*17, 133, 185
  sovietism   5*n*14, 94*n*9, 104*n*22, 156, 173
Cominel, George C   24*n*48
comparative economic systems   1, 166*n*12
congruence testing   25*n*49
Connelly, John   170*n*20
consequentialism   17, 17*n*37, 19, 20, 21*n*42, 22, 22*n*45, 28, 33, 63, 181, 184
conservatism   57*n*1
  free-market   138
constructivism   11*n*26, 52, 165
contextual analysis   34*n*63

counter-revolution   13*n*27, 14*n*28, 33, 38*n*3, 40, 43, 44, 45, 45*n*10, 46, 46*n*11, 57*n*1, 86, 89*n*34, 110, 182, 182*n*33, 183, 184, 185*n*36, 186
  bourgeois   40, 44, 182, 184
  (counter)revolution   15, 23, 44, 182
    epigonic   33, 44
  counter-revolutionary terror   29
  Stalinist   185, 186
coup d'état   43*n*8, 44*n*8, 74
Crimean War   71*n*22
crisis   19, 44*n*8, 66, 67*n*14, 68, 71, 92*n*4, 100, 103, 104, 113, 149, 158, 170*n*20
  at the highest level of power   71, 152
  chronic   66, 66*n*13, 68, 100
  economic   67, 70, 152, 157, 159
  endless. *See* stagnation (economic)
  political   68, 69, 70, 71, 106, 152
  social   68, 69, 106, 152
Cromwell, Oliver   77, 90
Cuba   186
Czarnota, Adam   27*n*55, 57*n*2, 58, 58*n*3, 59, 59*n*4, 60, 61, 62, 72
Czech Republic   105*n*23, 134, 150
Czechoslovakia   13, 105, 150, 156

Dąbrowski, Marek   120, 121*n*35
Dahrendorf, Ralf   52*n*19, 117*n*32
Danton, Georges   32
Davidson, Neil   13*n*27, 16, 16*n*33, 16*n*34, 16*n*35, 17, 17*n*37, 18, 19, 20, 21*n*43, 22*n*43, 28*n*56, 44, 158*n*3, 182, 183, 183*n*34, 187
democracy   16*n*35, 30, 77, 83, 84, 102*n*18, 160*n*6, 165, 172*n*24, 175
  bourgeois   37, 82
  dearth of   139*n*57
  democratic opposition   140
  democratic republic   63*n*9, 79, 158
  democratisation   7*n*21, 30, 150, 160*n*6
  direct   160
  institutions of   14*n*28
  owner   102*n*18
  parliamentary   102*n*18
  political   76
  radical   79, 91
  social   2, 5*n*14, 41, 48, 94*n*9, 94*n*10, 110, 114, 132*n*47, 144, 162, 170*n*20, 171, 171*n*22, 175, 176*n*27, 180*n*30
  withering away of   160*n*6

INDEX   209

deproletarianisation 132
determinism 178
    historical 177
    technological 95n11
Deutscher, Isaac 95n10
Dissent (magazine) 37n2, 48, 50n18
Djilas, Milovan 93, 93n6
Dow, Sheila C 26n53
doxography 34
Drewnowski, Jan 5n14
Dreyfus, Alfred 44n8
Dryszel, Andrzej 106n23, 118n33, 121n35
Dubček, Alexander 102n19
Dühring, Eugen 66
Dunn, John 36n66
Dymski, Gary A 166n12
Dzielski, Mirosław 137

Eastern Europe. *See* Central and Eastern Europe (CEE)
Economic Action 114
economics 1, 6n19, 36, 95, 99, 120, 139, 147n69, 161, 173, 174, 188
    academic 1, 3, 3n9
    French 162
    history of 6
    institutional 170n21
    neoclassical 95
    Nobel Prize in 102n18, 143n64
    Polish 2, 3, 6, 6n17, 6n19
Edward the Confessor 87
Egypt 87
Eley, Geoff 28n56
elites
    desertion of 84, 142, 153
    ruling 69, 71, 97n14, 109, 110, 111, 111n27, 123, 134, 136n51, 141n61, 147, 150, 151, 152, 159, 177n28
    technocratic-managerial 134, 135
Engels, Friedrich 22n44, 28, 29n57, 29n57, 31, 64, 65, 66, 66n13, 74n27, 75n29, 79n30, 83, 181
England 1n5, 66n13, 75n29
Enlightenment 27n54
entrepreneurs (businessmen). *See* bourgeoisie
European Community. *See* European Union (EU)
European Union (EU) 122, 168, 178

Evans, Richard J 28n56
exploitation 15n31, 46n12, 67n16, 79, 81n32, 94n8, 95n11, 101n18, 163
    mode of 67, 67n16, 185
Eyal, Gil 134, 136

Fabre d'Églantine, Philippe 88
Falkowski, Mieczysław 4n11
Faulkner, Neil 185n36
Fetscher, Iring 71n23
feudalism 8n22, 16, 18, 19, 26, 65, 70, 83, 90
Filtzer, Donald 184, 185n37
Finland 49, 105
First World War 49, 163, 169n19
Fitzpatrick, Sheila 183, 184, 184n35, 185n36
Fordism 162
Foster, John Bellamy 3, 6n17, 100n16
France 21n42, 26n50, 27n54, 44n8, 75n29, 80, 86, 88, 89, 90, 146n68, 152n2, 153n2
(free-)market economy. *See* capitalism

Gabryel, Piotr 145
Galbraith, John K 3n9, 167, 173
Gardawski, Juliusz 132, 132n47, 147, 148
Garibaldi, Giuseppe 83, 90
Garlicki, Andrzej 107
Gazeta Wyborcza (daily newspaper) 42n6
Geistesgeschichte 34, 168n15
Geremek, Bronisław 120, 124, 125n39
German peasant war 27, 87, 89
Germany 37, 51, 69, 83, 92n3, 102n18, 162, 165, 172n24, 182, 186
    West 8n22, 105, 117n32, 150, 165
Gerschenkron, Alexander 11n26, 143n65
Gerstenberger, Heide 17n37
Glasman, Maurice 53, 92n2
glasnost 113
Goldstone, Jack A 25n49
Gomułka, Stanisław 4n13, 42n6, 114, 120, 120n34, 124, 124n38
Gorbachev, Mikhail 102n19, 106n24, 109, 113
Gramsci, Antonio 29n57, 80, 80n31
Great Britain 21n42, 110, 120, 153n2
Great Peasants' War. *See* German peasant war
Gregory, Paul R 143n65
Grinberg, Daniel 27, 31
Guardian (daily newspaper) 120
Guesde, Jules 44n8

Habermas, Jürgen   13, 15*n*31, 16*n*31, 160
Habsburg (dynasty)   37, 48
Hankiss, Elmer   14*n*28
Hardy, Jane   14, 14*n*30
Harman, Chris   21*n*43, 158*n*3
Hayek, Friedrich von   176*n*27
hegemony   28, 30, 62, 80, 80*n*31, 81, 82, 133,
    135, 143, 153, 154
  bourgeois   136
  co-   80
  natural   28, 63*n*9, 80
  revolutionary   31, 80, 81, 81*n*32, 82
Heilbroner, Robert L   162
Herer, Wiktor   172*n*24
Herling-Grudziński, Gustaw   56
Hilferding, Rudolf   6, 6*n*18
Hill, Christopher   28*n*56
Himmelweit, Susan   65*n*12, 66*n*12, 67*n*15
Hirszowicz, Maria   170*n*20
Historical Materialism (academic
    journal)   17*n*37
historical narrative   34*n*63
historiosophy   36*n*66
history   6, 7*n*21, 11*n*26, 25, 26*n*53, 27*n*53,
    27*n*54, 28, 33, 34, 36, 36*n*66, 42*n*6, 43*n*7,
    51, 67, 86, 87, 88, 90, 101*n*18, 121*n*35, 142,
    151, 155, 163, 164, 172*n*24, 174, 175, 179,
    182, 183*n*34
  Comparative Historical Analysis
    (CHA)   25*n*49
  economic   4
  of economic thought   4, 6*n*19, 34*n*63, 36
  of economics. *See* economics
  of ideas   1, 4, 26*n*52, 27*n*54, 33, 34, 36*n*66,
    155, 168*n*15, 170*n*21
  of Poland   9*n*24, 41, 125, 143*n*65
  the end of   88
Hobsbawm, Eric J   17*n*36, 20*n*40, 28*n*56
Hohenzollern (dynasty)   37
Hołda-Róziewicz, Henryka   4*n*11
Hungary   13, 37, 100*n*15, 105*n*23, 112, 134, 156,
    159*n*5, 174
Hutchful, Eboe   12

iconoclasm   85
idealism   176*n*27
ideology   7*n*21, 11*n*26, 26*n*50, 30, 32, 51, 55, 83,
    85, 109, 141, 144, 151, 156, 157, 159, 170*n*20
  bourgeois   168*n*16, 187
  de-ideologisation   156

impoverishment   38, 39, 46*n*12, 49, 50*n*17,
    96*n*12, 107, 125*n*39
India   105
inequalities   15*n*31, 38, 39, 105, 127*n*40, 166*n*13
  income   105*n*23
  (socio-)economic   4, 9*n*24, 70, 105, 106,
    106*n*23, 152, 154
inflation   107, 120, 123*n*37, 126, 146
Institute for Training Scientific Cadres
    (IKKN)   31*n*60, 169*n*20, 170*n*20
institutionalism (institutional
    economics)   5, 170
intellectuals   10, 31*n*60, 45, 84, 109, 139,
    139*n*54, 140*n*60, 141, 142, 142*n*63
  humanistic   134, 139
  Solidarity   159
intelligentsia   11*n*26, 32, 38, 39, 40, 55, 56, 62,
    81, 84, 85, 130, 137, 139, 139*n*54, 139*n*55,
    139*n*56, 139*n*57, 140, 141, 142, 143, 143*n*65,
    153, 154, 160
  Eastern European   11, 160
  Solidarity   100, 109, 139, 140
International Monetary Fund (IMF)   104, 115,
    121*n*35, 121*n*35, 122, 137, 145, 145*n*66, 146,
    147, 147*n*68, 155, 159
Italy   71*n*22, 80, 83

Jacobinism   88
Janczak, Hieronim. *See* Kurowski, Stefan
Japan   27, 46*n*12, 53*n*20, 92*n*3, 105
Jaruzelski, Wojciech   102*n*19, 106*n*24
Jefferson, Thomas   90
Józefiak, Cezary   115, 116

Kabaj, Mieczysław   96*n*12
Kalecki, Michał   1, 3*n*10, 4, 4*n*12, 4*n*13, 5, 6,
    6*n*17, 6*n*18, 7*n*20, 161, 161*n*7, 166, 166*n*12,
    169*n*19, 173, 173*n*26
Kaleckianism   5, 166*n*12, 169
Karwowski, Ewa   1*n*3, 1*n*6, 2, 4*n*12, 5*n*15, 6*n*17,
    9*n*23, 95*n*10
Katznelson, Ira   109, 140, 140*n*59
Kautsky, Karl   171*n*23
Keynes, John Maynard   3*n*9, 5, 111*n*27, 173,
    176*n*27, 180
Keynesianism   6*n*17
  left-wing   5
Khrushchev, Nikita   102*n*19
King, John E   166*n*12
Kisielewski, Stefan   138, 146

INDEX   211

Klaes, Matthias   35n65
Klaus, Vaclav   150
Kleer, Jerzy   178, 178n29
Klein, Naomi   97n14, 149n71
Kochanowicz, Jacek   27, 31
Kołakowski, Leszek   5n14
Kołodko, Grzegorz W   3n9
Kołodziejczyk, Ryszard   47
Konat, Grzegorz   3, 3n9, 4n12, 6n17, 6n18, 6n19, 54n22
Koredczuk, Józef   30
Kornai, János   92n2
Kościuszko, Tadeusz   158
Kovács, János M   11n26
Kowalewski, Zbigniew M   40n4, 57n1, 67, 67n16, 68, 95n11, 184, 185, 185n37, 186, 186n38, 186n39
Kozłowski, Paweł   1n1, 2, 4n14, 10n25, 35n65, 36n65, 36n66, 170n20, 170n21, 176n27, 182n33
Krusiński, Stanisław   4
Krusińskites   4
Kryshtanovskaya, Olga   12
Krzywicki, Ludwik   3, 4n11, 6, 6n18, 168n16, 171, 171n23, 176n27
Krzyżanowski, Adam   3n9
Kuczyński, Waldemar   52n19, 113, 130n45, 136n51, 146, 147
Kula, Marcin   24, 24n48, 25, 25n49, 27n53, 28
Kulas, Piotr   139n54
Kultura (magazine)   170n20
Kumar, Krishan   13
Kurczewski, Jacek   127n40
Kuroń, Jacek   9n24, 93n6, 108, 131, 132, 136n51, 141n61, 149
Kurowski, Stefan   108, 121

La Fayette, Marie Joseph de   90, 91
Labour Focus on Eastern Europe (magazine)   48
Łagowski, Bronisław   45, 45n9, 45n11
Lakatos, Imre   34, 35, 35n65
Lange, Oskar   1, 4, 4n10, 4n12, 37, 38, 38n3, 46, 48, 54, 54n22, 95, 170n21, 170n21, 173, 173n26, 176n27, 178
Łaski, Kazimierz   5n16, 173, 174
Leder, Andrzej   12n27, 13n27
Lenin, Vladimir I   16n35, 31, 57, 57n2, 68n18, 70, 70n20, 70n21, 73, 74n27, 75n27, 89, 133, 177n27

Łepkowski, Tadeusz   31, 57n1
Leszkowska, Anna   97n14, 123n36
Lewandowska, Eliza   48n15, 93n4, 167n14
Lewandowski, Janusz   150
liberalism   63n9, 79, 83, 91, 109, 132n47, 140, 149
  bourgeois   137
  conservative   109, 110, 140, 150
  democratic   93n7, 135, 136
  neo-   94n9, 109, 140, 141, 150
  social   139n57, 170n20, 171, 171n22
Lipiński, Edward   37n2
Lipton, David   119, 121n35
Lowenthal, Richard   52n20, 53n20
Lubczyński, Krzysztof   41, 169n17
Lukács, György   52, 170n21, 177n27
Łukawer, Edward   2
Luxemburg, Rosa   1, 1n4, 4, 4n12, 5, 6, 6n17, 35n65, 51, 169n20

Maas, Harro   34, 35
Magala, Sławomir   26n50
Małachowski, Aleksander   129, 130n45
Marcuzzo, Maria C   34n63
marketisation   117n32, 126, 158, 178
martial law   73n23, 101n17, 104n22, 106n24, 107, 108, 112, 140, 160
Marx, Karl   5, 6n17, 17n37, 18, 22n44, 29n57, 31, 32, 51, 64, 65, 65n12, 66n12, 69, 75n28, 76, 89, 161n8, 162, 163, 173, 177n27, 180
Marxism   5, 6, 14n28, 16n35, 21, 21n42, 22n45, 24n48, 26, 27, 28n56, 31, 31n60, 32, 46, 54, 64, 65n11, 66, 66n12, 67, 67n14, 68, 70n20, 71n23, 74, 75n29, 95, 95n11, 101n18, 161n8, 163, 165, 168n16, 169, 169n20, 170n21, 171n23, 172, 174, 176n27, 177n27, 177n28, 185n36, 187
  Capital-centric   17, 17n37, 18, 19, 20, 21, 21n42, 22, 23, 32, 184, 185n36, 186, 187
  Marxism-Leninism   168, 171
  Neo-Marxism   14n28
  Polish   6n19
  Political. See *Capital*-centric Marxism
  Post-Marxism   14n28
  revisionist   31n60, 140, 168n16, 169, 169n17, 170n20, 171
  Russian   16n35
materialism   177n27
  dialectical   177n28
  historical   22, 163, 177n28

Mazowiecki, Tadeusz   52n19, 118, 131, 136n51,
       138, 147, 150
McChesney, Robert W   100n16
Meade, James   102n18, 167, 173
means of production   95, 113, 162
   collective ownership of   168n16
   private ownership of   162
megasystem   102n18, 172, 172n24
Meiji Restoration   27
Meiksins Wood, Ellen   19, 175, 176
Meller, Stefan   27, 31
Merkel, Jacek   145, 145n67
Mikołajczyk, Magdalena   170n20
millenarism   87
Minc, Bronisław   169n20
mode of production   16, 16n33, 18, 21n43,
       22n43, 26, 59, 64, 65, 65n11, 66, 66n12,
       67, 67n16, 68, 68n17, 95n11, 183, 185
   ancient   65
   Asiatic   65
   capitalist (bourgeois)   65, 67n14, 185
   feudal   65
   tensions and contradictions in   59, 60,
       61, 64, 66
   tributary   16
Modzelewski, Karol   2, 93n6, 140, 149, 170n20
Monopoly Capital School   6, 6n17
Monthly Review (magazine)   6n17, 10
Mooers, Colin   14, 14n29, 16, 20n39, 24,
       28n56, 158, 158n3, 158n4, 159, 159n5, 160,
       161, 181
Moore, Barrington   17n37
Morawski, Witold   9n23
Mujżel, Jan   115
Myrdal, Gunnar   7n21, 8n21

Nagy, Imre   102n19
National Bank of Poland (NBP)   121n35
Netherlands   105
New Economic Mechanism   112, 174
New Left Review (magazine)   13
Nişancioğlu, Kerem   17n37
Nolte, Ernst   13
nomenklatura   12, 37n62, 55, 94n9, 94n10,
       99, 100, 102n19, 104n22, 106, 106n23,
       109, 133n48
   enfranchisement of   55, 101n17,
       133n48, 142
North, Douglas C   3n9

November Uprising   28
Nowe Życie Gospodarcze (magazine)   14n29,
       14n30, 37, 39, 47, 49n16, 54
Nygaard, Bertel   21n42, 22n44, 152n2, 153n2

Obywatelski Klub Parlamentarny
       (OKP)   120n34, 124, 149
Olesiak, Kazimierz   125, 137
Olszewski, Henryk   27n54
Orsi, Pier L   17n37
Osiatyński, Jerzy   2, 120n34
Ost, David   179n29
Overton, Richard   87n33

Paine, Thomas   86
Paris Club   119
Paris Commune   85
Paszyński, Aleksander   120
paternalism   53n20
peasants   18, 70, 75n29, 87, 97n14, 132, 159n5
perestroika   10, 113
Petras, James   160
philosophy   34, 35, 42n6, 171n21, 176n27
   of science   7n21, 34
   twentieth-century   34n64
pluralism   78, 112
   political   12
   social   108
Polanyi, Karl   8n22, 173n25
Polish Academy of Sciences   169n20
   Institute for the History of Science,
       Education, and Technology of   4n12
Polish People's Republic (PRL)   9n24, 30,
       93, 97, 98, 99, 100n15, 103, 105, 106, 111,
       112n28, 137, 143
Polish United Workers' Party (PUWP)   7n21,
       30, 99, 109, 133n48, 140n60, 141, 159, 160,
       169n17, 170n20, 170n21
Polish Workers' Party (PPR)   7n21
political economy   1, 3n10, 4, 5, 5n16,
       6, 117n32
political science   139, 151, 179n29
politocracy   134
positivism   168n16, 169n16
Pospiszyl, Michał   13n27
Post, Charles   17n37, 18, 19, 20, 21, 186, 187
poverty   69, 70, 123n36, 164, 175
price liberalisation   104, 114, 119, 123n37, 125,
       126, 136, 154

INDEX   213

private property   10, 12
    rights   134
    socialisation of   102n18, 172n24
privatisation   12, 55, 96, 96n12, 97, 104, 112,
        115, 116, 117n32, 118, 119, 128, 132n47, 133,
        133n48, 134, 135, 150, 178
    clientelistic   133n48
    corruptive   133n48
    grassroots   154
    mass   150
    quasi-   55
    uncontrolled   133
process tracing   25n49
proletariat. See workers
Proudhon, Pierre-Joseph   88
Prusek, Andrzej   177, 177n28
Puritanism   90
putsch   43n8, 44n8, 74, 152
Putterman, Louis   166n13

Rabaut Saint-Étienne, Jean-Paul   87
Rae, Gavin   1n6, 3, 5n15, 7n20, 143n65,
        163n10, 176n27
Rakowski, Mieczysław   104, 113, 114n29, 118,
        119, 120, 126, 137
Reagan, Ronald   102n19, 110, 176n27
Reaganism   144
reconstruction (history of ideas)   5, 23, 24,
        26, 33, 34, 35, 36, 93, 100, 152, 155, 156,
        161, 181, 182
    historical   34, 35
    rational   34, 34n63, 34n64, 35,
        35n65, 168n15
Redshirts   83
reform
    crucial   4n13, 7n20, 166n13, 167
        of capitalism   4, 166n12
        of socialism   4, 52n20, 166, 166n12,
            167, 167n14
    economic   10, 101n17, 104, 108, 112, 112n28,
        113, 131, 136n51
    from above   27, 29, 44
    radical   117n32, 166n13
    reformism   9n24, 28, 29, 84, 113, 166n13,
        168n16, 169n16, 171n23, 172n23
    reformist impotence   71, 103, 108, 154, 157
    social   83
religion (clergy)   18, 89, 90
    reactionary role of   62, 153, 155

revisionism (theory of revolution)   17, 17n37,
        18, 18n38, 21, 32
revolt   43, 43n8, 44n8, 74, 97n14, 152
    workers'   42, 43
revolution
    American   86, 90
    anti-communist   15
    betrayed   40n4
    bloodless   15
    bourgeois   9n23, 10, 11, 11n26, 12, 12n27,
        13, 13n27, 14, 14n28, 14n30, 16, 16n35,
        17, 17n37, 18, 19, 20, 21, 21n42, 21n43,
        22, 22n44, 22n45, 23, 24, 25, 26, 27, 28,
        29, 30, 31n61, 32, 33, 37, 39, 40, 42, 43,
        44, 46, 48, 48n13, 48n14, 49, 50, 50n17,
        50n18, 53, 54, 57, 58, 58n3, 59, 59n4, 60,
        61, 62, 63, 63n9, 64, 66n12, 67, 68, 71,
        72n24, 73, 75, 75n29, 76, 77, 78, 79, 80,
        82, 83, 84, 85, 86, 87, 89, 90, 92, 125, 128,
        130, 144, 152, 154, 155, 156, 157, 158, 158n3,
        161, 181, 182, 183, 183n34, 186, 187
    bourgeois-democratic   16n35, 51, 184
    cycle of   77, 84, 184
    early   181
    epigonic   8, 8n22, 9, 9n23, 10, 14, 15,
        16n32, 21, 22, 23, 24, 33, 35, 37, 37n1,
        38, 39, 41, 42, 45, 45n9, 48, 50, 52,
        54, 54n22, 55, 93n5, 96n12, 106n24,
        125, 128n43, 130, 139n55, 155, 156, 168,
        169n19, 172, 176, 180, 181, 181n31, 183,
        184, 187, 188
    imitative   50n18
    late   181
    model of   25, 27n53, 33, 35, 57, 58, 60,
        61, 62, 63, 63n9, 67, 69n19, 71, 73, 75,
        83, 89, 100, 106, 107, 129, 144, 152, 153,
        154, 155, 156, 157, 161
    of continental Europe   37, 130
    quasi-   12
    theory of   17n37, 20, 25, 54, 181, 186
    without bourgeoisie   11n26, 12n27,
        14, 14n30
    burghers'   48n13, 54
        epigonic   47
    capitalist   10, 38, 38n3, 39, 41, 79, 93, 130,
        186, 187
    new   187
    civilisational   15
    communist   13, 187

revolution (cont.)
  completion of   62, 85, 86, 88, 153, 155
  conservative   13
  controlled   15
  creeping   15
  Cultural (in China)   164
  democratic   15
  detonator of   59, 60, 61, 73, 74, 125, 126, 152, 154, 158
  direct causes of   10, 59, 59n4, 60
  Dutch   57, 85, 89
  English   57, 90, 147n68
  European   13, 18n38, 25
    Eastern   158, 187
    of 1848   58
  evolutionary   15
  external aspect (factor) of   62, 82, 144, 146, 153, 155, 159
  February Revolution of 1848   29n57, 80, 86, 90, 146n68
  freedom   15
  French   20n40, 21n42, 24, 24n48, 25, 26n50, 48, 57, 79, 85, 86, 88, 89, 90, 147n68, 152n2
  from above   16n32, 27, 29, 29n57, 29n58, 52, 53, 53n20, 54, 57, 63, 63n8, 75, 76, 106n24, 112, 128n43, 130, 135n49, 152, 158, 166n13, 183, 183n34, 184, 184n35, 186
  from below   29n57, 57, 63n8, 73n25, 183n34
  gentle   15
  German of 1848   51, 77
  in incomes   125n39, 127, 128n42
  in the majesty of the law   15
  in the theory of revolutions   180
  Latin American   87, 90
  legal and constitutional   15
  liberal   15
  liberalist   15n31
  limits of   16n35, 78, 81, 112, 137, 152
  market   15
  model of   128, 155
  moral   15
  negotiated   15
  October (in Russia)   185
  of 1989   15
  of a new beginning   15
  of common sense   15
  of freedom   15
  outburst of   59, 59n4, 60, 61, 63, 73, 75, 126, 128, 152, 154
  over-dreamed   12n27
  passive   29n57
  peaceful   15
  peaceful revolution of Solidarity   15
  personnel   15
  Polish   15, 15n31, 130, 143, 144, 146n68, 181
  political   21n43, 32, 69, 182, 183, 184
  proletarian   10, 39, 40, 40n4, 42, 44, 46n11, 54, 130, 163n10, 182, 184, 185, 186
  quiet   15
  rationed   15
  refolution   15
  revolutionary consciousness   30, 59, 60, 61, 71, 71n23, 72, 83, 84, 107, 110, 112, 152, 154, 159
  revolutionary leaders   80, 90, 91, 153
  revolutionary (political) staff   62, 81, 83, 84, 153, 154, 160
    cult of   62, 91, 153, 155
  revolutionary project   43n8, 60, 61, 62, 63n9, 68, 78, 79, 85, 88, 112, 119, 121, 122, 152, 154
  revolutionary propaganda   62, 86, 88, 148, 149, 150, 151, 153, 155
  revolutionary situation   31, 59, 59n4, 60, 61, 68, 68n8, 69, 70, 70n20, 71, 71n22, 73, 84, 103, 105, 106, 152, 154
    pseudo-   44n8
  revolutionary terror   30, 89, 89n34, 153
    economic   62, 89, 153, 155
  Russian (second)   12
  self-limiting   15, 45
  social   22n43, 43n7, 65, 184, 187
  socialist   13n27, 27, 45, 51
  Solidarity   9n24, 15, 38, 38n3, 45
  Spanish   87, 90
  structural causes of   59, 60, 72
  systemic   15
  technocratic   16n31
  theory of   17n37, 26n50, 26n53, 31, 32, 52, 181, 184
  velvet   15
Risorgimento   83
Robespierre, Maximilien   76, 90, 91
Romania   13
Romanov (dynasty)   37
Romme, Gilbert   88

INDEX   215

Rorty, Richard 34, 34n64, 35, 35n65, 168n15
Rosati, Dariusz 105, 119
Rothschild, Kurt W 5n16
Round Table 104n22, 106n24, 115n30, 121,
    141, 163
  Agreements 37n2, 42n6, 115n30, 117n32,
    118, 139n57, 163
  talks (negotiations) 99, 107, 114, 115, 116,
    118, 125, 137, 138, 139, 160
Rupnik, Jacques 12n27
Russo-Japanese War 71n22
Rzeczpospolita (daily newspaper) 104, 113,
    118, 121, 121n35

Sachs, Jeffrey 52n19, 96n12, 114, 119, 120,
    121n35, 124, 147n69, 149
Sadowski, Władysław 172n24
Sadowski, Zdzisław 2
Sadura, Przemysław 17n36, 177n28
Sady, Wojciech 34n64
Saint-Just, Louis de 88
Sakwa, Richard 16n31
Salmonowicz, Stanisław 26n53, 28, 31,
    48, 48n14
Samary, Catherine 44
Sandelin, Bo 8n21
Savelsberg, Joachim J 11, 12
Savoy (dynasty) 83
Scandinavia 8n22, 46n12, 102n18, 105, 172n24
Schaff, Adam 170n20
Second World War 8n22, 30, 162, 184
Sejm 104, 113, 126, 129, 131
Sekuła, Ireneusz 104, 114, 115, 136, 137
Self-Governing Republic (political and
    economic programme) 109,
    132n47, 140
Sen, Amartya K 3n9
shock therapy 96, 100, 108, 110, 114, 115, 118,
    119, 126, 128n44, 131, 153, 159, 164
Siemek, Marek J 170n21, 171n21
Sierakowski, Sławomir 9n25, 102n18, 106n23,
    162n9, 172n24, 177n28, 180
Siermiński, Michał 40n4, 186n39
Sierpiński, Witold 6n19
Signorino, Rodolfo 36, 36n66
Simons, Thomas 146
Singer, Daniel 10, 11, 12
Skinner, Quentin 26n52

Skocpol, Theda 177n28
Słabek, Henryk 99, 106n25, 111, 136n51, 142
Smuga, Tadeusz 3
socialism 2, 5n14, 7, 13n27, 65, 94n10, 100n15,
    102n18, 107, 108, 109, 112, 114n29, 117n32,
    136n51, 140, 157, 166n12, 171, 172n24, 173,
    173n26, 177n28, 184, 185, 186
  crucial reform of. *See* reform
  degenerated 94n10
  democratic 7n21, 94, 94n10, 171
  despotic 5n14
  market 101n18, 166n13, 173n26, 174,
    175, 178
  national 171n22
  real 8, 16, 21, 23, 26, 33, 39, 42, 47, 52,
    53n20, 55, 67, 68, 68n17, 92, 93, 94,
    94n10, 98, 99, 100, 101, 101n18, 103,
    103n20, 105, 106, 106n24, 107, 107n26,
    108, 109, 115, 117n32, 118, 126, 128n44,
    132n47, 144, 145n66, 154, 157, 166n12, 167,
    180, 182, 184, 187
  state 5n14
sociology 22, 23, 38, 132n47, 136n52, 175
  comparative historical 25n49, 33
  French 162
  of science 7n21
Solidarność (Solidarity) 4n10, 9n24, 15,
    40, 42n6, 43, 45, 46n11, 55, 106n24, 114,
    115, 116, 119, 120, 126, 131, 137, 138, 139,
    140, 140n60, 142, 142n62, 142n63, 145,
    147n69, 148, 149n71, 150, 151, 154, 158n4,
    159, 159n5, 160, 163n10
  anti-democratic character of 160
  Carnival of 73n24
  opposition 99, 109, 139
  Second 151
Soros, George 118, 119
Soviet Union. *See* USSR
Spain 49
Spring of Nations 69
stagnation (economic) 66n13, 100, 100n16,
    102, 103, 106n24, 108, 111, 153, 158
Stalin, Joseph W 156, 177n28, 184,
    184n35, 185n36
Stalinism 13n27, 21n43, 169n20, 182, 183, 184,
    185, 186
Staniszkis, Jadwiga 55, 55n23
Stankiewicz, Wacław 2, 3, 3n8, 6n19

state   11n26, 15n31, 16n33, 20n39, 21n42, 21n43, 22n43, 27n54, 53n20, 75n28, 78, 94n9, 114, 116, 117n32, 120, 136n52, 140, 142, 152n2, 153n2, 159, 164, 165, 166n12, 175, 177n28, 185
  bourgeois (class)   9n24, 38, 39, 54
  burghers' class   48
  capitalist   187
  financial bankruptcy of   70, 71, 106, 152
  intervention(ism)   53n20
  media   141n61
  -owned enterprises (sector)   96, 99, 101n17, 104, 112, 118, 124n37, 127, 132n47, 133n48, 142, 150
  patronage   11n26
  power   75n27, 75n28, 139n55
  rapid change in   60, 61, 62, 73, 74, 129, 152, 154
  welfare   7, 7n20, 49, 135, 162, 163, 166n13, 167, 169n19
Ste. Croix, G. E. M. de   94n8
Steinmetz, Max   182n32
Stiglitz, Joseph E   3n9, 9n25, 164, 166n13, 180
Stone, Bailey   18n38
Stone, Lawrence   28n56
strike   38, 42, 77, 78, 97n14, 158, 158n4, 160, 162, 164
  agrarian   78
  committee   159n5
  mass   38, 77
  political   77, 78, 152
  school   78
subjectivism   7n21, 176n27
substitutes. See Gerschenkron, Alexander
Suchocka, Hanna   150
Surdykowski, Janusz   15n31
Sweden   1n5, 92n3, 102n18, 117n32, 172n24
Sweezy, Paul M   6n17
Switzerland   1n5
Szelényi, Iván   11, 11n26, 16n31, 134, 136
Szelényi, Szonja   11n26
Szlajfer, Henryk   6n17, 143n65
Szomburg, Jan   150
Szwarc, Karol   2
Szymborska, Hanna   1n3, 4n12, 6n18, 9n23

Tabin, Marek   6n19, 9n24

Taiwan   46n12
Tanewski, Paweł   112n28
Tatur, Melanie   12
Taylor, Edward   3n9
Teschke, Benno   17n37, 21n42, 22n45, 28n56, 66n12, 187n40
textual exegesis   34n63
Thatcher, Margaret   110, 124, 176n27
Thatcherism   144
Tittenbrun, Jacek   96, 97, 98
Tocqueville, Alexis de   32, 86
Toporowski, Jan   1, 1n3, 1n6, 2, 3n10, 4n12, 5, 5n15, 5n16, 6, 6n17, 6n18, 7n20, 9n23, 95n10, 173n26, 181n31
totalitarianism   156, 157
Townsley, Eleanor   16n31, 134, 136
trade unions   45, 46n11, 97n14, 98, 104, 113, 127, 131, 132, 138, 142, 143, 143n64, 144, 151, 162
transitional system (formation)   13n27, 94, 102n18, 172n24, 185
Trautwein, Hans-Michael   8n21
Trotsky, Leon   182, 184, 185n36
Trotskyism   94n10, 95n10, 169, 184
Trzeciakowski, Witold   107, 137
Tu i Teraz (magazine)   58n3, 61, 74
Tygodnik Solidarność (magazine)   55
Tymowski, Andrzej W   8n22

unemployment   9n24, 38, 39, 46n12, 118, 119, 120, 122, 122n36, 124, 159, 164, 172n24, 175, 178
United States (USA)   1n5, 92n3, 102, 110, 134, 144, 145, 146, 151, 179n29
upheaval   10, 11n26, 20n40, 40, 43, 43n8, 44n8, 74, 130, 184n35
  palace   43n8
  political   147n69
  social   43
USSR   10, 12, 13n27, 67, 102, 108, 113, 144, 156, 167, 177n28, 184, 185, 186
utopia   51, 80, 156, 167, 175
  communist   11
  conservative utopianism   88
  radical utopianism   88
  realistic   167, 172
  socialist   170n20

INDEX   217

value
   cognitive   21, 134
   disclosure   7, 7n21, 8n21, 32, 188
   judgements   36
   labour theory of   163
   law of   177n28
   use-   162
voluntarism   176, 176n27, 177n28, 179, 180

wage labour. *See* workers
Wałęsa, Lech   129, 131, 142, 143n64, 145n67, 146, 160
Walicki, Andrzej   92n2, 109, 161n8, 170n20
Washington Consensus   115, 145, 148
Washington, George   90, 91
Weber, Max   165
White, Stephen   12
Wielgosz, Przemysław   6n17, 97n14
Wierzbicki, Piotr   138, 138n53
Wilczek, Mieczysław   104, 113, 114n29, 116, 137
William of Orange   77, 90
William the Silent. *See* William of Orange
Winiecki, Jan   121
Winstanley, Gerrard   87n33

Władyka, Wiesław   61, 74, 158
workers   9n24, 10, 16n35, 37, 38, 38n3, 39, 40, 41, 44n8, 45, 46n11, 49, 52, 54, 56, 70, 75n29, 76, 77, 78, 79, 80, 96, 97, 97n14, 98, 101n18, 127, 130, 131, 132, 132n47, 133, 136n51, 137, 138, 139, 139n56, 143, 151, 159, 159n5, 162, 162n9, 164, 168n16, 169n16, 169n19, 177n28
   movement   10, 37, 40, 41, 43n7, 46, 77
   self-government   102n18, 117n32, 171, 174
workers' revolution. *See* proletarian revolution
World Bank   121n35
Wróblewski, Andrzej   118, 118n33, 119, 137
Wundrak, Richard   8n21

Yugoslavia   93n6, 101n18, 178

Żakowski, Jacek   124, 125n39, 141n61
Zapata, Emiliano   91
Zybała, Andrzej   140n60
Zybertowicz, Andrzej   27n55, 57n2, 58, 58n3, 59, 59n4, 60, 61, 62, 72
Życie Gospodarcze (magazine)   51

www.ingramcontent.com/pod-product-compliance
Lightning Source LLC
Chambersburg PA
CBHW070620030426
42337CB00020B/3861